2 ||||| |||||| ||| ||||||||||| |||||||| ||

W9-BXE-581

A12901 803996

10/10

DEMCO

The Best American Short Plays

2006–2007

The Best American Short Plays

2006–2007

edited with an introduction by
Barbara Parisi

I.C.C. LIBRARY

APPLAUSE THEATRE & CINEMA BOOKS
An Imprint of Hal Leonard Corporation
New York

The Best American Short Plays 2006–2007
Edited with an introduction by Barbara Parisi

Published in 2010 by Applause Theatre & Cinema Books
An Imprint of Hal Leonard Corporation
7777 West Bluemound Road
Milwaukee, WI 53213

Trade Book Division Editorial Offices
19 West 21st Street, New York, NY 10010

Printed in the United States of America
Book composition by UB Communications

ISBN 978-1-55783-747-9 [cloth]
ISBN 978-1-55783-748-6 [paper]
ISSN 0067-6284

www.applausepub.com

To William and Gloria Parisi,
Rochelle Martinsen,
and my husband—
Michael Ronald Pasternack

contents

foreword
by Mark Medoff

My first play, an early version of *The Wager*, was "A Play in 10 Scenes." It ran about 50 minutes. That was 1967. When *The Wager* opened as a "new play" in New York in 1974, it had become a two-act, then a three-act, then a two-act.

In the '90s, I wrote a play without an intermission. It ran ninety-something minutes. *Prymate*, originally two acts opened on Broadway in 2005 without an intermission. *The Same Life Over*, which I will begin directing this year, is seventy-eight pages and will be done without an intermission.

I love keeping the audience in their seats, as we do with movies, and love building plays that continually ascend a flight of stairs without respite. (Those plays also serve to save an audience from having to buy those $12 orange drinks at standard intermissions.)

I haven't intentionally written a one-act play since the several that followed my first effort with *The Wager*. Several of those are published by Dramatists Play Service. A couple are done with some regularity. (One of them, *Doing a Good One for the Red Man*, caused the great Horton Foote to rip me to pieces in San Antonio one summer day following a reading to a fairly conservative audience of Texans who didn't like me allowing an Injun to gun down two decent white folks at a roadside souvenir stand "out west.")

I know I learned my first, crucial lessons about playwriting from one-acts—especially those of Edward Albee, Samuel Becket, Harold Pinter, Eugène Ionesco, N. F. Simpson. I studied at the font of their imaginations, and what imaginations they were! They inspired and amazed me; most of all, they liberated me.

In a review of one of my early plays in the *New York Times*, the reviewer referred to me as Harold Pinter's "American little brother." I was honored to be labeled such. (The first play I directed, when I decided directing was a good job for me, was Pinter's *The Birthday Party*.)

I first turned to playwriting in my mid-twenties. There was a new community theatre in Las Cruces, New Mexico, and an actor involved in the group, a grad student in the English Department at New Mexico State University, in which I was a new instructor, said, "Why don't you write a play and we'll put it on."

I did and they did and my life changed course forever. The collaboration of separate spirits put me in mind of a lifetime of team sports, where the combined efforts of a group of people made for an extraordinary kind of interdependence.

I learned that contemporaries of mine, young playwrights in New York at the beginnings of careers (people named Wilson and Melfi and Sheperd and MacNally), were seeing their early work done at two places called Café Cino and Café La Mama. I wanted my work done in those cafés, but had no idea in a universe before faxes and FedEx and the Internet and instant communication with anyone anywhere in the world how to get my work to whomever one needed to get it to in order to have it considered for production in New York, the capitol of American theatre.

I was in New Mexico, where following the first production of the ten-scene *The Wager*, a young colleague in the English Department at NMSU, said to me, "You have talent, but you can't make it in the American theatre from New Mexico."

I was nothing if not brazen; ignorance of the way the theatre world worked aside, I said, "Oh, yes, I will."

Within a few years, I made my way to a production of *The Wager* at HB Studios in the West Village, thanks to the cousin of my dentist, an aspiring director named Kenneth Frankel, who worked for a Broadway producer named Elliot Martin, who had enough interest in the play to farm it out for a trial run to Herbert Berghof and Uta Hagen, who were in the business not only of training actors but of supporting young, living playwrights.

(Though Ken Frankel lost the directorship of *The Wager*, he did direct my second full-length play, *When You Comin' Back, Red Ryder?*, which was produced at the Circle Repertory Theater, started by the young director Marshall Mason and the aforementioned Wilson [Lanford].)

My wife, Stephanie, and I slept on a friend's floor on 14th Street. With the support of HB Studios, my father and mother, the director Frank Geraci, and four wonderful young actors, my life in the theatre was launched with a maiden experience that was nothing if not the most fun in the history of the world.

When asked then, some forty-plus years later, by Barbara Parisi to contribute to this anthology, I rolodexed through the manuscripts I have in progress to see if any might lend itself to a thirty- or ninety-minute version.

No.

But I have a hard time saying no to people who are doing good things for living writers, as Barbara is. Without a play in mind, I said, "Sure." I was prepping to direct a movie at that time and told Barbara I was really going to be tied up until near the end of the year but would try to get her something by the August deadline.

So I turned myself to a play I began a few years ago, then started over as a novel. The novel is long and covers the Boomer Generation from birth to social security; but I thought there are a couple of threads that happen in the current moment (post-millennium) that might be made into a play of under an hour. I also thought I would surely learn something about my characters by focusing on a small section of the tapestry.

I found, as a respite from prepping the movie, working on the piece I've included here, to be stimulating and relaxing. As I had been ordered by my producing partner to quit screwing around with the movie script (which I wrote), building a one-act play satisfied the daily urge to write something while I waited to get on the movie set and run an army. (Even at near seventy, I need more things to accomplish than I can logically accomplish.)

I remember liking the one-act play—as a writer, a director, an actor. My mentor told me long ago, in my late teens, when I was an aspiring fiction writer, that a short story needed to start in the first line, whereas a novel could begin at a more leisurely pace—a chapter, even two. As a teacher, I've taught my students what my teacher taught me. Often, in teaching playwriting and screenwriting, I limit plays to under an hour and screenplays to ten–fifteen minutes. I marvel at the ability of the best of my students to start briskly and create an event that happens and resolves in a short period of time.

So here are sixteen plays that would be fascinating to see in a series of evenings, perhaps with a company of actors and several directors and one scenic and lighting designer. Let's all meet somewhere—Natchez or Boise or Sacramento or Las Cruces—and settle in with some interested folks for a week or two and put on some shows.

Introduction
by Barbara Parisi

This is my third edition as editor of The Best American Short Plays, and as in the past, it has been an exciting and rewarding process selecting the plays for this edition. Previously, in my introductions, I have explored the concepts of writing one-act plays and themes of one-act plays. In this edition, I have decided to focus on the importance of plot and story development in the creation of characterization in the process of writing a one-act play.

Plot is defined as a narrative storyline of events that create meaning and effect. A story is a chain of events coming from the plot or a series of plots. Aristotle defines plot as the arrangement of the incidents not the story itself but the way the events are presented to the audience, which is the structure of the play. The elements of the plot are: exposition, foreshadowing, inciting force, conflict, rising action, crisis, climax, falling action, resolution (denouement).

The plot and the subject (what the story is about) are not the same. Content is the arrangement of events in the story. The playwright develops a plot by arranging events in his story. The plot expresses the meaning of the work. A plot should be plausible, have elements of surprise, be suspenseful, have foreshadowing and be logical.

Plots develop through characterizations, conflicts with others, and conflict with self. Plots need to create suspense through uncertainty of threats or outcomes. Plots should provide coincidence, mystery, and surprises. A character's problem within a story gets resolved through the plot.

In an article from the *Playwrighting Seminars* edited by Richard Toscan, entitled "Plots: They Come in Pairs," playwright Marsha Norman states: "I used to think that you could just start to write and see what happened. Now I find that if you do that, it doesn't turn out; you may not get anywhere that's interesting. There are drives to plays. Sometimes I think of them as pieces of machinery. With a destination, lots of things come into focus for you as a writer."

Richard Toscan defines a suspense plot as the what-happens-next of a play. He says suspense plots keep the audience with you and justifies the emotional conflict. He believes the suspense plot is to get you as much mileage as you can with very little effort and your energy is to be invested in the emotional plot. Playwright Wendy Wasserstein is quoted in Toscan's series is an article entitled "Emotional Plots":

> I don't write from an outline—I have an idea where the play is going to arc to or land on.... With *The Sisters Rosensweig* I wanted a woman to turn to a man and say, 'I love you like I've never loved anybody,' a woman who's never said this before. That's not in the play, but it's where the play's going.

Toscan believes emotional plots deal with emotional consequences of events, and it is why playwrights do what they do. He believes that physical activity can substitute for suspense plots.

In Richard Toscan's series, in an article "Elevator Plays," he describes playwright Mark Medoff's play *When You Comin' Back, Red Ryder?* as an elevator play. An elevator play can be set anywhere that is isolated and the characters can't leave. Toscan believes this is a good technique to structure a plot. Playwright John Patrick Shanley states: "I'm an emotional writer. I write because I do not want to stay where I am.... It's an uncomfortable place and therefore very powerful."

What drives a playwright to write a moving plot and how do they do it? In developing the plot, a writer must take these steps:

- Identify the main character. Who is the protagonist of the short play?
- Create a thorough physical description of the protagonist. Include in your description how the protagonist responds to situations.
- Define and describe the character of the protagonist. This is a description of how the protagonist thinks; his or her motivation; and how he or she reacts mentally, psychologically, or morally to situations.
- Identify the the antagonist (the character opposed to the protagonist) in your short play.
- Give a thorough physical description of the antagonist.
- Describe the character of the antagonist.
- Briefly describe the main conflict of the short play.
- Briefly summarize the rising action of the short play.
- Identify the climax of the story.
- Briefly summarize the resolution of the conflict.

If you have a subplot, a writer might consider these key steps:

- Briefly describe the characters involved in a subplot in the short play.
- Briefly summarize the conflict, rising action, climax, and resolution of the subplot.
- Would you recommend it or not?

A one-act/short play is the gem of theatre. For many centuries, short plays have been performed in schools, churches, barns, parks, fairs and festivals, and small theatres. In the twentieth century, they were used by amateur performers and not professionals in the theatre. In recent years, with notable playwrights writing short plays, the commercial theatre has professionally produced short plays as evenings of theatre. Through their plots, short plays tap into our beliefs, values, attitudes, anxieties, fears, happiness, joys, hopes, aspirations, and dreams, dramatizing our ever-changing human condition.

For my introduction, I have asked the playwrights to share their plot, theme, and inspiration for writing their one-act play.

Mark Medoff

In *DeBoom: Who Gives This Woman?*, one generation is inevitably superseded by the next. It's difficult and maddening to come to grips with the way life is arranged: we are born, we make myriad mistakes, we die.

The plot of *DeBoom* reveals Geoffrey DeBoom, defrocked film and theatre critic, teaching at the University of New Mexico film school. His estranged wife, Cassandra Rosenblum DeBoom, is a research professor 200 miles away at New Mexico State University. Cass informs Geoffrey that their daughter Maxine has become engaged and is arriving in Las Cruces with her affianced that evening. Geoffrey flies to Las Cruces, remembering and bridling. He has a great deal of difficulty coming to grips with what he perceives as the loss of his daughter to another—and unworthy—man.

Amelia Arenas

The five monologues in *And Then* stem from one question: is it possible to empathize with a character who has done the unthinkable? The ancient Greeks did more than that: they *sympathized* with some characters that we would consider monsters. That's the case with Medea.

Indeed, Euripides' *Medea* is a catalogue of horrors. It is also the first literary attempt to look into the mind of someone who has broken the most sacred human laws. Maddened by love for Jason, a Greek hero, Medea, a barbarian princess, steals her land's sacred treasure, the Golden Fleece, murders her brother, and escapes with her lover. For years, Medea follows Jason in his adventures—a woman among men. She also bears him two sons. But Jason's plans change: he abandons Medea and takes a new bride. And here's where Euripides picks up the story: Medea begs Jason to come back to her but he scorns her. So, exiled, humiliated, a hated foreigner, she murders Jason's bride, then the girl's father, and, finally, her own children.

Reading Euripides' version of Medea's story one has the keen sense of what it must be like to fall prey to mad love, cultural alienation, tormenting guilt, bitter solitude, and the lust for revenge. But Euripides offers no apology for his heroine—not even an analysis of her motivations. Instead, he invites us to walk into her chilling shadow.

And Then is a modest homage to a keen psychologist and to a man profoundly curious about women—a writer unafraid to delve into the darkest human emotions without trying to explain them, and who imagined and conveyed his characters' experiences with breathtaking specificity.

The monologues in *And Then* were inspired by real people whose lives, as the title suggests, took a sudden, apparently unexpected turn. But they're not portraits; rather, they are an effort to witness through the experience of five contemporary women aspects of Euripides' legendary heroine that still haunt us.

Hanadi is a twenty-eight-year old Palestinian lawyer who decides to blow herself up along with twenty-two strangers in a Haifa restaurant. Mary Kay is a sixth-grade teacher who falls madly in love with one of her students. Lynndie is a young American soldier who becomes a torturer in the notorious Abu Ghraib prison. Susan is a young housewife who drives her car into a lake and watches her two children drown. Leonora is a rich, middle-aged woman tormented by jealousy and solitude, who plots the most self-destructive kind of revenge: a suicide that will look like murder.

Zilvinas Jonusas

Homophobia and suicide are the main themes of the play. I've lost too many friends to homophobia. With this play I want to remind the public that homophobia still exists.

The plot of *The Cleaning* reveals Vlad—also called Josef K.—who receives a strange message under his door. He brings this message to an unknown place. Suddenly he is caught in a spotlight and "The Voice" starts asking him questions. The witness Leni is called. Josef K. knows Leni as well as Leni knows Josef K. She says that Josef K. should be punished because he is a homosexual. Leni's accusation triggers Josef K.'s memory. He confesses why he was not able to give Leni her biggest wish in life, a child. Leni is not convinced, but it is too late. The decision by Josef K. has already been made. Leni finds scattered pages of Josef K.'s paper that he brought with him. She thinks that she will find the answer in the papers, but... her accusation is her punishment. Leni is asked to return the next day.

Amy Fox

Breakfast and Bed was inspired by an experience of a friend of mine. In a spirit of experimentation, my friend, who considered herself straight, went home with a young woman she met at a party. She woke up the next morning seemingly alone in a strange apartment, only to encounter a "roommate"— the mother of the woman she had picked up. This struck me as a dramatic situation worth exploring in a short play. I was curious about the potential interaction between these characters—a thirty-something woman freely exploring her sexuality crossing paths with a slightly older woman whose life has been more prescribed. The play gave me an opportunity to consider the ways in which our beliefs about sexuality have become more flexible, and how that might create both pressure and opportunities for women of two different generations.

Rich Orloff

When asked to discuss the theme and message of *The News from St. Petersburg*, I must confess my first response is: DO I HAVE TO?!!! I'd much rather write a play than write *about* a play. Especially *meaning*. My goal is to take an audience for a ride, not to make them think. If they enjoy the wit and are engaged by the characters and story, I'm satisfied. Delighted. Thrilled!

In *The News from St. Petersburg*, set in 1905 Russia, an aristocratic couple, their servant, and their doctor all have intense responses to a rumor of a people's revolution ending the Tsarist republic of Russia. When I wrote the play, I was inspired both by a desire to parody Chekhov's plays and characters (and those deliciously long Russian names) and by reading about the Bloody Sunday massacre in St. Petersburg. (Sasha's speech on the subject is historically accurate.) As humans, we often desperately cling to the status quo, refusing to acknowledge that change is inevitable. No wonder history continues to surprise us.

Wait a second, did I just reveal a message? I swear, it was an accident! It took umpteen drafts and several readings and productions just to get the jokes right. Okay, *maybe* there's a theme in the play, but *pleeeze* don't tell anyone. I'd rather folks discover it on their own. When they're not busy laughing, that is.

Scott Klavan

In *Double Murder*, a couple is trying to poison each other but the fundamental parts of their characters get in the way. The man's diffidence, the woman's assertiveness stops them just at the point of fatal success. The reason their marriage doesn't work is the reason they can't end it. At sea, in need, they shift roles and personality traits. The confident woman gets support, the inept man gains confidence. The result is a congenial atmosphere, a brief emergence of affection. But in celebrating, drinking their health, they kill themselves. An accident, on purpose? Victory or defeat? Modern men and women, in conflict with each other, and within themselves, fumble through love—and murder.

Jeni Mahoney

Running in Circles Screaming was really inspired by a period of my own life in which, for a variety of reasons, I found myself on the butt-end of people's careless remarks; I knew they weren't trying to hurt me, but it hurt nonetheless. The more I experienced this, the more I realized how common it was, and the more I realized I was probably as guilty of doing it as anybody else.

In the play, two women, Lou (Louise) and Heather, meet on the playground: watching the kids, sharing stories of mommy-hood and the workings of the universe, but when Heather shares her disappointment in having a boy rather than a girl, Lou turns out not to be the soul sister she was looking for. Heather ends up leaving the playground miffed and snubbed, never knowing that her new friend Lou isn't a fellow mommy at all, but she wishes desperately that she were.

When I first started writing the play, I wrote it very much from Lou's point of view. She just wants to be at the playground like any other mom: she wants to belong. But as time went on, I really came to have compassion for Heather as well. She is just as invested in her disappointment as Lou is in hers. Heather is like a lot of people (people we all know, I suspect) who very easily fall into seemingly harmless, though vaguely judgmental, chit-chat as some form of, as Heather puts it, "being friendly."

As much as this is a play about people who are struggling with disappointment, I don't think it's a sad play. All of these people come to the playground to enjoy themselves: to feel alive, to share, to laugh, to play. I think if I had to name one thing that I wanted an audience to take away from *Running in Circles Screaming*, it is the feeling they have in that moment of realizing what Lou is doing at the playground.

Peter Maloney

Here is a brief description of *Witness*.

I: The actor sets out early one morning for an audition. Emerging from the subway, he wonders at the black smoke streaming from a hole in one of the city's two tallest buildings. He continues on to the casting office, but when no other actors show up, the audition (for Bud Lite) is cancelled. Returning to the street, the actor sees that where minutes ago there were two towers, now there is only one. He watches, with the gathering crowd, as that building collapses...straight...down...in slow-motion. Broken glass sparkles in the bright air like confetti in a snow globe. The actor is reminded of a scene in an action film. Déjà vu.

II: As in another film, a neighbor of the actor tells of being abducted by aliens in the middle of the night. Of being lifted from his Upper West Side block in a spaceship. Of being subjected to humiliating examination by beings from another world. The actor asks why other residents of the block failed to hear the spaceship as it arrived and left, and the abductee, a responsible composer of popular music, declares: "Oh, you *heard* it, but you *forgot* you heard it."

III: The owner of a video store in Baghdad is swept up by American soldiers, imprisoned at Abu Ghraib, and subjected to months of physical and mental abuse. He is unable, because of his deep shame, to speak about what has happened to him. Needing, desperately, to speak of it, he finds a way to do so through the prism of his passion: American movies.

IV: In his essay "*Shahadah*," (Witnessing), Victor Danner explicates a statement of the Prophet Muhammad, saying: "The created Universal Spirit is the luminous center of the entire creation, which then issues from its central point like rays of light moving in different directions. One of those rays of light intersects with the plane of man's soul, in the innermost heart."

V: Taking refuge in madness, Kasim constructs an alternate reality in which his captors' intrusive light, the light-ladder from Spielberg's mother ship, and the Prophet's "luminous center of creation" are all one.

Lauren Feldman

The theme of *Asteroid Belt* reveals a college student and her parents grappling with fate's challenge of time and space. Although I think there could be others. The plot takes us through that journey.

I wrote this play when I was young and scared and figuring out the world and my place in it—and I was thinking about mortality and the desire to be known, to have mattered. What I like about this piece is how intimate and intense the speaker's relationship is to the audience; how much they are genuinely needed. Also, it was my first play.

Liliana Almendarez

Glass Knives was inspired by college life and how students, when they are away from home for the first time, find freedom. However, how does that freedom translate when that student goes home? This piece was inspired by many different stories from my undergraduate days at SUNY Oswego. Up until I wrote this piece, I had been writing short comedy skits. This was the first impulse to write a longer piece that had both humor and heart to it.

In *Glass Knives*, a student goes home after one semester of college. She finds it difficult to re-acclimate to her home environment after being on her own for the first time. Daughter and family struggle to find some middle ground in order to relate to one another once again.

Adam Kraar

Hearts and Minds was in part inspired by my work over the past six years teaching acting and speech at the NY Institute of Technology, which has students from virtually every continent of the world. I'm fascinated by the complex mix of cross-cultural misunderstandings, clashes, and connections. I love the students' bone-deep decency, and am gripped when I see this decency smash up against their ambitions and fears.

In *Hearts and Minds*, an idealistic speech teacher strives to touch the conscience of a relentlessly practical student from Russia, by getting him to empathize with other students. Teacher and student end up educating each other about what they are willing to sacrifice for their values.

I hope the play will provoke audiences to see the contradictions involved in pursuing the American dream, including the strange and sometimes comical collisions of high ideals and huge ambitions.

Julie Rae (Pratt) Mollenkamp

The themes in *In Conclusive Woman* are truth, perseverance, survival.

The plot takes us on a journey with award-winning artist/teacher Julie Rae through the contemporary cultural whirlwind of relationships and power, women and men, subject and object, love and chaos, as she reveals the life of a sexual survivor, fat chick, momma's child, beloved teacher, abandoned wife, failed mother, surgical crash test dummy, fabulous post-forty party girl, and twenty-first-century semi-wise woman.

My inspiration is how telling our secrets allows us to grow and find peace despite the painful and life-changing events that happen to each of us. The decision to love the scars of our past makes for a significantly more joyous and satisfying life experience. "It's not the shit that happens to you; it's how you choose to deal with it."

Mike Pasternack

The theme of *Mixed MeSSages* is that nothing is black and white; everything is shades of gray, and things are never what they seem to be on the surface.

The plot takes place in World War II, during the Battle of the Bulge, with an American soldier having a series of particularly bad experiences. He is wounded, left for dead, and then almost executed by his own countrymen. Later, he finds himself in the middle of the infamous Malmédy massacre, but survives and seeks refuge in a farmhouse. While there, he is treated by a German medic in the SS. The two men soon learn they have more in common than one might first believe.

My inspiration stems as a tribute to my deceased father, a decorated World War II veteran. I used a few of his war stories as a basis. Some of the events in the play actually happened to my father during the war. I also wanted to debunk some of the stereotypes associated with the era (German medics did defy orders and aid wounded Allies) and give the whole thing a *Twilight Zone*–ish twist. Through this and other writings, I keep my father alive.

Victor Gluck

My inspiration for *Amouresque* and *Arabesque* was when I first read Anthony Hope's short story "Love's Conundrum" in one of Thomas Costain's *Stories to Remember* collections. I immediately saw it as a play. I adapted it for the stage as *Amouresque*, "an Edwardian comedy of courtship," and left it in the drawer for three decades, figuring it was too short to be of any use. When Francine L. Trevens chose to direct it as part of a Lunchtime one-act play festival, she called me and said, "Are you going to write a companion play or do I have to find something?" I immediately came down with bronchitis and was ordered to stay home from work for a week by my doctor. With the time cleared on my calendar, I went back to the original collection of Anthony Hope short stories I had located and found another story that could take place on the same set. In six days I had adapted this as *Arabesque*. At one time I considered making it part of a trilogy. When I told Francine, she said, "Don't tell me you would call it *Humoresque*!" which discouraged me from continuing with the idea.

I have always thought that I would have been happiest in the Edwardian era, that last time period of gracious manners and elegant living. Of course, one would have had to be well off in those days to have enjoyed that time period. Although the original Anthony Hope stories are set in Britain, I reset them in Massachusetts, probably under the influence of the novels of Edith Wharton and her summer home, the Mount, located in the Berkshires, where she often entertained her good friend Henry James. In *Arabesque*, the relationship between Julian Lowell and Audrey Liston is intended as a parody of James and Wharton.

As to the theme or message of the plays, I think Shakespeare said it best in *A Midsummer Night's Dream*: "The course of true love never did run smooth." In addition, I believe that in love, most people do not know their own best interests. My father, who was a psychologist, brought me up on the theory that most people end up with what they most want. Set in 1907, *Amouresque* and *Arabesque* are both comedies of courtship that take place during the same weekend at Margaret Hudson's country house not far from Cambridge, Massachusetts. In *Amouresque*, a young girl has fallen in love with an absentminded philosophy professor who teaches at a men's college and who is too involved in his studies to notice her. She attempts to awaken his interest by offering him a philosophical proposition to solve. Typical of his thinking, he deals with it just as he would one of his classroom cases.

In *Arabesque*, during the same weekend at Mrs. Hudson's, another guest is bestselling, self-styled "authoress" Audrey Liston, who writes romantic fiction (unlike Mrs. Wharton). She is immediately attracted to Gerald Gardiner, a handsome, athletic scion of a leading Boston family. He, however, is pursuing a flighty, self-willed debutante, who is leading him on a merry chase. Audrey's friend, Julian Lowell, a cousin of Mrs. Hudson, watches amusedly from the sidelines while Audrey pretends that she wants Gerald's help on her new novel in order to pique his interest in her. Julian, a writer of serious work for a limited audience, and more than a little jealous of her enormous success, steps out of character long enough to warn Gerald that Audrey takes her characters from life, but after that Gerald is on his own. I have written two additional Edwardian comedies of courtship, which under the umbrella title *Weekends in the Country* make up a full evening in the theatre. These two plays, *Come Kiss Me, Sweet and Twenty* and *Love Before Breakfast*, share the same hero and can also be performed on the same set.

Jules Tasca

The impetus for creating *The Birth of Theater* began when it occurred to me that many people are unaware that theatre did not begin with the Abydos passion plays of ancient Egypt or the complex works of fifth-century BCE Greek playwrights.

Theatre began when humanity began. It has its roots in the mimetic urges that are part of our species. When I was a college student, I was told that it is a conjecture that theatre commenced with the imitation of the hunt for the tribal members who, because of youth or old age or gender, could not participate in the most dangerous and exciting activity of the primitive world.

Since that "conjecture" was taught, anthropologists have discovered in tribes that had never had any contact with our modern world—for example, certain tribes in New Guinea—the old conjectures were accurate. Groups were found doing exactly this: with masks and costumes and spears, they put on plays that re-created what hunting parties experienced when they left the safety of their villages to bring fresh meat to their families.

In the conceit of the play, I tried to capture, in their nascent state, the advent of what an actor feels, what a director does, and what a theatrical ensemble experiences. These ancient forbearers of today's theatre artists created an art form that has evolved into the theatre of today. I'd hoped that this short play would give them a small measure of thanks.

The Best American Short Plays

2006–2007

DeBoom: Who Gives This Woman?

Mark Medoff

Mark Medoff

Mark Medoff is a playwright, screenwriter, and director. He received a Tony Award for *Children of a Lesser God*, as well as London's Olivier Award for Best Play. He was nominated for an Academy Award and a Writers Guild of America Best Adapted Screenplay Award for the film script of *Children* and for a Cable ACE Award for his HBO Premiere movie, *Apology*. He received an OBIE Award for *When You Comin' Back, Red Ryder?*

Among his movies are *Clara's Heart*, *Off Beat*, and *City of Joy*. Medoff directed and co-produced the documentary film, *Who Fly on Angels' Wings* (2000), and directed the feature film, *Children on Their Birthdays* (2001), based on the story by Truman Capote. Among other awards, it received the Houston World Film Festival Award for Best Family Film. In 2006, he directed the short film *100 MPG*, and, in 2007, he directed *Boom*, a training film for the military. This summer, he directed the feature film *Refuge*, which he wrote from a story by Phil Treon and him.

His latest play, *Prymate*, ran briefly on Broadway in 2005. Most recently, he directed the new musical *Extinction: A Love Story* by Bob Diven and *The Men of Mah Jongg*, a new play by Richard Atkins, that ran at New York City's Queens Theater in the Park in December 2008.

Medoff has also written one novel, *Dreams of Long Lasting*, and has received many academic honors. He was Reynolds Eminent Scholar in the School of Theatre at Florida State University, 2003–2006. He is now distinguished lecturer in playwriting at the University of Houston and artistic director of the Creative Media Institute for Film and Digital Arts at New Mexico State University. He formerly taught at NMSU for twenty-seven years and was co-founder and artistic director of the American Southwest Theatre Company and head of the Department of Theatre Arts for nine years.

In 1974, he received NMSU's highest faculty honor, the Westafer Award. In 1980, he was honored with the Governor's Award for Excellence in the Arts, New Mexico's most prestigious artistic honor. In 2005, he received The Kennedy Center Medallion for Excellence in Education and Artistic Achievement.

3

• • •

[GEOFFREY DEBOOM, *61, alone onstage, speaks to us.*]

DEBOOM   Used to be I slept six hours and erupted into the day, my mind as febrile at the moment of tremulous waking as it would be in the epicenter of the day's quakes.

Now, I sleep and wake and sleep eight, nine, ten hours and have no desire to get out of bed except for the middle-of-the-night urination—and then only for the sake of my decaying kidneys (27% function last test)—the lack of desire to rise and go forth abetted, no doubt, by the fact that I have nothing to look forward to, or to be fair—not that fair is of much interest to me anymore—that I look forward to nothing.

I roll off the Posture Pedic so as not to precipitate a back spasm that would put me back to bed for a couple of weeks, forced to choose among self-analysis, pop books, bad music, or, worse, movies.

So, I would rather go to the university than stay home. Thus, mobility, such as it is, has value.

I engineer the four-step journey across carpet into the bathroom, favoring the titanium and plastic right knee over the left one with its shards of chipped bone and cartilage roaming the joint like Rice Krispies through molasses.

Load my toothbrush with whitening paste and crane myself toward the toilet with stiff arms on the seat, dropping lead-like the last few inches as my arms give out to gravity.

Avoid the mirror. Pee lefty, brush righty.

Wait for my indolent bladder to drain. Pee, squeeze, squirt, squeeze, sit, wait, wait, dribble, squeeze, squirt.

I stopped frequenting the student bathroom down the hall from my garret in favor of a trek to the faculty lav several corridors over, following a whiz between two undergrads who imagined life would always be thus, their bladders emptying in a tsunami of malted urine.

They left me chained to the urinal like Prometheus, long after they'd zipped, washed (one of them), exited (lunch, ball game, sexual encounter?), while I stood and sprinkled and spritzed for a couple of hours, guilty of what wisdom has taught is mankind's most egregious sin: growing old.

I drive off the toilet on a silent "Hut!," aware that no matter how many last little squeezes I exert on my prostate, before I am upright my penis will emit a last squirt that will saturate a quarter size circle in the crotch of my Jockeys. (Tip: black underwear.)

Limp the road of life now with wet pants. On a panel at a civil rights conference last year on the failure of the movie industry to do much about diversity (and in a superficial effort at disclosure—not there as a supporter of affirmative action, political correctness, or the glories of the melting pot; I was there to say the industry was not a moral conglomerate but a financial one that didn't care about diversity unless it paid in dollars). Wearing cream-colored Zanellas. Knew, following the pre-speech safety whiz, I'd spritz a 25-cent piece right before taking the stage. Wore a Kotex Mini Pad.

Diapers pretty soon.

Rinse toothpaste—two cupped palms of water, left above right—always two, going back to age eight and the onset of compulsive behavior: Save the family, give thanks to a benevolent Savior, request not to die young. Shake out the toothbrush, restore it to its place in the receptacle next to Cass's unused, firm Oral B.

I had figured in twisted Cartesean fashion: She has a toothbrush at my condo; therefore, she'll come back to me.

Must tackle my image in the mirror (daily query delivered to no one but me: What is my father doing in there?) and resist with the modicum of self-control still available the desire to smash my head through glass, plaster board, and studs to the outdoors.

Imagine my father's and my communal head, connected by a tendon or two, yo-yoing from the second floor.

Next, a moment's loathing of the once sculpted but now flaccid pecs (pubescent breasts, really), the reedy biceps, their rippling, dry overskin like stretched, faux snake skin, the leavened baguette in the midriff that defies the hundreds of crunches I do daily.

My eyes drop to the ellipse-shaped pouches under my eyes that don't go away since squirrels started depositing their nuts there a decade back. Not tiredness, according to a woman at a book signing, she with parchment skin stretched like loomed silk over the front of her skull and tacked behind her ears, but, she whispered so that only the first five or so in line behind her could hear, the walnuts are just fat deposits which can be removed in an hour operation in a doctor's office.

Tropical forests of hair festoon along the helix, tragus, lobe of my ears, sprout like roach antennae from the tip of my nose. Every two weeks, with tweezers, I stand here wearing my reading glasses and pluck the antennae black filament by black filament, each pluck sending through my neural network a little electrical reminder of my putrefaction.

There is the hair on my head that only recently began thinning on top and receding into my temples. Good chance death will beat baldness.

The human body, helpless to resist, humiliates the living thing that was itself.

I have contemplated suicide a thousand, ten thousand times. I have stood on three separate Saturday afternoons at Barnes & Noble and perused the periodically updated tome that details for do-it-yourself sorts the best ways to get it done.

Tell myself I can't kill myself because of Cass and Maxine.

[*Dr./Professor* CASS ROSENBLUM-DEBOOM, *60.*]

CASS   Everybody's depressed, Geoffrey. Don't you think I have periods of depression?

DEBOOM   Of course, but mine isn't a period, mine is always, mine is unique in the world.

CASS   Geoffrey, is there none of your peculiarities that you can't romanticize?

DEBOOM   You're the geneticist who beat into me that we have different chemistries.

CASS   Why can't we just be mature and admit we've lost interest in each other and decide whether we can stand knowing that.

DEBOOM   [*To us.*] My life insurance might not pay off, as if that's an issue, since my daughter is rich and can take care of her mother, whether she wins a Nobel Prize or not, if she lives another hundred years.

But I know, though once unafraid if not brave, I am a coward now and don't have the guts.

A Southern Baptist gone public atheist, I am a closet Catholic. I fear there's a hell to which I'll be assigned for eternity with all the other perfidious misanthropes who set themselves up as judges of mass culture.

Terror keeps me alive, witness to my deterioration.

Dressed, deodorized, pomaded, I limp to the kitchen, listing to port, the left leg three-eights of an inch shorter than the right since the right knee was replaced with plastic and titanium. At the out-of-fashion tile counter I commence the ceremony of the pills. Seven supplements shipped via UPS once a month from a distributor in Dallas, then the replacement for the pill for arthritis that was destroying my kidneys and the one for high blood pressure followed by the one for the hyperthyroidism that is trying to keep the kidney function I have at its current short-of-dialysis level.

Skip the antidepressant for the eighteenth straight day.

I turn on my computer. Download e-mail. There are nineteen. Several from students with work attached; the *New York Times*; "Truthout," a Web site I use to keep track of liberal—pardon me, progressive—bullcrap; one from Max ("I need to talk to you, but we have to leave for the airport."), a couple of ads, three reminders of meetings at the Film School, two of which I'll duck though I've confirmed I'll attend.

Responding to e-mail has become my substitute for writing reviews, the thing I did for a living several times a week for thirty years, or writing the copy for my TV show, which I did for a decade and a half. I drag it out, to minimize the guilt of not working on the column I still write monthly for *Esquire*, until I can go to school but not be there so long that I'm bored or have to talk to people I don't want to talk to—which takes in pretty much everyone there. The phone rings at seven forty-two. I have no message, just the "beep."

CASS At least put a message on there that pleads for people not to leave a message. The silence is so infantile. I know you're there. Pick up.

DEBOOM Is Max all right?

CASS Maxine is fine. So am I—thanks for asking.

DEBOOM Sorry—you all right?

CASS Can you come down for the weekend?

DEBOOM Why?

CASS Maxine is flying in with her fiancé.

DEBOOM Her...

CASS Right.

DEBOOM When did—

CASS Last Saturday.

DEBOOM She told you last Saturday?

CASS She told me last night. He proposed last Saturday. She thought it best I convey the information to you.

DEBOOM Not a tennis player with a GED.

CASS She wants us to meet him together.

DEBOOM Just tell me whether he's some halfwit tennis—

CASS She didn't tell me. Don't drive that asinine car. Fly. But I can't pick you up. Rent a car. Stay at the Ramada, which used to be the Holiday Inn by the I-10 at University Avenue.

[CASS *hangs up.*]

DEBOOM   [*To us.*] Dial Max. [*Message: "It's Max." Beep.*] Max, it's Dad. So, congratulations. Call me if you have a long layover in Chicago. Or... I'll see you tonight. Your daddy loves you.

Yeah, yeah: Inevitable one day. Not that I see her often anymore. Those days are gone to the memory bin to be glorified and revised, in my feckless state, beyond all reality. She has a life apart from her daddy, as Daddy has from Mom.

Waiting in the security line to half undress—shoes, belt, jacket—and then to be wanded and patted down like pie dough because my prosthetic knee will set off the alarm, I check messages, hoping to get some kind of appetizer from Max.

[*He dials* MAX *again. "It's Max." Beep.*]

Dad again. I'm about to get on my flight. Thought I might catch you. Remembering the winery kid—is it him?

[MAXINE DEBOOM, *20s, tall, lithe, a professional athlete.*]

MAX   So he brought a gift! Mom, whatever they bring or don't, material or personal, you drive off everybody I bring.

CASS   All I said was I've been to that winery and they have a unique fermenting method.

MAX   Mom! I don't care! Somebody asks a question, how 'bout just don't answer once in a while! Fermentation, for godsake! Or politely suggest they find out for themselves. They're not asking you because they want to know; they're scared shitless because you know everything about everything and Dad stands there, towering over the earth like a monolith, scaring the crap out of them by his existence, and between the two of you, I'll never have a relationship with anyone but the two of you.

DEBOOM   You called your mom first—it's okay. See you tonight. Your daddy loves you.

[*To us.*]

First class is sold out, no upgrade, even after I opt for the craven ruse of cooperating with the desk jockey to figure out why I look familiar to her.

[*To the desk jockey.*]

I have a TV program about movies called *The DeBoomer Generation.*

I wait to board last. Fester past the fortunate eight who fill the spacious elite seats with their smug complacence toward me, hunched like Quasimoto, trudging as if I were in ankle shackles to the back of the plane, where I'll be crammed in three abreast with insufficient room for my failing body parts.

At my row will be a colossus who runneth over into my narrow tract, affording me the opportunity to make a memorable scene that I can leak to *Entertainment Tonight*. Flight attendant, didn't I hear there's a flab limit per passenger now? Why isn't this mastadon paying for two seats?

I have an aisle seat. There is no one in the middle. I have nothing to bitch about. My feelings are mixed.

Nothing is pure, I wrote about *East of Eden* after a festival of Steinbeck's books-into-movies in the late '80s, which I left renewed, with almost boyish confidence in my ideals, what I could do that others before me could not—of course could not, they were not me! I could define filmic art the way Lionel Trilling and Alfred Kazan had defined modern literature!

"Nothing is pure, but the film version of this novel brings us a confluence of words with actors, screenwriter, director, cinematographer, editor, composer that overwhelmed me anew by the complexity, the Aristotelian tractability of life made into art about life intractable."

And, yes, I can quote myself by heart if I have written it down.

Celebrity! From the Latin "to celebrate," as in: We celebrate them for no reason on earth other than our own pathetic lack of substance.

"You resent the wealth of the people you review," Stallone accused me following my review of the unspeakable *Rambo: First Blood Part II* (1985). So withering—and accurate—was my appraisal that it remains a film school staple, trotted out in countless film analysis classes the world over as "a perfect example," as one lily white professor at the University of Utah once wrote, "of calling a spade a spade."

Yes, Sylvester, I resent your wealth, your celebrity, your promiscuity, and your unearned political standing, but none of that has anything to do with the fact that you're an execrable actor in an excremental movie.

I had written: "The deceit in the conceit of an American avenger with steroid pecks, lathered in olive oil, wearing an undulating pubic wig, revising the abject failure of my nation in Vietnam made me laugh, made me sick. The actor wrote the script himself. For himself. It is a masturbatory exegesis on post-Vietnam American male impotence."

The review was the first time the *Daily News* had used symbols in its pages to mask someone's use of a perceived profanity. The closing sentence of my review: "Shame on the egregious makers of this propagandist, populist s***. We lost a war we should have won when we actually fought it."

My editor urged me to change "shit" to "excrement," a variant on excremental, which I had used above, but I insisted that was too polite a word and that I would accept the "s" followed by three *.

I realized at some point—an incremental understanding—that I despised the male of the species and that there was no word for it. There is misanthropy and misogyny for hatred of mankind and of women, but nothing to denote one's loathing of men, per se. Manthropy lacks the musicality of the other two.

In the early eighties, I was feminized by Cassandra Rosenblum-DeBoom and began to write respectfully of women. Streep, MacLaine, Pfeiffer. Even a kind piece after *The Witches of Eastwick* about Cher Bono, though I couldn't resist a riff on her competition with Michael Jackson in the torture of the flesh department. I was the first to point out that Nicole Kidman had the talent to be way more than the girlfriend of the modestly talented, big of nose and small of stature Tom Cruise.

Cass loved Cruise and thought less of Kidman, accusing me of favoring Kidman because she was the doppelganger of the six-foot, linear, curly-haired, monster-forehanded Maxine Abigail DeBoom.

Directors, producers, studio executives (virtually all men in my formative years) hated me for my perceived bias against their gender (and the gender virtually always at the center of their movies). I gained vigor from their united enmity.

My paper and network were threatened over the years with 162 lawsuits for libel (spoken) and slander (written). None ever went to trial. And none was settled out of court with cash. Only twice did people come after me physically. In the first case—Bruce Willis—a gaggle of bodyguards intervened before I squashed his nuts into canned peas. In the second case, I slammed Brian DePalma (whom I had decreed the worst director of the half century, either half), into an upholstered easy chair at a crowded Bar Mitzvah reception and told him I'd rip out his leftover hair, follicle by follicle, if he said one more pompous, self-serving, historically inaccurate word about his place in the canon of moving pictures. This incompetence had just razed Tom Wolfe's *Bonfire of the Vanities* (a book I admired and had said so, adding in the finale of the piece that Wolfe was the only writer I considered as intelligently acerbic as I, calling down a torrent of offended blather from the proletariat and snarly rebuke from lovers of the vituperative John Simon).

A while ago.

[CASS *sits at her desk, in her office.*]

Cassandra Rosenblum's door is open, her back to me.

She sips water from a quart plastic jug, from the springs at Evian (rumored to me by Nora Ephron to be mined from a faucet in a dollar store a few miles from Évian-les-Bains, on the south shore of Lake Geneva).

[*To* CASS.]

Dr. Rosenblum, I'd like to help you discover the cure for the common cold.

[CASS *finishes the sentence she's writing, clicks the pen to retract the point. She wears reading glasses. She rises, failing—or not bothering—to take her eyes off her blotter and whatever is written on the laptop there, then looks where she plans to walk for obstructions, then makes the four-step journey to where he waits, finally looking at him as she arrives. Embraces him as one might a telephone pole guaranteed to impart splinters.*]

Why aren't we together? Yes, I know: I made you stop smiling when you went to bed.

CASS   Thank you for coming, Geoffrey.

DEBOOM   Jesus, you got a face-lift.

CASS   Don't be ridiculous. Why, do I look good?

DEBOOM   You look so good that I know you got a face-lift.

CASS   And you let your hair go gray.

DEBOOM   Never could get that Just for Men a consistent shade of Troy Donohue blond.

CASS   Because you were in too big a hurry to do it right. I still can't get some of the stains off my bathroom tile.

DEBOOM   It took too long to do it right. I only did it because you didn't like it gray.

CASS   You looked sallow. Like now.

DEBOOM   Lift looks good—only noticeable enough to be noticeable by someone who stared at you a lot.

CASS   Nutrition and exercise.

DEBOOM   You hate exercise and nutrition doesn't do that. You have scars across the top of your skull?

CASS   I have a scar from my service in the Army of Israel. They don't do face-lifts that way anymore.

DEBOOM   How do they do them?

CASS   No idea.

DEBOOM   Then how do you know what they don't do anymore?

CASS   Everybody knows that.

DEBOOM You look damn good for your age, and pretty passable for any age over fourteen.

CASS Let's leave it at that.

DEBOOM "I know every etched line, watched each evolve in the irregular weather of our long relationship." That was a good sentence.

CASS You were still in love with me then, ten years, or faking it well for your readership.

DEBOOM I never faked my feelings for you.

CASS Oh, Geoffrey.

DEBOOM So, in spite of everything we've told her and everything to which she has borne witness: engaged, you think it's a tennis player? Some of them are heterosexual, right?

CASS I think you're thinking of figure skaters; seems to me, all the boy tennis players are hetero.

DEBOOM They'll only be in the same city for the four majors.

CASS They're renting a car.

DEBOOM Not some halfwit to hurt us?

CASS If you think, Geoffrey, how many times has she hurt you intentionally, ever in her life?

DEBOOM I kept a list.
[*Reads his open palm.*]
None. Maybe it's time.

CASS If they're on time, figuring luggage, the car, El Paso traffic, they'll be here for dinner. So, how about, maybe come at seven or a little later, not earlier, I won't be out of here till—

DEBOOM Where do you live?
She presses a lime Post-It note to my chest.
Cass hefts her briefcase. To my knowledge, she has never been late for a class. Conversely, she has never been on time for

anything else. She is the only person in my life I cannot imagine living without, though I am, and time grows shorter by a handful of seconds even as I speak the thought.

I watch half of me echo up a flight of stairs. Disappear, though her footfalls stay.

When I thought I could be a father, I wanted a jock, so wished, with predictable superficiality, a son. Came Maxine.

I put a racquet in her hand at twenty months. Before she was two, she could swing from both sides and even occasionally lay strings on a bounced ball from me, several feet away, on my knees. I committed myself to the future I wished for her, in part to battle an instinct that said if I didn't, I would live a life of suppurating and suffocating insularity and self-indulgence. By the time Maxine might have rebelled, she was too good at the sport and our friendship was too fierce for her not to chase my dream of her Immortality.

King. Evert. Graf. Navratilova. Venus and Serena. Bean Dip DeBoom.

When she was in junior high and high school in Manhattan, I went to the movies and wrote my reviews in the morning so I could be waiting outside her school at 3:45, armed with a ball bag and a stack of racquets.

[*To* MAXINE.]

Let me go with you.

MAX   Where?

DEBOOM   Follow you, tournament to tournament. I'll be quiet.

MAX   You have a newspaper column and a TV show.

DEBOOM   I'll quit. Let me coach you again.

MAX   Daddy, I have a coach. And an agent.

DEBOOM   And a nutritionist.

MAX   And a fitness trainer, right, yes.

DEBOOM   I could be all in one. No entourage. More cost effective.

MAX   Do you know how boring it would be to follow me?

DEBOOM   Oh, sure.

MAX   Do you?

DEBOOM   No.
[*To us.*]
In the exercise room of the Ramada Resort and Spa, *Thelma and Louise* is on Turner Classics. I turn it off. I had torn the movie apart—standard male movie with women playing the men. I got on the cross trainer and started skiing to nowhere.

MAX   Daddy, if you hate the movies so much, why'd you stop writing theater reviews?

DEBOOM   We will do anything to become celebrities, my darling. We don't care how we get there; we just want to be large and will adjust our morals and principles to fit the demands of the geography.

MAX   So they offered you movies as a reward and you stopped writing about the theater?

DEBOOM   You're being disingenuous, Maxine. I think you know why I stopped writing theater reviews.

MAX   Just wondered if it was the truth.

DEBOOM   If what was the truth?

MAX   That you wrote a piece for some conservative magazine—

DEBOOM   *Commentary*—

MAX   Yeah, that said masculinity was gone from the New York theater because most of the actors playing heterosexual men were homosexuals who weren't good enough actors not to seem gay.

DEBOOM   They couldn't fire me for that or they would have had a First Amendment problem. The First Amendment of the Constitution says—

MAX   Daddy, I'm in high school.

DEBOOM   Shortly after that piece appeared in *Commentary*, I wrote a rave of an Off-Broadway drama chockablock with heterosexuals. On the back of my review, the producers moved the play to Broadway at great expense. I re-reviewed the play and wrote that I couldn't imagine what had impressed me the first time—it was an entirely ordinary play. The play closed after sixteen performances. My editor took that opportunity to take me off the theater. He said they didn't want the same critic reviewing theater and film. And movies were less holy at the time.

MAX   You helped to make them holy.

DEBOOM   I wasn't promoting the sanctity of film but of DeBoom.

MAX   It wasn't your fault that we're nuts for film and not so crazy about literature anymore. And is that so terrible? I mean, promoting the sanctity of yourself in whatever you do? Have you ever known anyone who was, whatever the word would be, selfless, unselfish?

DEBOOM   Your mother—the closest.

MAX   Really?

DEBOOM   Oh yeah.

MAX   But you could say her need to be unselfish is a sickness and her need to be selfless is just as bad as—

DEBOOM   Max. You're sixteen, you can cut the competitive crap with your mother. You can trust her with your one and only life.

MAX   Something has happened. Between you. What?
    [*To* CASS.]
    Another man?

CASS   No.

MAX   Daddy?

DEBOOM   A woman? No.

MAX   No, does Mom have another man?

DEBOOM   I don't think so. At least not that I'm ... Is there another man?

CASS No.

MAX Why are you treating each other this way?

DEBOOM How am I treating your mother?

MAX Like someone who refers to his wife as "your mother." Like you hate her.

DEBOOM Hate—really?

CASS When his cocktail of medications misconnect, I get stupid.

MAX You're implying he's a drug addict??

CASS Are you waiting for me to tell you what I did to make your father disinterested in me?

MAX It might be useful to me if I'm ever stupid enough to get involved seriously with someone.

CASS Your father acts as if he's the only person in the world who's depressed and we should all suffer him because he's suffering that.

MAX Daddy?

DEBOOM I don't hate anything about your mother, Max. What do I even dislike? She smokes outside the house but comes inside stinking of them, she's habitually late, she's indecisive ordering in restaurants but maniacally decisive in everything else.

MAX So, what—

DEBOOM It's me, not your mom.

MAX Is this like your midlife crisis?

DEBOOM May be.

CASS Your father and I haven't had sex in a year.

MAX I don't need to know that.

CASS Then stop asking questions that elicit answers you don't want to hear. I noted your father's dwindling interest in me sexually, which happened concurrent with his growing disgust with his place in the larger world, the one in which he was revered and reviled as a critic of the culture. I never begrudged him his public recognition though I was—am—involved in something of infinitely greater importance.

MAX Maybe a little begrudging, Mom.

CASS Fine. But I didn't blame him, I blamed a culture so shallow as to be . . . something. I don't know how to complete that metaphor.

DEBOOM Your mom wants to try some time apart.

MAX Separate, you mean?

CASS Your father says he's in a black hole.

MAX Why would you want to be without each other at this time of your lives?

CASS We're seeking ground on which we can be friends again.

MAX Can't either of you just talk in human sentences! You were such good friends. What does that mean, a black hole?

DEBOOM Don't worry about it.

MAX Like dead matter so dense you can't see light?

DEBOOM No. It passed. I see light.

MAX You swear?

DEBOOM Yeah.

MAX What light do you see?

DEBOOM You.

MAX What happens when I get married and . . . not go away . . . I've gone away . . . but have my own family?

[MAX *and* CASS *recede.*]

DEBOOM [*To us.*] Each month for a year an egg dropped and did not become fertilized. We went to two doctors; each came to the same conclusion. Cass dove into the genetics of my sterility like a deep-sea diver. She dismissed as primitive the popular protocols of hormonal control of spermatogenesis and delivered what the

Columbia Journal of Medicine called a seminal paper on the hypothalamic, pituitary, gonadal axis. Privately, her theory was that my infertility came from my father's forebears, who, unknown to me, had produced every other generation Down syndrome children who were put away in institutions.

We took Maxine home on June 4, 1984; she was two weeks old.

Cass wanted to adopt from Israel. Though I felt I should let her have whatever child of whichever gender from whatever continent she wanted, she had a colleague at Columbia studying the increasing abandonment of children in America out of our generation and opted for homegrown.

That she was blond was partly accidental. Insofar as the agency took requests, we asked for a white female. That she grew tall was good fortune; she assumed my genes had dominated her stature.

Cass, I believed, knew who our child's birth parents were. I didn't want to know. I could remember on occasion that she was not genetically mine but not often.

We decided we would not tell Maxine she was adopted.

I was a young theater and film critic; I knew nothing about genetics.

[*To* CASS.]

You are essentially setting out to prove we have no free will. The "nature-nurture" argument for you is "nature," period.

CASS   Yeah, I don't know, maybe. I'm throwing some stuff out there. I need a Nobel, that's the point. A few years, we may be able to tell you who the fucking terrorists are going to be when they're four or five. . . . I know you know that I would like, in the second half of my life, to be of monumental consequence.

DEBOOM   I follow the map to her house, a place in which I have not known her.

CASS   Hello, Geoffrey. Come in. I got a bottle of cabernet—I hope it's decent.

DEBOOM   I don't drink.

CASS   I didn't mean to ruin your fun. Have a glass of wine.

DEBOOM   It's all right for you to have been right about the drinking. Are they here?

CASS   On the way up from the airport. What shall we do while waiting?

DEBOOM   "Hang ourselves." I'm kidding.

CASS   Are you?

DEBOOM   Yeah, yeah. That's an exchange from *Waiting for Godot*. Which I believe leads Vladimir or Estragon to say: "It'll give us an erection." And the other to respond: "Let's hang ourselves immediately."

CASS   Mm. Help me make the salad. Trim the radishes, wash them; hearts of palm in the refrigerator—slice about yay-wide.

DEBOOM   When did you stop loving me?

CASS   I haven't stopped loving you. But I've reached a place where I only love you as much as you love me. The marriage worked for a long time because of its inequity.

DEBOOM   Meaning?

CASS   We both loved you best.

DEBOOM   Stop respecting me then?

CASS   When you declared yourself a moral eunuch without normal feelings of love and regret, your reasoning was so sound I bought in.

DEBOOM   Good critic—if that's not an oxymoron—has to preach his views with conviction.

CASS   And I got tired of feeling so much of what you said to me in earnest sounded like you'd written it out before I knew to ask a question or make an observation. I realize you wield the language to obscure your feelings, those things you claim have been buried since childhood by your need to be admired and make your parents love you, despite the fact that it always seemed clear to me they both adored you. Trite, trite, trite, Geoffrey. You are, in fact, painfully prosaic and ordinary.

DEBOOM That's redundant: prosaic, ordinary.

[MAX *and* HECTOR LEON DE SOTO, *32*.]

MAX Daddy, Mom, this is Hector Leon de Soto, my fiancé.

DEBOOM Your distant relative Hernan ended up in Mississippi at a river searching for a shortcut to China.

HECTOR LEON That wasn't very bright of him, was it?

DEBOOM [*To us.*] On Cass's back patio, purple mountains before us, we eat, and following the inevitable question about who the hell this person is who proposed to marry my daughter, this:

HECTOR LEON Dad was an immigrant. He started out selling pre-owned vehicles, but he had a gift. Is that the wrong word— Maxine says you're a stickler for words. A knack—is that better? Dad had a knack for selling and I hope I've inherited that knack and can take it to the next level.

DEBOOM And what does that mean, the next level?

HECTOR LEON Well, Dad owns three dealerships now that sell seven makers of premium automobiles and trucks. I manage the BMW store. Needless to say, you have any interest in a fine German automobile . . . Our cost, of course.

CASS What about the great gas mileage debate?

HECTOR LEON That cars should get better mileage so as to lessen our addiction to foreign oil?

CASS Mm.

HECTOR LEON Frankly, Mrs. DeBoom, I don't think anybody really cares. Otherwise, don't you figure we'd have done something decades ago or yesterday or, certainly, no later than quitting time today? Mostly the uproar comes from fanatics, and I think people in my business want to defy those people just on principle.

CASS   What principle is that?

HECTOR LEON   That the celebrities who stand behind those fanatics don't actually save or ration or conserve on anything, Mrs. DeBoom, so why should the rest of us?

DEBOOM   Because we should?

CASS   I go by Dr. Rosenblum, Hector, but why don't you call me Cass.

HECTOR LEON   Thank you, I'm happy to do that. If you don't mind, I go by Hector Leon, not just Hector.

CASS   All right, I think we're set to go.

HECTOR LEON   Now, what do you drive, Cass?

CASS   A Volkswagen. Where did you go to school, Hector Leon?

HECTOR LEON   I went to Loyola of Chicago, ma'am—Cass—when Maxie was at Northwestern.

MAX   We wonder how many times we passed around Evanston and didn't know whom we would become to the other.

HECTOR LEON   But I'm a tennis-a-holic, so I went to a Loyola-Northwestern match. I thought she was amazing, but those jocks, you know, the ones with that kind of talent, they didn't have a lot of interest in the people like me interested in business.

MAX   But then we both moved to New York and I went to look at the condo in Washington Heights and he was there to look at it at the same time.

HECTOR LEON   Fate.

MAX   He challenged me to two out of three.

HECTOR LEON   I took a game—though I think she threw it my way.

MAX   Absolutely didn't. You earned it.

HECTOR LEON   Tried to—tell you that. Where did you and Dr. DeBoom meet?

CASS   He's not a doctor—but just call us Cass and Geoffrey, Hector Leon, please. Geoffrey was just back from Vietnam and in the first year of grad school in journalism at George Washington University. I was just recently back from Israel.

MAX   Where she fought in the Six-Day War.

HECTOR LEON   You actually fought?

CASS   Yes, I did.

HECTOR LEON   What did you—

MAX   She doesn't talk about that.

HECTOR LEON   That's a conversation killer, Cass.

[*To* DEBOOM.]

Max said you were carrying a lot of baggage from Tehran.

DEBOOM   She shouldn't have said that. Because it isn't true.

HECTOR LEON   Wow, your parents, Maxie, are like the embodiment of "strong, silent type."

CASS   Geoffrey never really addressed what happened during his time as a hostage in Tehran, because he thinks it's heroic to seem above normal emotions.

DEBOOM   Whatever she says is, Hector Leon, is.

HECTOR LEON   I hear you, Geoff.

CASS   He's kidding. He knows I only know what I know.

DEBOOM   My wife was the healthiest-looking human physical being I'd ever seen. Dark skin and big eyes and shaped like a long-distance runner.

CASS   Shaped more like a shot-putter now.

DEBOOM   No, you're not. But what killed me, Hector, and ultimately— Leon—gave me life was she was the most giving, the most cohesive and coherent human being I'd ever met. Still is.

HECTOR LEON   You think you'll get back together?

CASS   Why don't you just ask what you want to know, Hector Leon?

HECTOR LEON   And you, Cass, were just a housewife at first?

DEBOOM   Just a housewife?

HECTOR LEON   You know what I mean?

DEBOOM   Wife, homemaker, mother, researcher, teacher, avid student of the building blocks of life.

HECTOR LEON   Max says that Mr. DeBoom mostly raised her—I mean, given your schedule being so packed and all and Mr. DeBoom writing his reviews at home.

DEBOOM   All of life for both of us was meant to keep Max safe. I'll do the dishes.

MAX   No, Mama and I will. You and Hector Leon go in the living room.

[DEBOOM *and* HECTOR LEON...*alone.*]

DEBOOM   Where did you say your father was from?

HECTOR LEON   Brazil.

DEBOOM   You sure?

HECTOR LEON   Am I sure where my father emigrated from?

DEBOOM   Mm.

HECTOR LEON   Yeah, I'm pretty sure.

DEBOOM   But not entirely.

HECTOR LEON   No, of course I'm positive. Why?

DEBOOM   Was he ever in Tehran?

HECTOR LEON   Iraq?

DEBOOM   Iran, Hector. Leon.

HECTOR LEON   What I meant. No—why would he be?

DEBOOM   Maybe he chose to fight for his adopted country.

HECTOR LEON   Between you and Cass—what happened?

DEBOOM   You look like someone I knew in Tehran. You know where Iran is?

HECTOR LEON   Why aren't you doing that anymore—being a critic, having your own TV show?

DEBOOM   Got tired of it and terrible at it, and the people who paid me got tired of me being terrible.

HECTOR LEON   What should I see? I mean, I see everything, but are there films coming out I should be on the lookout for?

DEBOOM   No. Don't go to the movies. They stink.

HECTOR LEON   Not all of them. I mean, I think there are brilliant movies being made every year.

DEBOOM   No. They all stink. Read a novel.

HECTOR LEON   Even the old ones?

DEBOOM   Books or movies?

HECTOR LEON   Movies.

DEBOOM   Some of the old movies don't stink. "It is time to be old, to something-something." Who was that?

HECTOR LEON   I don't...

DEBOOM   Eliot was: "I grow old, I will wear the bottoms of my trousers rolled."

HECTOR LEON   What about *Citizen Kane*?

DEBOOM   Masturbatory exegesis about all that is loathsome about the male subjects of movies and the men who make them about men they imagine to be like themselves.

HECTOR LEON   You're kidding, right?

DEBOOM   No.

HECTOR LEON   *Citizen Kane*?

DEBOOM   Thus spake Geoffrey DeBoom.

HECTOR LEON   So you can't get me on a movie set?

DEBOOM   Why would you want to get on a movie set?

HECTOR LEON   To see how it's done.

DEBOOM   Selling cars is important. Making movies isn't.

HECTOR LEON   I disagree. I mean, I agree what I'm doing is of consequence, but film is the art form of my generation.

DEBOOM   And in a few years, everybody your age will be making movies in their bedrooms and flooding the Internet with them. The particularity, the specificity, the uniqueness will be gone. The special among your generation will be the people who serve: the plumbers, carpenters, car dealers.

MAX   We've been stuck in planes and airports all day. We're going to go for a run on the ditch banks. We'll be back.

[*They go.* DEBOOM *turns to* CASS, *who rinses dishes, wearing yellow gloves.*]

DEBOOM   I need to borrow your computer.

CASS   Why?

DEBOOM   Look something up.

CASS   What?

DEBOOM   I don't know. A line from a poem or book or from someone.

CASS   Don't read my e-mail.

DEBOOM   Why, what's in there?

CASS   That's not the point. The point is it's none of your business.

DEBOOM   You could have cut right to "it's none of your business."

CASS   I just don't trust you—and, yes, I could have left out "just."

DEBOOM   You Google, I'll rinse.

CASS   You remember everything.

DEBOOM   Not always. Anymore. Sometimes it takes until the next day.

CASS   And you can't wait.

DEBOOM   Why should I when there's Google.

CASS   What do I put in?

DEBOOM   "It is time to grow old." No. It's . . . "It is time to be old" something-something . . .

[*He rinses. She Googles.*]

CASS   Ah. Wow. Google. Wow. That was two wows but . . . Emerson, "Terminus," a poem.

DEBOOM   Terrible poem.

CASS   How do you know?

DEBOOM   I just remembered.

CASS/DEBOOM   "It is time to be old, / To take in sail . . ."

CASS   . . . "The god of bounds, / Who sets to seas a shore, / Came to me in his fatal rounds, / And said: 'No more!'"
[*To him.*]
Time to grow older. To give way to the next generation. Move.

[*She nudges him from the sink, puts her yellow gloves back on, looks at one of the plates he rinsed.*]

CASS/DEBOOM   You call that clean?

[*She resumes rinsing.*]

DEBOOM   Weren't we much more in love?

CASS   When?

DEBOOM   Then. Where they are.

CASS   I would lie in bed in the dark and as I closed my eyes for the night, grateful beyond words that we were together, I would smile.

DEBOOM   I put one leg over you, you put your face into my shoulder. Your breath on my skin would slow so fast, become even and . . .

CASS   I was safe.

DEBOOM   But I made you quit smiling.
[*To us.*]
She made her Intro to Biology class, a hundred of them, read *A Portrait of the Artist as a Young Man* for discussion in their lab sections.

So I reread it and sat in the back of the lab section she ran. I was, then, unemployed after thirty years as a film critic in print and television, living off the tidy sum of money I'd made investing in the dot-com explosion, thanks to a stockbroker who recognized the dot-com emperor was naked before anyone else, but didn't tell anyone until the day after he told me we were going to sell everything.

She had a lab of a dozen baby-faced sophomores in hooker clothes (the young women) and voluminous shorts and capacious T-shirts (the young men) follow her on the page, hoping through a combination of visual and aural stimulation to make them comprehend the incomprehensible. "Pity," Joyce writes, "is the feeling which arrests the mind in the presence of whatsoever is grave and constant in human sufferings and unites it with the human sufferer."

Whut? She told her students to stop romanticizing their youthful suffering and, as Joyce wrote, "to go to encounter for the millionth time the reality of experience and to forge in the smithy of" their souls "the uncreated conscience of" their "race."

[*To* CASS.]

There isn't one of your young aspiring scientists capable of the pursuit of greatness.

CASS Of course there is.

DEBOOM You're deluding yourself.

CASS You haven't heard an idea or seen a single experiment any of them has done.

DEBOOM Doesn't matter.

CASS You can't tell by looking.

DEBOOM Yes, I can.

CASS Would you like to read some of their abstracts on our current DNA research?

DEBOOM God, no.

CASS Please get a job, Geoffrey.

DEBOOM I'm probably jealous of your creativity. You have more creativity in a single test tube than I have in all the glassware in my cupboards.

CASS Is that a good metaphor?

DEBOOM No. What are you doing these days?

CASS Simplicity itself. A kit you'll be able to get at the drug store, take a saliva sample from your own mouth, drop the solution on it, and know in seconds whether you have any of half a dozen influenzas.

DEBOOM I thought you told me there are no medications for flu.

CASS There aren't. But by making the ID, you can at least keep yourself away from others.

DEBOOM Okay.

CASS Jesus, Geoffrey, make something big that I do little. Please.

DEBOOM I'm sorry if you think that's what I'm doing. I know you're among the vanguard of those who will unlock the secret of human life on earth.

CASS You can go back to your hotel, if you want.

DEBOOM Let me ask you something. Hector Leon…
[*To us.*]
Max and Hector Leon return wet from their run. Hector Leon heads for the shower. Max stretches in the kitchen, asking without speaking that we speak to her about her proposed husband.
[*To* MAX.]
If you love this guy, this man—

MAX Hector Leon.

DEBOOM Hector Leon. Have you Googled him?

MAX What?

DEBOOM His family.

MAX As a matter of fact—yes, of course I have, Daddy.

DEBOOM And ... Brazil.

MAX What about it?

DEBOOM Live with him awhile. A few years before you get married.

CASS Because he's Brazilian?

MAX His family's very traditional; they won't let us share a room when I visit. He has to stay in a hotel when he comes into the city overnight.

CASS He may pay for the room, but I'll bet he doesn't use it except to collect the chocolates off the pillows.

MAX We can't be in the same town, Mommy, and not hold each other when we go to sleep.

DEBOOM You're telegenic, you're articulate—you can have a career in television. You can affect a generation of girls, travel the world promoting the value of sports for women. Don't commit death by car dealer, my angel.

MAX I want to be loved, Daddy.

DEBOOM You are adored, Max.

MAX Him. I want his love and adoration.

CASS Marriage, Maxine, it's ... in the end, not terrible, but it's so implausible. And adoration—my God, adoration, that's ... just so ephemeral.

MAX So what do I do? Go from guy to guy? Have a child by myself? Whose sperm do I use? Is that what you'd wish for me?

CASS I don't know, Max. I'm not a good person to ask.

MAX Then why are you talking? Why can't you have the good sense to lie! I need something positive from you.

CASS Love as hard as you can, for as long as you can.

[DEBOOM *takes* MAX *in his arms.*]

DEBOOM   Okay, there are exceptions.

MAX   Yeah.

DEBOOM   Seriously.

MAX   Right.

DEBOOM   I hope he understands what he has in you and can stand to stand in the shadow of your grace.

CASS   Let her find it out for herself, like everyone else.

DEBOOM   Why?

CASS   Because that's the way life lives, Geoffrey.
[MAX *laughs.*]
Jesus, my mind is going. Why did she say that? When did you say that?

MAX   I don't remember exactly. I mean, I remember but . . .

DEBOOM   She was playing in the Twelve and Under finals at Boca Raton and the girl she beat said it wasn't fair that Max hit her forehand like a man. And Max shrugged and said, "That's the way life lives."

MAX   Would you talk to him about what he really wants to do? He's embarrassed to broach it to you.

CASS   Selling cars isn't what he really wants to do?

MAX   He's a terrific writer.

HECTOR LEON   [*Entering.*] Your daughter flatters me, Geoffrey.

MAX   Shower.

[*She goes, exchanging a look with her fiancé that is the passing of a baton in a relay race.*]

HECTOR LEON   I was encouraged by my writing teachers into taking an MFA in poetry, so I started at NYU. I got through last year, the first year, but I lacked the confidence to overcome my parents' objections.

DEBOOM   Is that what it was?

HECTOR LEON   What do you mean?

DEBOOM   I Googled you while you guys were running.

CASS   Why?

DEBOOM   Unless there's another Hector Leon de Soto—

HECTOR LEON   Okay, stop.

DEBOOM   Does my daughter—our daughter—know you're selling cars because you're under indictment at NYU?

HECTOR LEON   You think I'd withhold that from her?

DEBOOM   Sure.

CASS   What the hell's happening here?

[MAX *steps into the doorway; she's been listening around the corner.*]

HECTOR LEON   I'm going to tell your folks about the indictment.

MAX   It's going to sound bad, Daddy.

DEBOOM   Accused of raping and trying to murder one of his freshman comp students? I'm sure he had a good reason.

MAX   It was her, she who tried to rape and kill him. He was just defending himself.

DEBOOM   Nice twist.

MAX   Dad! Hector Leon may be the only true genius I've ever met. People—even the faculty—were so jealous of him.

DEBOOM   "Talent," you may recall your mother telling both of us often, "isn't an excuse for self-indulgence."

HECTOR LEON   I make no excuses—I am what you see, Geoffrey, Cass.

DEBOOM   Nobody is what you see, are you crazy? Maxine, why do you keep picking these guys?

MAX   Dad, I mean it!

DEBOOM   Hector Leon? What's he accomplished to have two names?

MAX   Stop it, you sound like a crazy person! Go on, baby.

HECTOR LEON   What I have to say needs some preamble.

DEBOOM   Jesus—really?

MAX   My dad hates preambles.

HECTOR LEON   The young woman's story, according to her: I tell her I've forgotten her term paper at my apartment. According to her, I ask her to stop by. She does. I hit her with a cattle prod and drag her—

CASS   I'm sorry, you—

MAX   She said he zapped her with an electric cattle prod, dragged her to the bathroom, heaped her into the tub and raped her. Then, according to her, I apologize, solicit her promise not to tattle, and let her go. She calls the cops immediately, they come and arrest me. Despite lip service to the contrary, I am guilty till proven innocent.

DEBOOM   And your version?

MAX   She flirts with him all semester, shows up at his house to dispute the grade on her term paper, which he returns at the final class along with everyone else's; she offers herself in exchange for an A in the course as she's desperate to get into law school. He resists, she persists, he defends himself.

DEBOOM   Just happens to have a cattle prod handy.

MAX   He was training his pet.

DEBOOM   Caribou?

MAX   Labrador. It was low voltage.

HECTOR LEON   She had a gun.

DEBOOM   She came to your house to get her term paper packing a gun?

MAX   Yes.

DEBOOM   "What we have here is failure to communicate." *Cool Hand Luke*, 1967. Good movie. Except Newman constantly repeated that gesture, movie after movie, where he pinched the bridge of his nose with thumb and index finger to indicate ironic world-weariness.

MAX   Dad.

DEBOOM   She brings a gun. He resists, she persists, he defends himself.

MAX   The D.A. wants Hector Leon to settle, but if he doesn't, they'll have to take the matter to trial. The D.A. says guilty or innocent, he'll lose in court.

HECTOR LEON   You ever been to the slam, Geoff?

DEBOOM   Jail, no, not exactly.

HECTOR LEON   You've been there or you haven't?

DEBOOM   I haven't been to jail.

HECTOR LEON   You figure you're tough enough for jail but I'm not. Whereas I look at you and figure you better never do time because you haven't got a chance in hell of becoming anything in the slam but someone's big, blubbery boy.

CASS   Are you two serious?

DEBOOM   I think we are. But you're probably right, Hector; I'm past the ability to defend myself against the black behemoths of prison as mythologized by bad movies.

HECTOR LEON   I took karate for ten years, so I don't think I'd have the same problem.

DEBOOM   Karate.

HECTOR LEON   She's not the first female—or male, for that matter—to show up unannounced at my door.

DEBOOM   Why? You're a pretty average-looking guy.

HECTOR LEON   And that's a pretty transparent remark, Geoff.

DEBOOM   Though it happens to be the truth.

HECTOR LEON   I don't initiate personal relationships with my students. She didn't like her grade, but I gave her the benefit of the doubt with the B and she knew it. She wanted an alibi to show up. She was pissed I didn't want her, always talking in class but always stating the obvious as it was revelatory, perched in my front row in her short skirts and pastel underpants.

DEBOOM   Does my daughter have any idea how different a person you are from the one she thinks she's marrying?

MAX   Daddy, I'm sitting here.

DEBOOM   I know.

MAX   So ask me.

DEBOOM   I did.

MAX   I adore the man. I believe the man.

DEBOOM   Can your attorney broker a plea bargain or a settlement?

MAX   The de Sotos have offered a fair settlement, but we're afraid that when Hector Leon becomes the face of the dealership in the commercials that someone will drag all this up. We need your help.

DEBOOM   What can I do?

MAX   Write an in-depth piece for *The Times* about the truth, how we just naturally assume the man is guilty in a case like this, but here you have this brilliant, complex man who—

DEBOOM   First of all, I have no way to determine who's telling the truth unless the young woman will talk to me, and why should she? Secondly, the *New York Times* isn't any more interested in me writing for them now than when I was thirty-five.

CASS   The *Daily News* then.

DEBOOM   I quit them the same day I left my TV show, remember?

CASS   *Esquire.*

DEBOOM   They've gone young businessman.

HECTOR LEON   I am a young businessman.

MAX   *Men's Journal, Vanity Fair, Premiere.*

DEBOOM   I'm not writing for *Premiere*—I have standards.

HECTOR LEON   *PLAYBOY.*

CASS   Nobody reads the articles.

[*She and* DEBOOM *laugh, a joke from their teens.*]

DEBOOM   He can't sell his life rights, if he's found guilty.

MAX   Dad—he won't be found guilty.

CASS   He wants to sell his life rights?

MAX   That's not the point, Mother. He wants to be presented as a three-dimensional person.

DEBOOM   I was the king of one and two dimensions.

HECTOR LEON   A good piece gets you on *Larry King*.

DEBOOM   He hates me.

HECTOR LEON   Why?

CASS   Because Geoffrey vilified him as—and I believe I'm quoting accurately here—"the limp dick of contemporary vapidity, the cultural icon of self-serving bloviation."

DEBOOM   I should have said "limp penis."

HECTOR LEON   What does "bloviation" mean?

MAX   *Charlie Rose* then.
[*Off her father's disinterest.*]
Primetime Live, 60 Minutes. He needs a platform to sell his screenplay.

DEBOOM   Oh, Jesus, no, please no.

HECTOR LEON   I'd like you to read it; if you like it, which I'm pretty—

DEBOOM   No, no, Christ, no!

HECTOR LEON   I can't spend my only life selling cars, Geoff. And nobody reads poetry today.

DEBOOM   Nobody reads it, but people keep publishing enormous, pretentious gobs of it.

MAX   The money's in screenplays, Daddy, you know that.

DEBOOM   What kind of a poet/car dealer concerns himself with money?

HECTOR LEON   Max says there's no law an artist has to suffer in poverty.

DEBOOM   Poverty—what poverty? Max makes a fortune every year.

HECTOR LEON   I'm not living off Max. I can support her just fine, certainly until I sell my first—

DEBOOM   Writing a screenplay is not a worthy undertaking for a man who controls hundreds of BMWs!

MAX   You're making fun of him.

DEBOOM   I'm having no fun.

HECTOR LEON   Just read it and give me your true thoughts. Max says it's too lyrical.

DEBOOM   One lyrical self-serving individual to another: I can't imagine what would compel me to spend the next week of my evaporating life analyzing your screenplay about cattle-prodding some rapacious teenie-bopper.

MAX   So, are you saying you won't help us, Dad?

DEBOOM   Oh, Max.

MAX   I need to know.

DEBOOM   How many drafts have you done—how long have you been writing on this?

HECTOR LEON   I started it in jail, while they were holding me—it took my father a few hours to get over from Jersey and bail me out. I finished the first draft the following day.

DEBOOM   You wrote a screenplay in two days?

HECTOR LEON   It just poured out like vomit.

DEBOOM   Lyrical, indeed.

[MAX *holds up two, long yellow legal pads that appear to have been submerged at some point in water, dried, then written upon.* DEBOOM *looks, doesn't touch.*]

You wrote a screenplay in two days, in longhand, that you want me to read?

MAX   It's very balanced, Daddy. He tells both sides, the teacher's and the student's, two characters treated with equal empathy. It's complex. Brad Pitt and Katie Holmes above the title.

DEBOOM   Brad Pitt is a white guy, Hector is Latino, Hispanic, Chicano, Mestizo, Spicano, Cubano—but not Anglo.

HECTOR LEON   Max says it needs Brad Pitt. She says he likes you.

DEBOOM   Why don't I burn him a call, tell him I'm shipping off a coupla legal pads for him to take a gander at, written by my prospective son-in-law, the car dealer/poet who is under indictment for—

HECTOR LEON   I really don't understand your hostility at me, Geoff.

DEBOOM   Yeah, look, great talk, good night, everyone, see you tomorrow—what are we doing tomorrow—are we doing something tomorrow?

MAX   We'll hang out. Take a hike over Baylor Pass, eat some Mexican.

HECTOR LEON   An honor to meet you, Geoff.

MAX   [*Hugging her father.*] Daddy.

DEBOOM   Sweetheart, he's guilty. Bail while you can.

[*But* MAX *presses the screenplay on her father.* CASS *walks* DEBOOM *out.*]

CASS   Maybe this is our punishment for thinking or pretending we were good parents.

DEBOOM   We were very good parents. What do we do here?

CASS   There is the possibility that he's telling the truth. For Max's sake, we have to embrace that possibility.

DEBOOM   Isn't it clear he's guilty—you with your logical mind? Deduce!

CASS   Induce. Inductive logic—as, truthfully, the premise that he's innocent is supported by his and Max's pronouncements, but those pronouncements do not guarantee the premise.

DEBOOM   Fine—but the screenplay?

CASS   That cannot be the issue here, Geoffrey. We'll hike in the morning, we'll be with him, we'll know. Be here at nine.

[*She kisses his cheek. He tries to get arms around her but she's gone. From the darkness he hears hyena laughter.* MAX. *Tickle laughter. His daughter being tickled by* HECTOR LEON.]

DEBOOM   [*To us.*] Wrath heaped on me by the *Times* of New York and Los Angeles when I reviewed my guy Oliver Stone's *Wall Street* for my assessment that fifty years from then, the Boomer Generation's greatest contribution to history would be sociopathic greed and institutionalized dishonesty.

I look under the sheets for bugs, stains. Get in with Hector Leon's screenplay, thinking I'll read the first and last ten pages and make up various damning, indecipherable baloney and squelch the love of my daughter's life, the criminal poet car salesman, and earn my ex-wife's eternal and entire enmity.

I awaken, slog through my routine, go to the restaurant. Where Maxine and Hector Leon are seated at a table for four, a carafe of coffee between them. Despite the hour, they are eating tostadas and salsa.

HECTOR LEON   Max said you get up at six, we came at six-thirty.

MAX   [*Pouring coffee.*] What did you think?

HECTOR LEON   The truth, please.

DEBOOM   [*To us.*] The Oracle of Delphi foretold Laius, King of Thebes, that his own son would murder him. Laius, in a move that could instruct many a parent in danger of death by child, nailed Oedipus' feet to a mountain.

[*To* HECTOR LEON.]

I thought you said you were writing both characters equally.

HECTOR LEON   I did. I thought I did. Didn't I?

DEBOOM   No. Allison comes off as a moron, Alfredo as a reasonable, if eccentric, genius.

HECTOR LEON   Allison's got some school smarts, but why's she married at twenty, and pregnant?

DEBOOM   Maybe she got married because she was pregnant.

HECTOR LEON   No, she got married, then she got pregnant. Who with any brains does that at twenty?

DEBOOM   Maybe she was in love.

HECTOR LEON   To think she was going to be happy with some unformed dope just out of his teens?

DEBOOM   She should have chosen you.

HECTOR LEON   What?

DEBOOM   Isn't that what we think when we see someone we find attractive attached to someone else? What's she doing with that idiot when she could pursue me?

HECTOR LEON   She did choose Alfredo. But he was a terrible choice, and, trust me, I told her so—he did, Alfredo, on page 34—struggling artist, self-absorbed, anti-marriage, doesn't want kids. Said she couldn't help it, she was drawn to the essence of what he warned her against.

DEBOOM   I really hope you recognize that as self-serving nonsense, Hector, but I'm afraid you don't. Leon.

HECTOR LEON   He's just being honest.

DEBOOM   Sure. Okay, Allison's term paper subject: "The case for vigilantism in the twenty-first century." That's the crux of her character, man.

[DEBOOM *flips pages.*]

Here, read from here.

[*To* MAX.]

Read, Allison.

[*To* HECTOR LEON.]

You read, Alfredo. Lemme hear it.

HECTOR LEON   Here?

DEBOOM   Yeah.

[MAX *is up for whatever might illicit her father's support. She pats the table close to her.*]

[*Side by side, they read from his screenplay. Goes like this:*]

ALFREDO   You remember an old movie called *Death Wish*?

ALLISON   You're kidding, right?

ALFREDO   The movie for those who feel powerless against the sociopaths of color among them. So, you're Allison Coopersmith, the new Charles Bronson.

ALLISON   First of all, Mr. Delgado, there were criminal palefaces in that movie as well as scumsuckers of color.

ALFREDO   Whom would you execute, Miss Coopersmith?

ALLISON   There are so many people, I don't know where to start.

ALFREDO   With me maybe?

ALLISON   People like you, for sure.

ALFREDO   What sort of people do I represent?

ALLISON   Pompous smarty-pants who pretend to have talent nobody else thinks they have who play like they're better than people who are probably a lot more talented than they are but they harass because somebody said, hey, go teach this class of dopey undergrads that are hopeless examples of the TV-X-Box-Never-Read-a-Book generation.

ALFREDO   What about the eternal hope that formal education can make people better?

ALLISON   I believe it. You don't. You are just so, so cool. Oh, don't deny it. You are. You think. Guess what? You're not. What you are is just a Mexican of average intelligence pretending to be a smart white guy, but who really doesn't know what he's pretending to know, and I know that even if the others in class don't. I'm sick of not being able to tell the truth about people just because they belong to some supposedly oppressed, distressed, or suppressed minority.

ALFREDO   Wow.

ALLISON   And Mexico's a time bomb. It will implode in our lifetime.

ALFREDO   Really?

ALLISON   We'll be slaughtering you at the borders. The Mexicans will be the new Jews. You know the Jews?

ALFREDO   Heard of 'em.

ALLISON   That's not what I meant; it was a rhetorical question—of course you do. The point is the Holocaust of the twenty-first century will be "just south of the border, down Mejico way."

ALFREDO   Know the song, haven't heard the theory.

ALLISON   My fiancé says even silence is taken as an offense in the presence of certain people. If you don't embrace their crackpot beliefs with a standing ovation, you're evil! Not stupid, not misguided—you are evil!

ALFREDO   So in your new version of *Death Wish*, you'd kill a lot of Mexicans.

ALLISON   The ones in the hairnets with their crotches around their ankles, not the ones that want to get green cards and work their asses off to make up for the Negroes who are too good to do menial labor anymore.

ALFREDO   Negroes?

ALLISON   Yes, yes, Negroes. They're their own problem—not me, I'm not their damn problem! So, hey, you kept my term paper on purpose.

ALFREDO   Why would you say that?

ALLISON   Because you have the hots for me.

ALFREDO   Not anymore.

ALLISON   But you did.

ALFREDO   I was kidding.

ALLISON   Then why didn't you have my term paper at your office? I'll tell you: Because you couldn't very well seduce me there.

ALFREDO   So why'd you come here?

ALLISON   See where it leads.

ALFREDO   Maybe precipitate something you could use against me.

ALLISON   May-be. It's my fiancé's night to go out for steak with the boys. Talk about massive irrelevance: a group of men together, drinking, eating raw meat, and telling jokes about women. They're all MBA students in business. Ten years from now, corporate scandals in the making.

ALFREDO   Why are you marrying him?

ALLISON   He's just so darn cute.

ALFREDO   His baby or someone else's?

ALLISON   You think I'm promiscuous?

ALFREDO   I don't know what that means anymore. Men dress like little boys in short pants with their underwear sticking out, women dress like whores reborn from the sixties.

ALLISON   You see my belly button? Huh, you see it? No!

ALFREDO   I don't think you have a fiancé. Whose baby is it?

ALLISON   You're a mean person.

ALFREDO   You didn't wear underwear.

ALLISON   What?

ALFREDO   You came to class without underpants.

ALLISON   How would you know whether I wear underwear to class if you weren't looking up my skirts?

ALFREDO   Why would you sit in such a way that I could look up your skirts?

ALLISON   I'm allowed to wear what I want—to be in style!

ALFREDO   Then I'm allowed to look at what you're wearing, aren't I?

ALLISON   I too am a person, even though I'm paying out the nose to go to your stupid university!

ALFREDO   You talked a lot in class but always spoke the obvious as if it were a revelation.

ALLISON   We were graded on class participation! You just wanted people to regurgitate back whatever you said! I didn't!

DEBOOM   Stage direction: "Alfredo tries to ease her out the door and she attack him."

HECTOR LEON   Attacks.

DEBOOM   "Attacks him."

HECTOR LEON   Typo, sorry.

DEBOOM   "She falls and tears up her knees. She jumps on him. Tears at his pants, manages to get his belt undone, his zipper down, his member in her hand. He throws her off. She grabs the serrated carving knife off the counter, comes at him. He hits her with the dog-training electric prod."

ALFREDO   Sorry, sorry. Hey, I didn't want to do that, but you . . .

ALLISON   I care for you.

ALFREDO   Yes, yes, thank you, Allison, that's very flattering. Go home now.

[*To us.*]

Trying to remember . . . American theater was rife with nudity in the seventies, but has there been a play where someone holds someone's member onstage? And in my generation's retreat from its youthful excesses to insentient prudery, would we stand for it now? And why is it that handsome men assume their right to any woman is part of their inheritance?

MAX Daddy...

DEBOOM "He eases her out the door. She's light-headed, and lands on her knees. Short skirt, no panties. He locks the door. Watches her through the curtains. She gets in her car, takes off."
[*Riffling pages.*]
And then cops show up. Accuse him of rape, assault with a deadly weapon. He counter-accuses her the same. Max.

MAX What, Dad?

DEBOOM Does this strike you as a representation of reality?

MAX Dad, this is good.

HECTOR LEON I understand you don't want to lose your daughter, Geoff, but don't stoop low.

DEBOOM I don't want to lose my daughter, but I know that's unfair; however, I don't have to give her up to someone unworthy of her, and I'm concerned you don't have a social conscience.

MAX Damn it, Dad. You should see him with little kids.

DEBOOM My screenwriting students write skits, they write anecdotes, they write special-effects-driven drivel about vampires. And, yes, I've used the alliterative "special-effects-driven drivel" before. My Ph.D. students vomit up their opinions, as if to have some is to make them worthy of being read or heard. This is not interesting because it's you protecting you. Great writers, even pretty good ones, don't protect themselves.

MAX So, just tell him what he needs to do.

DEBOOM He has to represent both characters equally, to care for each equally. He can't glorify the "Hector" character.

HECTOR LEON This is the way she was, damn it, Geoff.

DEBOOM   Well, that may be interesting life, but it's lousy fiction, because I do not believe your main character and no one is speaking for the second character; therefore, I will not sit there with his one-sided view of the world for two hours.

MAX   He'll work on it. Will you read it again?

DEBOOM   Send me the script, typed and in proper format, maybe I'll read it again.

HECTOR LEON   I don't know how to thank you, Geoff.

MAX   We're going out to the club, Daddy. I'm giving a clinic. You want to hit with me?

HECTOR LEON   I thought I was.

MAX   I can hit with both of you.

DEBOOM   I don't have shorts or sneakers.

HECTOR LEON   I can lend you.

DEBOOM   [*To us.*] I join Cass in the bleachers at the university courts, which are packed with kids in baggy shorts and T-shirts, backward hats, and their parents.

[*They watch imaginary balls go back and forth across the net.*]

CASS   She said you treated him like one of your students.

DEBOOM   Well or badly?

CASS   Disdainfully. You've lost the will?

DEBOOM   What will?

CASS   To live? Is that what this—

DEBOOM   We're just a pile of genetic chemistry, according to you. Without medication, my genetics own me. I'm off my antidepressant—three weeks. The beast is loose.

CASS   You stopped taking your—

DEBOOM   Yeah, I thought if I get off the antidepressant, I might be able to get an erection and I could pursue you again.

CASS Geoffrey, you have a job, responsibilities—or if not—bills, loans, a mortgage.

DEBOOM I'll sell my house. I can live on the proceeds.

CASS No.

DEBOOM Don't tell me no! You've chosen for yourself, Cass. I'm doing the same. Nobody's going to be hurt by this except me.

CASS You're already planning to suffer. Do you not care whether you live any longer, Geoffrey?

DEBOOM I'm pretty disinterested. I'm no fun to be around. Neither you nor Max wants to spend time with me, and why would you? I don't want to either. But I have to, as long as I'm present.

CASS Are you dying?

DEBOOM Well, not from anything I know about except a kind of terminal malaise I know I shouldn't inflict on others but can't seem to help doing.

CASS I started wondering last night why you would want us to be together again when we both know we've lost respect and feeling for each other unless you were dying and needed a caretaker.

DEBOOM We both will.

CASS What?

DEBOOM Need caretaking while we do the actual getting dead. We should do that together.

CASS No. And, Geoffrey, you know...you do know what it would do to Max if you killed yourself.

DEBOOM She'd get over it. She has Hector Leon. "Youth is wasted on the young." Know who said that?

CASS No idea. Someone with a sense of irony.

DEBOOM Someone really bitter about the arrangement of life. Mark Twain. Like him, I don't like the arrangement.

CASS Which arrangement is that exactly?

DEBOOM   You're born, you make myriad mistakes, miss myriad opportunities, and start to disintegrate physically. You lose your sex drive, your hair, your muscle tone, your joints wear out, you get shorter. It's Max's group moving into position. Ours has had its day, culminating in the atrocity of George Bush.

CASS   Speak for yourself.

DEBOOM   Okay, mine has had its day, and I should get out of their way, not obstruct the path of those oncoming, the time they have to traverse it is so short. They just don't know it.

CASS   I don't feel that way, Geoffrey. I don't feel I should step aside. I feel I have good years left. A decade, maybe more, of research and teaching, enjoying Max, her life, Hector Leon's, grandchildren.

DEBOOM   That's good, Cass. I'm glad for you.

CASS   Did you lie about his screenplay?

DEBOOM   No.

CASS   To influence Maxine's feelings because you don't want to give her up, and you can't see that you've already lost the little girl you pretend she still is.

DEBOOM   Maybe I lied.

CASS   Because what I read seemed pretty damn good. At least, an aspiring writer who should be encouraged. Mentored.

DEBOOM   I am capable of any deceit.

CASS   You have to see him as a three-dimensional person.

DEBOOM   I'm the king of one to two dimensions.

CASS   Geoffrey, please, give it a rest.

DEBOOM   Sure. I sleep on your side of the bed now.

CASS   Why?

DEBOOM   I don't know. Closer to the bathroom.

CASS   The sad reality of longevity is that we grow tired through familiarity, and the unchanging, even when it's good, yearns for tension, and tension must have its release. We need to get a divorce.

DEBOOM   We're legally separated.

CASS   I dream I'll meet somebody who will stir me—I want to be thoroughly fucked again before I die, Geoffrey—and why continue to pretend we might get back together?

DEBOOM   It protects me.

CASS   From what?

DEBOOM   Unwanted advances.

CASS   You're kidding.

DEBOOM   Have you slept with anyone since we split?

CASS   I don't think that's your business.

DEBOOM   You can tell me.

CASS   No.

DEBOOM   I take that to be a yes.

CASS   It seems impossible, but it's true.

DEBOOM   Which—what?

CASS   We're at the end.

DEBOOM   [*To us.*] Thwong, THWONG, thwong, THWONG—balls against cat gut—iambic, as the highs schoolers hit the unaccented shot and Max hits the accented one, the inflected beat barely discernible like a good poem.
[*To* CASS.]
The feeling of missing you is palpable; it has mass in my chest.

CASS   Oh shit, let's get it done with, the ache in the heart and the belly and the infernal legal work. I wonder if the sad reality of marital longevity is that time inevitably brings most couples to where we are.

DEBOOM   You didn't need that adverb.

CASS Thank you.

DEBOOM You know how many couples in our self-indulgent generation are divorced?

CASS Our generation had the guts to announce the un-sacredness of marriage.

DEBOOM You don't miss anything about us?

CASS I do occasionally have the missing feeling. But I don't have that loving feeling anymore.

DEBOOM Righteous Brothers, 1969.

CASS That feeling, the missing me, it's missing what we were, not what we are. What we are can no longer reach back to touch what we were.

DEBOOM Maybe the feeling, the thing we define as love changes with age, or should. Maybe we have to redefine it.

CASS Not together, Geoffrey. I'm sorry.

DEBOOM [*To us.*] I have a row to myself on the flight back to Albuquerque. The flight attendant is young and black and doesn't see me, even when she smiles and shuffles peanuts to me, takes my drink order. "That's a Diet Coke for...no one." There's a message from Cass to call her when I turn my phone on.

CASS Maxine wants the wedding to be in New Jersey. His family has an estate on the water. It's traditional for the bride's parents to pay for the wedding but his mother would like them to pay for the whole shebang.

DEBOOM We have money. We'll do what's proper.

CASS No, we don't really. Let them do it.

DEBOOM Okay.

[*To us.*]

And so, there is my implicit approval of my daughter's marriage to a man I don't want her to marry. Giving up, giving in?

Maturity? My head feels overgrown with vegetation running amok cartoon style. Need weed-eater. Scythe. Tarzan—that cry that not only Cheeta the chimpanzee understood but every kid in America: Someone has to be fearless enough to frustrate our predatory selves.

[*The Tarzan cry.*]

"Aaah-ahhh-ah-aaaaaaahhhhhh!"

[*To us.*]

I read his screenplay again. He listened, somehow learned something from our conversations that allowed him to improve the piece. I managed to tell him it is actually something someone might want to produce.

They are married in New Jersey, the day after my sixty-second birthday during the university's Christmas Break. Much of the tennis world is there. At the end of my walk of my daughter down the aisle, the minister asks, "Who gives this child?"

"Her mother and I do," I say, knowing that can't be done.

Who shares this woman?

I lift my daughter's veil and kiss her cheek and place her hand in Hector Leon's. Take my seat beside her mother.

CASS Our baby.

DEBOOM Yes.

[*Lights fade to black.*]

• • •

And Then

Amelia Arenas

Amelia Arenas

Amelia Arenas is primarily known as an art historian. Her books (*Is This Art?*, *The Masterpiece and Its Shadow*, *A Brief History of Looking*, *Woman at Easel*, and *Look!*) focus on the relationship between art and the public.

She also writes about popular culture and classical literature. Her work as a playwright and director includes *Hell* (2005–2006) and *Confessions* (2008–2009), two pieces in a trilogy about the Western concept of the self inspired by the writings of Dante, Saint Augustine, and Freud. *Dreams*, the last piece, is projected to appear next year.

A one-woman play, *And Then*, was first performed by JoJo Hristova in 2007.

**five monologues about contemporary women
inspired by Euripides' *Medea***

characters

> **HANADI**, a terrorist
> **MARY KAY**, a teacher
> **LYNNDIE**, a soldier
> **SUSAN**, a housewife
> **LEONORA**, an heiress

And Then was conceived as a one-woman play. Costume changes take place onstage. They are set against a backdrop of projected fine-arts and mass-media images and choreographed to sections of Cherubini's *Medea* sung by Maria Callas.

• • •

I. Hanadi

[*She reads from a piece of paper in front of a video camera. A Palestinian flag hangs in the background.*]

This is the last statement of Hanadi Jaradat, your martyr, spoken before the Haifa operation.

Allah, Father of all things! Allah, the merciful . . . !

[*She drops the sheet.*]

I was there.

The fire spread from my breast like thunder.
But not a single one of those strangers died
before I did.

I was prepared.

Now they call me a terrorist.
Yesterday, I was Hanadi.

* * * * *

And what ever happened to him—
that good-looking, well-to-do boy
I was supposed to marry?

And what about that other one.
Remember, Mother?
The one Father never let me talk to.

* * * * *

I feared the strength of a man's arms
and my mother called me cold
because I couldn't stand the noise of children.

I wanted a man's stiff flesh.
Not his claws.

But that husband and those children
I was to have one day
blew up with me last night.

Last night . . .

My hunger for love
was not as great as my rage.

* * * * *

They said that mother collapsed
when she saw my picture in the news.
She thought I was working late . . .

Mother!
Don't look at those pictures!
You won't find your child there.
She's a ghost now.
She will be climbing the chestnut tree
in your backyard forever.

* * * * *

Father,
Remember how you never let me go out?

I hid under the covers all night
with a tiny mirror in my hand,
playing with that dried-up lipstick
I found in Mother's trunk.

I wanted to be like the woman in those pictures—
the one your father married and died young.
The one from Jordan.
The one with the big hat
and a cigarette in her hand.
I used to think that
if I looked at her long enough without blinking,
I could make her smile.

You never let me go out, Father.
I was supposed to hit the books
and quit dreaming about faraway places
and pretty ghosts.
And I did what you said.
Didn't I?

But, last night,
I joined an orgy.
An orgy that will go on till the end of days.

* * * * *

As far back as I can remember,
you've said again and again
"This land is ours!
We have to be better than them.
They are the sort that suffers out loud.
We are the sort that remembers."
Did you understand my death, Father?

Now you say that you won't ever mourn me
because I made you proud.
Weren't you proud of me back then?

Do you ever cry for me now, Father?

* * * * *

And you, neighbor?
I once walked by your streets,
and you looked at me with a sly glance.
I covered my head with a black scarf
but I painted my lips bright red.
You hid your girls in your houses
and your sons smoked under the elm tree
while I was earning a living.

* * * * *

Look at me now, neighbor!
LOOK!
Don't turn the TV off!

You don't have to peek
through a crack in your window anymore.
I am the girl your sons could have never married.

You can look at my mangled corpse and cry.
Now I am your martyr.
I am a scar you'll flaunt.

Look at me, neighbor!
LOOK!
Memorize my horror.
I died for YOUR sons—
the ones who squatted all day long
waiting for a job,
when I was at work.

* * * * *

I didn't put on the pretty dress
and go to that party,
just as you said, Father.
I obeyed.
I dressed myself in the pride of your fathers.
And I took with me
those loud words you spoke.

They were all with me last night.
They were the fuel that turned me
and those strangers
into a wave of blood.

* * * * *

Remember the wounded pigeon
we brought home?
Remember how you made him better?
We called him Ibrahim.
Remember how, a few days later,
when I returned from school,
we found him stiff in that cardboard box?

Remember how I begged you,
"Father, make him better!"

But you didn't.
You couldn't.

We buried him in our backyard.

I sat on your lap and cried.
But you didn't dry my tears.
You said,
"The salt of sorrow shapes the soul."
You told me it was time to do my homework.

* * * * *

And Fadi?
OUR FADI!

He blew up with his homework in his hand.
And you could not bring him back either.

* * * * *

I wish you had held me in your arms a little longer…
I wish I was buried in that cardboard box.

Father!
Don't look away now!

Watch me!
I am a cloud of stench.
Be proud of me!
Listen to me!

ALLAH, FATHER OF ALL THINGS
be proud of me!

THIS is my wedding day!

* * * * *

II. Mary Kay

He was so sweet, Daddy.
So smart,
So...different!

I can still see him hanging around
the school yard
waiting for me after class...

I helped him with his homework.
He even babysat for my kids sometimes.
Such an artistic kid, you know?
But he had trouble with math.
I taught him how to divide decimal fractions.

This kid was my lover, Daddy.

MY LOVER.

I'll do anything
to smell the sweet scent of his mouth again—
chewing gum and beer.
To lick the salt off his chest.
To feel with my cheeks that hairless skin.
That pounding heart...

He was a man of twelve.
My husband was a forty-year-old child.

* * * * *

But you made me marry him.
One day I had a few beers in college
and got pregnant.

There was nothing to do.
You were a senator.
We were CHRISTIAN.

So here I am, Daddy.
In jail,
I have nothing left to lose.
All I have is time to think of him.
My little prince . . .

I'd rather be here than
in that home you bought me.
I was a real prisoner then.

A divorce was out of the question.
Mother found my birth-control pills
and threw them in the garbage.

I had four kids with HIM.
One after another.

My kids!
I miss them so much . . .

They've now erased
their mother from their dreams.
And all those toys,
All those bedtime stories.
All those songs . . .

Birthdays.
Christmas.

* * * * *

Why did you have to die on me, Daddy?
You were the only one who understood me.

Remember how you used to take me with you
to all those Republican conventions?
I always wore pink, just as you liked me to.
You even taught me how
to write my own speeches.

* * * * *

Mother fixed my curls.
Tight.
And my skin hurt.
The pink dress had so much starch in it!
But I was proud to be there with you.

You never introduced me as Mary Kay.
You said to everyone,
"Here's my little girl!"

That's what I want to be called
from now on.

I've seen my name printed so many times,
so many strangers have pronounced it
that it's no longer mine.

That's what I want on my tombstone:
"HERE LIES DADDY'S LITTLE GIRL"

* * * * *

You were so handsome!
You bought us so many beautiful things...
And you were on TV all the time,
And Mother had a talk show of her own on the radio.

Mother.
Your wife.
She never once kissed me.
And when she made my braids,
she pulled my hair so hard...
She always smiled with anger.

But you had another one.
Her picture was all over the news one day.
Remember?
She was so young...
She got pregnant.
And then you wrote a check
to get her and her baby
away from our perfect world.
She was your student, Daddy.

* * * * *

You never ran for the Senate again.
You started to drink again.
And I was left all alone with Mother.
Playing house in the dark.

Once, in church,
I saw her tears.
Her mascara was beginning to run.
When she realized I caught her,
she looked at me hard and smiled.
She put her sunglasses on,
walked out,
and kept smiling,
she smiled hard,
shaking hands all the time.

* * * * *

Daddy, I miss him so much!
I'll be in jail for years.
I'm a sex offender.
I'm a child molester.
I'M A RAPIST.

They say I'm a monster.
Do you think I'm a monster, Daddy?

* * * * *

Why don't they leave me alone?
All those TV cameras...
It's not like before.

I can't sleep anymore!
I only want to have those sweet black eyes
scanning my body.
I want to be left alone with my longing.
With the memory of his small body
learning to conquer my own.

* * * * *

I broke parole.
We made love in my van.
I bore him two children.
And they don't let me see them.

They say he now goes out with girls his age.
My hair is already getting gray.
When I get out of here
I'll be a middle-aged criminal.

But I'll be free to love him again.
He'll be waiting for me.
Won't he, Daddy?

I'll be waiting.

* * * * *

III. Lynndie

[*She's in a dive somewhere. She's drinking from a beer can. She's quite drunk.*]

Hi there!
I'm Lynndie England.
PRIVATE England!
I'm an American soldier!

Oops, sorry! I was an American soldier.
And I kicked ass, damn it!
But where the hell am I now?

The stupid lawyers don't even let me talk in court.
I could say a thing or two about my "superiors"...

I'm fucked, man,
I'm toast.
I'm twenty-one
but they'll put me away until I croak.

And, guess what? I'm pregnant.
As if I needed this...

* * * * *

Oh! Gimme a break!
We all did it.
So now I'm screwed because
somebody had a video camera
and because I have TITS!?

So, here I am.
A symbol of who-the-hell-knows-what.

Fuck everybody...

* * * * *

It was like porn, man.
I'm telling you.

Mike was there.
Watching it all.

I was crazy about him,
He was SO bad!
Such a dirty mouth . . .
One day he fucked my brains out
singing the national anthem!
It cracks me up...

I used to look at him and think,
wouldn't it be cool to be him?

* * * * *

They're making a big deal on account that I'm a woman.
It's not like I'd never seen a gun, OK?
I learned to shoot at nine.

Dad taught me how to hunt deer.
And I was good at it, too.
But then we had to drag the dead thing
into the van.
That was hard.

He let me ride in the back.
I wanted to look at the buck.
He was so big!
His eyes were still open.
His tongue hanging out from his mouth.

I touched him.
He was still warm.
A beautiful thing, you know...

If I live again, I want to be one of them,
you know. A big, motherfucker of a buck.
And I won't let anyone get me, damn it.
I'll fight back.

Anyway.
Dad would have killed me
if he'd caught me petting it.

I just wanted to know what the deer thought
when he froze, saw me point the gun at him
and heard the blast.

I asked Dad,
"What's gonna happen now
with the buck's kids and his wife?"
What can I say, I was just a stupid kid.

Dad cracked up.
I was so pissed!
I jumped out of the van.

He goes, "How can you be so dumb!
Deer don't have wives or kids.
They're not like us.
They're beasts.
We've been killing them and eating them
since God knows when.
So don't go stupid on me now.
Get in the van!"

I thought, "Wait.
We don't even eat the whole deer.
We dump most of it over the cliff and let it rot."

Anyway.
It's not like he was mad or anything.
Actually, when we got home he said,
"You're a swell kid, you know?
You wacked this one all alone.
Give Daddy a kiss!"

I hated Dad's kisses.
His mouth tasted like an ashtray full of whiskey.
But I liked the way he looked at me.
Not at home, when we were out.
When we were out I did not feel like a girl.

* * * * *

That day Mom was a mess
when she saw my dress all bloody.

Just like the day I said
I was joining the army.
What does she know?
She's always baking something.
Yakking on the phone with her friends.
Watching soap operas.
I had to get the hell out of that dump
or else I'd end up like her.

* * * * *

Man, if you had seen the party they threw me!
Billy left the gas station early,
Molly and Jake came
all the way from Norfolk.
And the kids from the factory came too.

Remember Andy and his cute girl?
What was her name again?
Was she plastered!
She was funny, though.

I still had a hangover when I got to the base...

So, I get into that plane.
And then,
Iraq, baby.
Wow,
what a mess.
You had to see it!
Bombs every day,
Everywhere.
And those sons-of-bitches Arabs
spat in our faces when we walked by their homes.
Two guys in my unit croaked.
Right there, practically in front of me.
They were not even fighting.
Just guarding the streets.

That's how these animals pay us back.
After we get that fat pig out of there
and we're trying to teaching them
how to live like human beings!

Animals! That's what they are!

Oh! You'll love this:
There, even the whores wear black veils!

* * * * *

They're shit.
They smell like shit.
They think shit.

But who the hell cares about any of this now.

* * * * *

One day we smoked a joint
and took the creeps out of their cages.

We got them naked.
I held one of them on a dog leash.
and put a panty over his head.
One of us took a leak on a guy's face
and all that...
So, what's the big deal?
The dogs were scary, though.
I'll give you that.

But, helloooo! It was IRAQ!
It's not like we were on vacation.
It wasn't a gangster movie either.
What do you think we got?
Stale hamburgers and flat beer.
And what was going on every day?
A LOT OF NOTHING.
Except another guy you just met got shot.
The rest was all,
"Yes, sir! Yes, sir! Yes, sir!"

Oh, please.
Somebody has to look bad
so that it all looks good, I GUESS.

* * * * *

But wait, what was I talking about?
Oh, yeah. The guy on the leash.
At some point, I look at him
and the coward covers his face
and starts crying like a baby.

Right there and then,
I thought of that buck I shot when I was nine.
He never closed his eyes.
He kept staring at me even after he died.

I still see him sometimes in my head
and I get all sweaty.
I wish I could talk to him and tell him,
"You're a real man.
Not like this scum here.
I didn't really mean to kill you, buddy.
I was just a kid.
I don't even like venison."

* * * * *

Hey, what are you looking at?
Did I offend you?
Well, pardon me, SIR.

* * * * *

IV. Susan

[*She stands in front of the TV cameras. She wears glasses.*]

I was stopping at a red light
and then out of nowhere
this black guy came
and got into my car.
And he had a gun.
And he pointed it at me.
And told me to drive.
And so I did.
When I asked him why
he told me to shut up
or else he'd kill me.

[*She takes her glasses off and sits down.*]

I called Mom.
She wasn't there.
I was drinking for days.
I took some pills
and I drove to the lake.

They were asleep.
So sweet, you know?
I wish you'd seen them...

I released the brakes,
and let the car go.

It was a full-moon night.
So pretty...
The car sank slowly, slowly.

* * * * *

The bubbles kept popping up
on the glistening water
like sprites in a fairy tale.

I was going to kill myself.
But I couldn't.
My dad shot himself when I was six
and I'm still waiting for him.

* * * * *

My kids.
My little kids...

I wanted to get them out of the water.
But I didn't.
And it's a good thing I didn't.
They're all right now.
They're with God.
They're little angels now.

They have nothing to remember.
Nothing to forget.

God will erase my kisses from their cheeks.
God will turn me into a faint shadow
in their never-ending dreams.

God will play with them.
(God knows how to play with kids.)
God will be their mother.

* * * * *

Their mother...

They had no mother.
They had a wreck of a human being for a mother.
Human garbage.

* * * * *

Human garbage made their breakfast every day.
Human garbage changed their diapers every day.
Human garbage took them to school every day.
Human garbage sang them songs softly
Every night,
Fell asleep smelling their sweaty heads.

Every night.

My sweet things...

* * * * *

Who am I?
I am the stupid high-school kid
who slept with every boy who said "hi!"
I am the woman crying her eyes out over a married man
who left her alone in some bar late at night.

My dad put a gun to his chest.
But my other dad put his fingers up my crotch
when I was nine-and-a-half.
And when I was ten.
And twelve.
And thirteen.

And fifteen.
And when I came back from prom night.

And you know what?
I LIKED IT.

And I liked that he liked it.

* * * * *

Whose little girl am I now?
I am a clerk in a supermarket.
I'm married to a nobody.
I'm fucking my boss AND my boss's son.
I'm living a life made of cardboard.
I'm a wet cardboard box
run over by trucks on the highway.

Past-due bills and arguments are my daily snack.

And when the night comes, what?
Awake.
Alone.
Just hearing the whisper
of their breath,
my two kids fast asleep.

The little things...

* * * * *

How can they possibly sleep through my anguish?
They don't know their mother is a whore?
A good-for-nothing.
A pathetic liar.
A failure at twenty-three.

* * * * *

I'd put them to bed and drive to Wal-Mart.
Spent a fortune on hair spray,
hair dye,
hair gel,

hair clips,
hair bleach,
hair-repair cream.

That's the mother I was:
A ghost with pretty hair.
No soul...
A body blistering with boredom and fear.

* * * * *

Where did I leave my soul?
In the playground?
At the shop's counter?
At the doctors'?
In some hotel bed?

* * * * *

In bed.
In bed.
In bed.

There, I was someone else.
I loved the taste of their mouths,
but I hated their faces afterwards.
And I couldn't stand the sight of my eyes in the mirror.
Was I me?

* * * * *

Who am I?
How could I?

* * * * *

Their heads smelled of sweat
and milk and candy bars.
They looked at me like dolls come to life.
They were so beautiful!
They smiled at me
as if I were the funniest thing alive.

But sometimes they cried,
and cried,
and cried.
Who the hell knows why.
But then they fell asleep.
And I stared at them, wondering:
What are you dreaming about,
little ones?

* * * * *

I loved them.
I hated them.
They were the shadows of what
I should have been.

[*Back to the TV cameras. She stands up and puts her glasses on.*]

I mean, I can't even describe
what I'm going through.
My heart aches so bad!
I can't eat, I can't sleep,
I can't do anything but think about them.

[*She takes her glasses off and sits down.*]

I loved them.
I hated them.

Damned kids!
My kids...
My darlings.
My angels.
My burden.
The ache in my groin.
The brats.
The sweet smiles.
The love of my life.

* * * * *

Listen to you, damned woman!

DAMNED,
DAMNED,
DAMNED,
DAMNED,
DAMNED WOMAN!

Burn in hell!

Your kids are with God now.
But you? You will be alone forever.
Dead in life.

God will have no time for you, doll.
You'll burn alive.
You'll burn until you're an old hag.

You know what you are?
You are nothing
but a thick, sour, simmering darkness.

[*Back to the TV cameras. She gets up and puts her glasses on.*]

I want to say to my babies
that your mama loves you.
That your daddy and your family love you.
And you guys, you gotta be strong,
'cause your mama and your daddy
are waitin' for you to come home.

She takes her glasses off, sits down and stares out, the body limp.]

* * * * *

V. Leonora

[LEONORA *sits, sipping a martini.*]

Arsenic.
Two hundred milligrams.
Twice a day.

It doesn't taste as bad as you'd think,
if you take it with a perfect martini.

10 milligrams of Valium.
Then, a long bath.
And another martini.

* * * * *

That Greek trainer at the gym
(what was his name again?).
Wait, I think he was Dominican,
or something of that sort...

What a hunk!
What a bore.
He kept saying,
"Take a break, babe!
There's plenty of what you want here."

* * * * *

Take a break, take a break,
broken heart!

Take a pill!
Have a drink!

* * * * *

[*The phone rings.*]

"Hello, dear?
It was GRAND, wasn't it?
We should do it again soon.
VERY soon."

"You're the best...
Ciao, bella.
Ciao. Love you!"

* * * * *

Here's something every girl should know:
Heartache is vulnerable to drugs
and booze.
Then memories fade,
and a bitter laziness takes over.

But if you drink when you wake up,
by lunchtime the memories catch up with you
and you have to cancel:

Two phone calls.

"Sorry, dear, I feel awful,
I didn't sleep a wink last night."

"I have to go to Connecticut tonight.
A last-minute thing, you know…"

* * * * *

"Darling, you're going to kill me.
I totally forgot!
I have an appointment with my new lawyer.…
Next time, dear.
Yes? Next time."

* * * * *

I feel awful.
I'm awful.
My soul is a burden
I can't carry in my flesh anymore.

If I could only sleep…

* * * * *

Leonora? Leonora!
Are you there?
Go away, Leonora,
go away!
Away, where?

Another pill. Another bath.

No. Not a bath.
Gin on the rocks.

* * * * *

If it were not three in the morning
I'd get a haircut,
or a manicure,
or a facial,
or go shopping,
or have a perfect lunch
with someone somewhere.

Do you call this a life, dear?

* * * * *

[*The phone rings.*]

"Hi, darling. I haven't seen you in AGES!
Let's go shopping!"

* * * * *

[*She hangs up.*]

Shopping, shopping, shopping...
It's like drinking, you know?
Just more expensive.

And then you look at yourself
in the glass door of the shop
before jumping into the cab,
and you're shocked.

Darling,
Where did your beauty go?

All that Botox,
all those collagen shots,
two face-lifts,
a tummy tuck.

Walk into your closet
and get into your usual drag.
You'll still look like shit.

How much perfume and fur
is it going to take
to hide your sagging soul?

* * * * *

You were so pretty once.
Wittiest thing around!
And such great parties, remember?
Necking with someone's husband
after theater and champagne,
and back home, furious fucking with the help.

("Oh, Daisy!
Would you be a perfect darling
and get me a couple of aspirin.
And a little vodka?")

Well, what can I say?
The good boys were all a bore.
A scotch or two and they'd put everyone to sleep
reminiscing about their days at Harvard
their Scottish grand-daddies
and all the wives they'd dumped.

* * * * *

He was different.
I didn't get bored.
He got me.
God! That mouth!
So slippery.
And that bite!

He made me bleed.
He ate me up.
And I cried for more.
Every time.

And I paid his bills.
All the time.

Are you ready for this?
I bought the tux he wore at our wedding—
a perfect Italian thing.
And next day I found the phone number
of the coat-check girl in one of the pockets.

The son of a bitch!

I went to the ladies room
and stared hard at my face.
You see these tiny spiderwebs
creeping around my eyes?
They only appear when I smile.

Bitterness becomes you, lady.
When you're tender,
you look like a hag.

* * * * *

The bastard . . .
So clever!

All that fancy talk about Truman Capote
and the Greeks,
and the Mediterranean sun,
and late Matisse
and William Carlos Williams—
who's he anyway?

Excellent blood!
Not a cent.

* * * * *

All the time breathing lies down my neck.

Stupid woman,
STUPID, STUPID, STUPID woman.
All along thinking:

This is it.
This is him.
I want nothing but him.
I want his teeth biting my nipples

* * * * *

What else do you want, love?

Three divorces.
A son who doesn't want to see you.
An ugly brat for a grandson
luckily put away in some boarding school.
And your daughter-in-law?
An investment banker from New Jersey
who looks like a frigid escort.
(Ha! New money.)

* * * * *

Listen, you think you're better than me,
don't you?
Dumb blonde with a microphone!
And you?
How much do you make in the back offices of FOX, dear?
Do you think you know me?

You're just hungry for a buck.
You worry about picking up the phone at home
because it may be Citicorp,
Chase Manhattan,
student loans.

You stupid people.
You STUPID, STUPID, STUPID people.
You think that fighting for
every penny in your pocket
makes you better than me,
just because I'm sad, and bored, and rich?

You have any idea, you little upstart
what it's like to be fifty
and have nothing to fight for?

* * * * *

It's three o'clock and he's not here.
Where is he?

He always comes back
smelling of whores.
Rips my dress.
Takes me on the floor.
And I don't care.
All I want is some love.
To make love...

DOES ANYBODY KNOW HOW TO UN-MAKE LOVE?

* * * * *

How many hands have you shaken?
How many names have you forgotten, Leonora?

How many times did you gulp enough Valium
to wake up in a pool of vomit?
It's really hard to kill yourself, as it turns out.

Not this time.

* * * * *

It's almost over.
The doctors don't know what's wrong with me.
Maybe it's all the booze.
Or just menopause...

The idiots!

I put everything under his name a month ago.
Last night I managed to make him angry.
We had a big fight.
I called the cops.

I just had my nails done
and I'll be wearing a glorious nightgown.

Two hundred milligrams of arsenic.
Another martini,
and I'll croak.
But he'll rot in jail.

Murder.
MURDER IN THE FIRST DEGREE!

Ah! Would you look at my skin?
Tony has been telling me for years,
"Honey, all you need is hydration!
HY-DRA-TION!"
But guess what?
Tears don't count.

[*She drinks up.*]

• • •

The Cleaning

Zilvinas Jonusas

Zilvinas Jonusas

Born in Lithuania, Zilvinas received his theatre education at the prestigious Vilnius University. While still a student, he was invited to join the Russian Drama Theatre of Lithuania, where he met the Russian director Yuriy Popov, and later joined with Popov to create the highly successful and innovative theatre show *Pop Off*, where he co-directed and choreographed all the theatre's productions.

Zilvinas' most prominent work in theatre as a director and producer includes *George Dandin or the Deceived Husband* by Molière, *Madame de Sade* by Yukio Mishima; as an actor, Comtesse de Saint-Fond, in *Madame de Sade* by Yukio Mishima, the title role of *Caligula* by Albert Camus, King Ignat in *Yvonne, Princess of Burgundy* by Witold Gombrowicz, and Kublai Khan in *Marco Millions* by Eugene O'Neill.

Zilvinas received his masters degree in media arts from Long Island University. His thesis, "Epistemologies of Death, Desire, and Disgust in the Films," was published by VDM Verlag in 2008.

setting

When the audience enters the theater (the performance space) they see a chair, a table, and a pair of shoes next to the table on the stage. There is a lamp with a circular metal shade above the chair. The placement of all these things should remind us of an electric chair. In the background there is a door. Harsh light is cast from under the bottom of the door. The stage is dark. Only the lamp above the chair is lit.

• • •

[THE CLEANING LADY *enters the stage holding a broom and a boom box.*]

THE CLEANING LADY   [*Unhappy.*] They left the shoes again. I told them to take the shoes. I'm not supposed to take care of the shoes. It's not my business to run around and take care of somebody's shoes. What do they think I am some kind of slave or something?

[THE CLEANING LADY *puts the boom box down and goes to pick up the shoes.*]

When will they get that a cleaning lady cleans, but never takes care of the shoes, never. It's not a cleaning lady's job to take care of the shoes. It is not. They never listen. Eh...

[THE CLEANING LADY *picks up the shoes and leaves the stage. A young man (later called* JOSEF K.*) enters the stage. He is wearing a black suit and is holding a piece of paper. The suit is way too big for him. It is as if somebody bought the suit for him hoping that he would later grow into it.*]

[JOSEF K. *is a little confused. He was not expecting to see the audience staring at him. He was definitely hoping to have a private interview. After a few uncomfortable moments with the audience he sees the table.* JOSEF K. *goes towards it and stops on one side of the table. He waits.*]

[*Nobody enters the room, so he starts playing with one of the buttons on his suit. The button falls down. As* JOSEF K. *starts looking for the button, suddenly there is a beam of light on him, as if the police have just caught him doing something illegal. From now on the light will follow* JOSEF K. *wherever he goes.*]

THE VOICE   Josef K.?

> [JOSEF K. *is startled by the sound of* THE VOICE. *He tries to find out where the voice is coming from and tries to understand whether or not that voice is talking to him.*]
>
> Josef K.?

JOSEF K.   I, I don't... You are talking to... oh, no, no, no. My name is...

[*He is cut off by* THE VOICE.]

THE VOICE   Josef K. You are a bank clerk.

JOSEF K.   No, no, no I don't work in a bank.

> [*Silence.*]
>
> There is some kind of misunderstanding. First of all I'm not Josef K. and this invitation [*Shows the paper.*] is not for me. I found it under my door this morning. I thought that this paper holds some kind of importance for somebody, so I brought it here.

THE VOICE   Does the paper have your address on it?

JOSEF K.   Yes it does, but since I am living in an apartment rented by another person I thought that it would be my duty to bring it to you personally and let you know that there is nobody living at this address.

THE VOICE   You are saying that nobody's living in your apartment?

JOSEF K.   No, no, no, that's not what I'm saying.

THE VOICE   Then the invitation is for you.

JOSEF K.   Well [*Pause.*] to tell you the truth I was not going to bring this paper myself, since I clearly understood that there was some kind of mistake at the post office. When I opened the door to put a note for the postman, I found two men waiting for me in the hallway. The two men forced themselves inside my apartment and demanded that I bring the paper to you personally. After I said that the paper is not for me and it is not my business to bring it back, they brought me here by force. Could you explain to me why I am here and what this means?

[*Silence.*]

I really don't understand why I got this and why those men took me here in such a manner.

THE VOICE   You are no doubt greatly surprised by this morning's events. Aren't you?

JOSEF K.   Of course. Of course I'm surprised, but not greatly surprised.

THE VOICE   Not greatly surprised?

JOSEF K.   Perhaps you misunderstand me. I mean...

[*Looks around.*]

I can sit down, can I?

[*There is no answer.* JOSEF K. *decides to sit down.*]

THE VOICE   This chair is for later.

[JOSEF K. *jumps up from the chair and returns to the point where he was standing before.*]

JOSEF K.   I mean, I'm, of course, greatly surprised, but when you've been in this world for over thirty years you get hardened to surprises, and don't take them seriously. Particularly not today's.

THE VOICE   Why particularly not today's? So you think what is happening to you is a joke?

JOSEF K.   I'm not saying I think the whole thing is a joke; the preparations involved seem far too extensive for that. All of you here, the papers and those two guards, indicate that the whole thing goes far beyond a joke. So I'm not saying it's a joke, no.

THE VOICE   That's right.

JOSEF K.   But on the other hand, on the other hand, it can't be too important a matter. I conclude from the fact that I've been summoned that those papers are definitely meant for somebody else and contain some ridiculous information which could be given by a man who's not serious.

THE VOICE   So you think the papers are not serious?

JOSEF K.   I don't know, but they are definitely asking for something I don't want to be involved with.

THE VOICE   What do you think those papers are about?

JOSEF K.   Well, I can't tell you exactly what those papers are all about, because for me they are a mystery as well. I could just suggest a thought, what I think they could mean.

[*Silence.*]

Well, first I am being accused of something and I have no idea what I am accused of.

THE VOICE   [*Suddenly.*] Take your pants off.

JOSEF K.   What? What do you mean?

THE VOICE   That's exactly what I mean. Take your pants off.

JOSEF K.   Can I ask you why?

THE VOICE   No. Here we are the ones who ask questions. If you're not going to take your pants off yourself, the two men will make you do it.

[JOSEF K. *takes his shoes off first. Then he takes his pants off, folds them, and places them next to the shoes on the floor.*]

The jacket too.

[JOSEF K. *takes the jacket off, folds it, and places it next to the pants. Now he is left wearing underwear and a shirt, which are way too big for him too.*]

THE VOICE   [*After a pause, with relief.*] Good. You are a man.

JOSEF K.   Well, I always was.

THE VOICE   Well, not in my notes.

JOSEF K.   What do you mean? . . . Oh, I'm sorry. I forgot . . . you— questions, I—answers . . .

THE VOICE   We would like to ask the witness to come in.

JOSEF K.   The witness?

[*The door opens and a young woman in her thirties enters. She is all dressed up in an office outfit that is a little bit too racy to be worn in an office environment. She looks more like she dressed herself in a little bit more sexually revealing/exposed way, as if she has a purpose to seduce as many men as she can. First JOSEF K. gets a little embarrassed by the presence of the woman, but then he sees the woman's face and quickly realizes that he knows her.*]

JOSEF K.   Leni?

[*The woman recognizes JOSEF K. as well, but shows no emotions.*]
What are you doing here?

[*Another light turns on above LENI's head where she stands.*]

THE VOICE   Do you recognize the accused?

LENI   [*Looks at JOSEF K., then coldly.*] Yes, I recognize the accused. His name is Josef K.

JOSEF K.   Leni it's me. I'm not Josef K. I'm ...

[THE VOICE *cuts off* JOSEF K.]

THE VOICE   Nobody gave you the right to talk when the witness is talking.
[*To LENI.*]
What would you say about him?

LENI   I think he should be punished.

JOSEF K.   What? Leni, why are you saying this?

THE VOICE   Please be quiet!
[*Coughs.*]
Why do you think he should be punished?

LENI   I think he is a homosexual.

JOSEF K.   Leni, I thought I could trust you. Is that what this whole masquerade is all about?

THE VOICE   Josef K., are you a homosexual?

JOSEF K.   What does it have to do with my case and all this?

THE VOICE   Answer the question. It has everything to do with your case and all this.

[*Speaks almost as if to himself, but is still perfectly heard by everybody.*]

I told you that I was afraid that you might become a lesbian, choosing this ridiculous profession.

JOSEF K.   Dad?

[*Silence.*]

Dad, is that you?

[*Suddenly there is a huge change in the lighting. A harsh spot light is directed to one of the audience members. It's loud and "happy." There is a feeling like a hundred TVs are playing commercials at the same time.*]

THE VOICE   [*In a different tone.*] The answer is correct. You've just won a free trip to Paradise Island!

[*Suddenly everything quiets down. The light is as in the previous scene.*]

LENI   He's not your dad. He's your judge.

JOSEF K.   [*To LENI.*] Judge?

[*Hoping that his dad is still there.*]

Dad? I don't understand.

[*To LENI.*]

He died nine years ago. If he's not my dad then how does he know? This . . . This was exactly what he told me then . . . I said to him, I was going to study the arts . . . He couldn't understand why. He couldn't understand why I wasn't choosing to be a doctor or a scientist. Then he looked at me and said that he's afraid that I might become a lesbian . . . I know it sounds funny. I and becoming a lesbian. He didn't know what to call it . . . My uncle . . . My father knew that his brother was . . . Or maybe he was afraid to call it by its real name. I felt like he was avoiding calling the devil himself . . . But I perfectly understood what he meant by "becoming a lesbian." I was seventeen then and the meaning of it was clear to me, as clear as a human tear could be.

LENI   He knows everything.

[*Shows to the paper.*]

I think you need to sign this paper as soon as possible if you don't want to be hurt even more. The sooner you sign, the less pain.

[*Suddenly in a different tone to* JOSEF K.]
Can you tell me why you said no when I asked you for a child?

JOSEF K. Leni, I told you that I can't have children with you.

LENI So, you mean, you were just pretending that you love me?

JOSEF K. No, I wasn't pretending, but I already knew that I can't have children.

LENI You're so egotistic. How of a big deal for you would that be? I saw you could do it.

JOSEF K. Leni, it's not about if I could do it. It's about being responsible.

LENI How can you speak about responsibilities when you are...

JOSEF K. I am what?
[*Pause.*]
You still don't understand, Leni.

LENI No, I understand perfectly. You can have children, but not with me.

JOSEF K. I will never have children, Leni.

LENI Why? Is there something wrong with your sperm or something, or did you catch AIDS already? What? I really want to know.

JOSEF K. I'm afraid that my children will be judged as I am.

LENI Nobody's judging you. It's all in your head.

JOSEF K. Then why am I constantly reminded that I'm not fit to live, that I'm a sick person, that God will punish me for my...Leni... I already knew from a very young age that there is something in me I won't be able to change. I knew it from the very first time I saw a naked man and had that strange feeling...
It happened on the beach when I was twelve. Every summer my mother, my brother, and I would go and spend our days there. One day I had the urge to go and look around. After I wandered away from my mother and my brother I found myself in the dunes with naked men lying all around me. The excitement of seeing those men took over me and I sat on a bench and started looking at them. A guy as old as I am now approached me. He sat

down on the bench next to me. He pointed to one of the older men on the dunes and said: "This man is not a good man. You should not listen what he says to you." And right after that he asked me if he could suck my pee-pee. It sounded very strange to me, but it was exactly what I wanted to hear at that moment. When I heard those words, I thought that all the water from my body had evaporated. My mouth was dry as the Sahara desert. After a moment of trying to say something, I just nodded, and followed him to the dunes to have what I wanted to have.

Time stopped then. Later I regretted what I did. I heard that it was wrong and that it's a deadly sin to have sex with men. But, surprisingly, at that moment it was so right that I completely forgot about time. I remember how we got undressed, I remember the guy asking me if I had done this before. Even though that was my very first time I knew what to do with the guy...

I remember how the guy came. I remember how suddenly I realized that my mother and my brother were probably looking for me. Without even saying a word I jumped into my shorts and ran to the sea to wash off all that excitement and guilt. My throat was even dryer. I tried to wash it down with the salty sea water, but it just got worse... God, I'm so thirsty.

[*The sound of pouring water into a glass is heard.*]

I saw my brother looking at me with a strange look as if he had seen me with that man. Later I realized that he actually did see me going after the man to the dunes... He just kept saying: "This man is bad. This man is bad."

From that day on, I was secretly visiting the same beach area (I could not stop myself from going there as often as I could.) Even if nothing would happen, I needed to see them. Every time after I would finish with one man or another I would run into the water to wash that something which was unwashable. Every time I would go home with that feeling that everybody knew what I was doing... I had to hide myself inside a thick shell. I dived into studying and sports. I made myself busy all the time just to forget who I really am.

The strange thing was that in the meantime I still was able to fall in love with girls. I thought that I am (was) "normal." But somehow I never wanted to touch a woman's body the way I liked to touch a man's. Somehow I never felt with a woman as close as I was with another man.

The real understanding of a man's love came to me much later. It came after I met you, Leni. I remember that day.

You were leaning next to a wall and were wearing exactly the same outfit as you are wearing right now. You were beaming that strange light which attracts men as bees to the honey. You approached me and asked if I would be interested in having a glass of champagne with you later. I said yes, and our evening finished in somebody's house. Even though we were sleeping completely dressed, my fingers were able to feel your wet desire. I believe we kissed each other the whole night. Then we had another "glass of champagne" night. I remember feeling my body erect for such a long time, that it was hurting me beyond words. But it was different. Something really important was missing. Later on I learned about your child. I really felt grown up then, even though I was only twenty-one at the time. I was already thinking about what a good father I could be to him . . .

One evening you introduced me to your best friend. That was when my whole life went crashing down on me, because I was thinking of getting married to you, but after that night . . . I had a rum with your best friend and realized that drinking champagne with you was just an image I wanted to have. Leni, my reality was rum, not champagne. I know you are probably disgusted by me right now, but your friend was who I wanted to be with for the rest of my life.

LENI   Why are you telling me all this right now? I knew that you were sleeping with my best friend. I asked you for a child.

JOSEF K.   You asked me for a child. You asked me for my DNA. It means that my homosexuality, my guilt might be transferred to another human being as a virus nobody wants to have. That means somebody will be judged and will be hurt and I will not be able to help them, because what I feel means nothing. Humans are not supposed to have feelings. They have to follow somebody's orders and rules. My feelings count for nothing, because they are not what a man is supposed to feel. Remember that day when your son suddenly grabbed your glass full of boiling-hot tea and spilled it on his face, remember? You could at least take him to the hospital and fix the burns he had on his face. Now imagine those burns inside of a child's soul. No doctor can help him heal it.

LENI   What does a child have to do with it?

JOSEF K.   Because as a child I already knew that I wouldn't be wanted. I knew that I would become a disgrace as soon as they found out about me. Already then I saw myself as those men on the beach looking for that different adventure. But there is nothing exciting about this kind of adventure. It is more like dancing with your loneliness. Because of that dancing you will be accused of something you never did. I was twelve, then, Leni, twelve... You're asking for my child. You're asking for a child who would grow up without a father, even more, without anybody who would understand why he is feeling this way, a child who would constantly be asking, why is this happening to me? Why can't I be like everybody else?

[*Looks at the paper suddenly.*]

How could I have missed that? Now I understand why I am here.

[JOSEF K. *suddenly puts on the jacket and the pants, leaving the shoes. He goes to the table, sits on the chair, and puts the paper in front of him.*]

LENI   What are you doing, Vlad?

JOSEF K.   I'm not Vlad, Leni. I lived my whole life as Josef K. I must be Josef K.

[*There is an electrical glitch. The beam of light which was following JOSEF K. throughout dies out.*]

LENI   Vlad?

[LENI *goes to the table and looks at* JOSEF K. *She picks up the paper. Suddenly there is the same beam of light on her face as the one on* JOSEF K.'s.]

THE VOICE Leni?

LENI [*Tries to understand who is talking to her.*] I don't...are you talking to me? My name is not Leni.

THE VOICE You will find your invitation under your door tomorrow morning. Be ready by seven o'clock.

[LENI *rushes out.* THE CLEANING LADY *comes in. She goes to the boom box, picks it up, and goes to the place where she found the shoes in the beginning.*]

THE CLEANING LADY Of course a cleaning lady always just cleans. Nothing else, just cleaning.

[THE CLEANING LADY *puts down the boom box, presses the play button, and prepares herself for the cleaning. After a moment she discovers the new shoes.*]

Shoot, they left the shoes again.

[*She recognizes the shoes. Tomasso Albinoni's Adagio in G minor starts playing.*]

Vladik? You're here too? Oh god, Vladik? How many more of you are going to come here? How many more?

[THE CLEANING LADY *picks up the shoes and goes toward* JOSEF K.]

So you're the last one for today, Vladik, the last one? Let me take care of you now, Vladik, let me take care of you. You were a good man, you were a good man.

[*The door opens and a huge pile of shoes spill into the stage.*]

[*Blackout.*]

• • •

Breakfast and Bed

Amy Fox

Amy Fox

Amy Fox is a playwright and screenwriter. Her plays include: *By Proxy, Summer Cyclone, One Thing I like to Say Is, Heights, Honeymoon Hotel,* and *Farm Boys* (co-writer). *One Thing I like to Say Is* was named a finalist for the 2006 Susan Smith Blackburn Prize, and has had two showcase productions in New York: (Clubbed Thumb, 2007; Cockeyed Optimists, 2009). *By Proxy* was commissioned by the Alfred P. Sloan Foundation in 2006, and was produced at CAP21 in May 2009. Amy's other plays have been produced or developed by the Ensemble Studio Theatre, Primary Stages, The Lark, Soho Rep, New River Dramatists, and the Blue Heron Arts Center. Her work has also been produced in London, San Francisco, Austin, St. Paul, Albuquerque, and Orlando. *Summer Cyclone* and *Heights* are published by Dramatists Play Service. She was a member of Youngblood for five years and is currently a member of the Ensemble Studio Theatre.

Fox adapted her one-act play, *Heights*, for the screen, and the resulting Merchant Ivory film was released in theatres nationwide in 2005. She has an MFA in fiction writing from Brooklyn College and teaches screenwriting at NYU's graduate film program. She lives in Brooklyn, New York.

characters

>ELOISE, late 30s
>LEX, late 20s

• • •

[*A small city apartment—living room/kitchen. ELOISE, late 30s, very attractive, is at the kitchen table, drinking coffee and smoking a cigarette. She wears a silk robe and her hair is in a towel turban. She is looking at LEX, late 20s, who is asleep on the couch, half dressed in clothes from the night before. A pair of black boots are in the middle of the floor. LEX opens her eyes. She sits up, covering herself and looking around, disoriented.*]

ELOISE   Hi.

LEX   Oh—hi.

ELOISE   Coffee?

LEX   Oh, no thanks.

ELOISE   It's good coffee. Hazelnut. If you like that.

LEX   I'm OK, thanks. I was just looking for...Chris.

ELOISE   There's orange juice.

LEX   That's okay. Um, is Chris here.

ELOISE   No. There's bagels...Chris had to go to work.

LEX   Oh.

ELOISE   We have that cream cheese, mixed with lox.

LEX   I'm okay—um, so Chris is—

ELOISE   At work. I could give you the number, if you want.

LEX   Um, okay. Sure.

ELOISE   I gotta look for it. I should have it memorized, but it's just one of those that doesn't stick, you know.

>You sure you don't want some coffee? Or a cigarette?

LEX   OK, some coffee.

[ELOISE *pours a cup of coffee and sets it down, instead of handing it to* LEX. LEX *sits down at the table.*]

ELOISE   That's right. A person's got to relax. Enjoy the morning. That's the way to live. Enjoy the night, enjoy the morning.

LEX   Sure.

ELOISE   Did you?

LEX   What.

ELOISE   Enjoy your night.

LEX   Yeah, it was...pretty good. So, roommates?

ELOISE   Sorry?

LEX   You and Chris are roommates?

ELOISE   Sure. I guess we are. As it were.

LEX   She didn't say.

ELOISE   Well, here we are. How's the coffee?

LEX   Good, thanks.

ELOISE   So let me guess. You went to one of those cat places, what is it called, the pussy cat something or other...

LEX   No—

ELOISE   Nanny's.

LEX   Lee's.

ELOISE   Oh yes, Lee's.

LEX   Have you been there?

ELOISE   No, what's it like?

LEX   I don't know. It's small, crowded, but kind of cute. Red velvet drapes, that kind of thing.

ELOISE   Like a lounge.

LEX   Yeah, in the back.

ELOISE   Good music?

LEX   Yeah, loungy kind of.

ELOISE   In the East Village, right?

LEX   Yeah, 5th Street. Right next to that vintage store, Roses?

ELOISE   I like that place. A couple months ago, I found this incredible flapper dress there. Red, with a fringe.

LEX   I love those. I always thought in a previous life, maybe I was a flapper.

ELOISE   Absolutely. What fun. And you have those big eyes.

LEX   Thanks…

> [ELOISE *holds out the coffee pot, offering more to* LEX.]
> Thanks.

[ELOISE *pours the coffee.*]

ELOISE   So was it crowded? Lee's? Oh, you said it was. It's just I really haven't been out to Lee's, or the pussycat place, so I'm just curious. How it works, what goes on.

LEX   Yeah, it was pretty much my first time. At Lee's, I mean.

ELOISE   Oh.

LEX   So I wasn't really sure how it would be. But mostly it's just a bar, you know. I mean that's what it is—a bar. You should check it out, if you want.

ELOISE   Do people dance, or just hang out.

LEX   Both, pretty much. We danced.

ELOISE   Chris? Really?

LEX   Yeah.

ELOISE   Huh.

LEX   What?

ELOISE   Oh, no, it's just she doesn't always feel like it. Or so she says.

LEX Oh.

ELOISE But, what do I know. I wasn't there.

LEX Well, we...danced.

ELOISE Sounds good. Chris didn't say much, this morning, but she never does. Seems like she usually has a good time, she always seems to *meet people*.

[LEX *takes this in, not sure how to react.*]

LEX Do you have that number?

ELOISE I'm surprised, actually, now that I think about it. I mean, don't take this the wrong way, but you don't seem like her type.

LEX Well. Look, I don't know what your whole set-up is here, but—

ELOISE I mean, you said it was your first time, right, at Lee's?

LEX Sure, but—

ELOISE Are you straight?

LEX What?!

ELOISE I'm sorry, she pretty much does her own thing, Chris, but I look out for her. Somebody's got to.

LEX She seems like she could look after herself.

ELOISE All I'm saying is I know some people go through a kind of phase, a time of exploration...

LEX Look, I don't know you—

ELOISE Which is fine, I just think if that's what it is, just leave Chris out of it. That's all I'm saying. Because she doesn't need that. To wake up next to a straight girl.

LEX Well, she didn't wake up next to anybody, did she. Because she went to WORK or wherever, and actually I'm feeling a little weird about this whole thing, so could you just give me that number.

ELOISE I mean, you're cute, that's not what I meant, when I said her type, you've got those beautiful flapper eyes. What I meant was...

LEX   What?

ELOISE   Never mind. Let's just have some breakfast.

LEX   I don't want breakfast.

ELOISE   Coffee then.

LEX   I don't want coffee. I want to go home and take a shower. I just want Chris's phone number.

ELOISE   Okay. Hang on.

> [*She gets up and starts going through a pile of papers. LEX gets up and follows her, waiting for the number.*]

> How old are you?

LEX   Thirty.

ELOISE   She's a baby. Twenty, did you know that?

LEX   No.

ELOISE   What did she tell you?

LEX   Thirty.

ELOISE   And you believed her?

LEX   I don't know.

ELOISE   She plays tough, but she's a baby. That's why I worry about her. Don't want to see her getting mixed up in some iffy situation. Somebody who doesn't know what they're looking for.

LEX   Look. I'm just gonna leave my number. And I don't know if you'll give it to her, but whatever.

[LEX *grabs a sheet of paper and scribbles down her number.*]

ELOISE   Of course I'll give it to her. Why wouldn't I give it to her.

LEX   Look, I have no idea what the deal is here.

ELOISE   You think I would do that? Confiscate your number?

LEX   You might.

ELOISE   Well, then you better take hers. Just in case. I think it's in here.

[*She dumps out the contents of her bag. A photograph of a little girl in pigtails is among the items.*]

There she is. Little sweetheart.

LEX   That's Chris?

ELOISE   Four years old.

LEX   You carry that around?

ELOISE   Wouldn't you? Look at that face.

LEX   Okay, look, I have to ask you, are you guys a thing? I mean, what's the deal.

ELOISE   A thing?

LEX   You and Chris?

ELOISE   Oh! No—

LEX   Because—there's this very weird vibe—

ELOISE   Hold on, there's no vibe, because . . .

LEX   Oh, yes, there is—

ELOISE   No—because—

LEX   What—

ELOISE   . . . I'm her mother.

LEX   What?!

ELOISE   It's true. She's my little girl. She moved home in December.

LEX   Home.

ELOISE   I don't know, she got dumped by some guy . . .

LEX   Some guy?

ELOISE   It happens.

LEX   Yeah, guys happen. But she doesn't like guys—

ELOISE   Not so much, it turns out.

LEX   I'm sorry, but I'm just a little disoriented. She said she was thirty, and this was her place, and—

ELOISE   Well, adjust.

LEX   What?

ELOISE   I mean, for God's sake, you knew her for what six hours? So not everything she told you is what you thought, fine, adjust. Integrate the new information.

LEX   Integrate.

ELOISE   That's what our brains do with new experiences.

LEX   Yeah, well, there's a little too much integration going on right now. Too much information to . . .

ELOISE   Right. I guess you're still processing last night.

[*Silence. *LEX* finally stands up.*]

LEX   I'm gonna go. Yeah. I'm gonna do my processing somewhere else.

ELOISE   I'm sorry. I shouldn't have . . . you don't have to go.

LEX   Yeah, well, just tell Chris . . . I don't know.

ELOISE   You still want the number? . . . I understand. I'll tell her . . . it's not her, can I tell her that, that it's because of . . . me. Or is it you.

LEX   It's really just . . . it's none of your business.

ELOISE   You're right.

LEX   I mean, none of this is your business.

ELOISE   I'm sorry—I guess I just thought you might want to talk to somebody.

LEX   To you?

ELOISE   No, of course not. I mean, I'm sure you have lots of people to talk to.

LEX   Yeah—sure.

ELOISE   I'm sure as soon as you're through that door you'll have your cell phone out ready to call whoever . . .

LEX   Yeah, it's really great, because whoever—always takes my calls. Always. Which is really great. If you do want to talk to somebody.

ELOISE   . . . Would you like some more coffee? You can stay a few minutes. We don't have to talk, we could just have some coffee. If you want.

[*The phone rings.* ELOISE *answers it.*]

Hello? Hi, Ted. Oh, sure. Um, yeah, that would be—okay. As long as it's funny, right? Never mind. I was kidding, or something. Sure, seven o'clock, bye.

[*She hangs up.*]

I have a date tonight. He wants to go to stand-up comedy. You're still here.

LEX   I guess I'm still . . . integrating.

ELOISE   Take your time. Here.

[*She pours more coffee.* LEX *slowly sits down.*]

It's not very romantic, stand-up comedy, is it? Chris hates it. Really hates it. Did she tell you that? Well, I guess she didn't tell you much. You thought she was thirty.

LEX   She seemed . . . mature.

ELOISE   Well, a lot can happen to a girl before twenty. I had Chris when I was eighteen.

[*She sees the phone number among the items from her bag.*]

There it is. The elusive work number. And here's ours.

[*She scribbles the numbers down.*]

LEX   She works where? She said, last night, she was an architect.

ELOISE   She's the assistant to the assistant to the architect.

LEX   Ah.

[*She picks up the phone number.*]

ELOISE   Do you think you'll call her? After all this? I mean, she's not the type to wait by the phone, but I'd like to give her some clue what to expect . . .

LEX   I don't think I should make any promises.

ELOISE   So you won't.

LEX   I don't know. I didn't say that. I said—

ELOISE   Come on, it's pretty clear. I just think it's only fair to be honest about things.

LEX   Look—I—

ELOISE   I mean it's your decision—no one is saying you have to call, but—

LEX   Look. I have a boyfriend.

ELOISE   Oh.

LEX   I mean, not entirely.

ELOISE   I see.

LEX   We're taking some time. So I can figure some things out.

ELOISE   Right. You did strike me as . . .

LEX   I'm trying to figure some things out.

ELOISE   Such as . . . if you like girls.

LEX   Pretty much.

ELOISE   How do you figure that out?

LEX   I'm not sure.

ELOISE   I'm always wondering how this happens.

LEX   I'm kind of taking it one day at a time. And I haven't really told anyone what's going on.

ELOISE   I thought you were looking for someone to talk to. I just had that feeling.

LEX   I don't know. I guess I thought last night would give me some kind of clarity.

ELOISE   Did it?

LEX   We were drunk—it's a blur. And a night like that can't just change everything, can it?

ELOISE   It would have to be a pretty special night.

LEX   George—that's my boyfriend—he's very logical—wants to analyze the situation from every angle. He's coming back to town tomorrow, from a job interview. Has to decide whether to move to Houston. He wants me to tell him where we stand. He asked me to do something definitive before he came back. Definitive.

ELOISE   I think about this a lot. How you would know. I mean, I'm curious, as a mom. Chris just rolls her eyes, when I try to ask her.

LEX   I don't know. Maybe for some people it's easier.

ELOISE   Chris first kissed a girl when she was thirteen. Then she started kissing boys. Till she met Julie. That was her first love, I think. She's been through four girlfriends and two boyfriends—I think she uses the guys really, for vengeance. But I don't know. I look at her and I don't know what to say. I don't know how to talk to her. Her world is so much bigger. But I want to understand it.

LEX   At least you try. I mean, my mom...she never really cared to ask.

ELOISE   I always wanted a daughter who would tell me everything. I just assumed I'd have some clue what she was talking about.

LEX   So you grill the girls she brings home. Is that usually what happens around here?

ELOISE   First time. It's just, I have so many questions. Everything is so wonderfully complicated these days. I don't know what my life might have been if I had that kind of freedom.

LEX   Well, I'm sure you could...

ELOISE   Yeah. You think there's still time?

LEX   Why not.

ELOISE   You're very brave.

LEX   Brave?

ELOISE   To just jump out there and test the waters....I don't even know your name.

LEX   Lex.

ELOISE   Eloise.

LEX   So...who's your date with. Tonight.

ELOISE   Ted. Third date. He's fine. Chris doesn't like him, says he smirks.

LEX   Does he?

ELOISE   Yeah.

LEX   Well, I hope you have a good time...

ELOISE   You know something? I don't want to go. He's boring. I hate stand-up comedy. And he's boring. There, I've said it. I'm totally bored. Jesus. I haven't been on a good date in a year! Jesus.

LEX   [*Laughing a little.*] I'm sorry...

ELOISE   It just gets worse and worse. The Teds, and those are the sweet ones. And the assholes...That's it. I'm not going.

LEX   Really?

ELOISE   I shouldn't go, right?

LEX   Well, if you don't like him...

ELOISE   That's it. I'm not going. We decided.

LEX   We did?

ELOISE   You're a lifesaver.

LEX   Okay.

ELOISE   Do you think I'm gay?

LEX   What?

ELOISE   Chris thinks so. I know she does. She's always dropping hints. She wants to know why I'm never dating anyone I like. And why I ask her so many questions all the time...

LEX   And why you end up having breakfast with some girl she brought home?

ELOISE   I don't like eating alone.... What?

LEX   Nothing. So these questions you're always asking Chris...

ELOISE   What it's like. How it's different, how it feels different.

LEX   I think it depends on the people.

ELOISE   Well, of course it depends on the people! I'm not so thick as that. But I want to know—I mean for you, for example, how does it feel to...

LEX   To...

ELOISE   Kiss someone. A girl. A woman.

LEX   I'm not sure if I've kissed a woman.

ELOISE   Oh.

LEX   But hypothetically, probably it would feels like...

ELOISE   Like?

> [*They look at each other. LEX kisses ELOISE—a tentative kiss.*]
> Why did you do that?

LEX   I thought you wanted me to.

ELOISE   Did you want to?

LEX   Yes.

ELOISE   It's the same, isn't it. Chris always said it felt the same, but I didn't believe it. But don't you think?

LEX   No, I don't. Not that time.

ELOISE   Oh. I don't know. Maybe it's different.

[*They kiss again, still tentatively. The phone rings. They break away. The phone rings again and again, the answering machine picks up.*]

CHRIS   [*On the machine.*] Hi, Mom, it's me. I'll be home like at 5. Oh, and sorry about this morning—the girl—I know that was totally weird.

[*A beep, then silence.*]

ELOISE   We can't do this.

LEX   I know.

ELOISE   It's too—

LEX   Yeah. I mean, Chris—

ELOISE   She's my daughter—

LEX   I should probably go.

ELOISE   Yeah. I guess that would be...

LEX   I'll just...put on my boots.

[LEX *struggles with the boots, while* ELOISE *watches, perturbed. The phone rings again.* ELOISE *can't decide whether to answer it. The machine picks up.*]

TED   [*On the machine.*] Hi, Eloise, it's me. Ted. I don't know if you recognize my—well, it's me anyway, Ted. So the comedy group, I know you were wondering about their reputation, they're called the Flying Buttresses, I know it's a weird name, but my friend says they're totally hilarious. In like a quirky way...

[ELOISE *reaches over and turns off the machine.*]

LEX   I'm sorry.

ELOISE   [*Sadly.*] For what?

LEX   I don't know.

ELOISE   Then don't be.

[*The phone rings again, a couple of times. Finally* ELOISE *grabs it.*]
Ted? Hi. This is not a good time.

[*She hangs up. She starts to laugh, but quickly stops, a pained expression on her face.*]

LEX   Okay. Well, okay. Bye.

ELOISE   Um—did you ever get the phone number?

LEX   For Chris? At work?

ELOISE   Or for here.

LEX   I kind of—don't know if I'll call.

ELOISE   Yeah. I'll tell her. Not to ... wait for anything.

LEX   Okay ... bye.

[*She goes, awkwardly.* ELOISE *looks after her.*]

ELOISE   Bye.

[ELOISE *goes to her closet and returns with a red flapper dress. She holds it up to herself, closes her eyes. End of play.*]

• • •

The News from St. Petersburg

Rich Orloff

Rich Orloff

Rich Orloff is a prolific author of short plays, mostly comedies, including four that have appeared in previous editions of *Best American Short Plays*. His one-acts have had over 600 productions on six continents (and a staged reading in Antarctica).

The News from St. Petersburg is part of Orloff's trio of one-act comedies, entitled *Ha!*, which also includes *The Whole Shebang* (published in *Best American Short Plays 1994–1995*) and *Oedi* (published in *Best American Short Plays 1997–1998*). *Ha!* is published by Playscripts, Inc., which has published sixty of his short plays in eight volumes.

Orloff's full-length plays include *Vietnam 101: The War on Campus* and the comedy *Someone's Knocking*, which have been produced at theatres and schools across the country, and eight other award-winning comedies (most of which are very good). You can learn more about Rich's plays, short and long, at www.richorloff.com.

characters

FYODOR, a landowner
ANYA, his wife
SASHA, their manservant
NIKOLAI, their good friend, the doctor
A COW OF NOBLE BIRTH (offstage)

place

The living room of a large estate, a few hour's horseback ride from St. Petersburg, Russia.

time

Late in the afternoon of Sunday, January 9, 1905 (old Russian calendar).

The living room is decorated in a plush but unimpressive style, as befits an aristocratic couple with mediocre taste.

• • •

[*As the play begins,* FYODOR, *a philosophical man of about fifty, sits in his easy chair, puffing a pipe, staring into the distance. His wife,* ANYA, *about the same age, is embroidering—something she is not very good at.*]

ANYA   [*Gives a long, deep, world-weary sigh. Then . . .*] The sky turns black so early in January.

FYODOR   The sky turns dark blue.

ANYA   Pardon me?

FYODOR   I always like to think the sky turns dark blue.

ANYA   What's the difference?

FYODOR   Black is gloomy. I like dark blue.

ANYA   Either way, the sky turns dark.

FYODOR   Yes, but it turns darker for you than it does for me. Life is all a matter of perception. I prefer to look at it through rose-colored glasses.

ANYA   I would think then the sky would turn purple.

FYODOR   [*Ignoring her remark.*] Do you know what Vladimir Nikolayich Trishnikov told me in church this morning?

ANYA   No, what?

FYODOR   He told me that Yevgeny Alekseyevich Trofimov-Pishchik was discovered embezzling from his own bank.

ANYA   How awful!

FYODOR   I never trusted the man.

ANYA   Why would anyone embezzle from their own bank? It is not a rational thing to do.

FYODOR   Perhaps Yevgeny Alekseyevich Trofimov-Pishchik is not a rational man.

[*We hear a cow moo in the distance.*]

FYODOR   Ah, Bessimka Bessinovna sounds in good spirits today.

ANYA   Guess what I heard in town yesterday. You won't believe it.

FYODOR   If I won't believe it, then why bother telling me?

ANYA   Just listen. I heard this on good authority from Charlotta, the servant girl of Boris Aekseyevich Kulibin and his wife, Nina Leonardovna. Apparently, Nina Leonardovna has been having an affair for five years with Semon Penteleyevich Rogov, ever since they danced together at the New Century's Eve party given by Mikhail Romanovich Ryabushinsky.

FYODOR   You don't say.

ANYA   There's more. Boris Alekseyevich knew about his wife's affair, but he said nothing . . . for business reasons. But last Tuesday, when Nina Leonardovna usually has her rendezvous with Semon Penteleyevich, who should Boris Alekseyevich see at the market but—Semon Penteleyevich! They were both so shocked they rushed back to the home of Boris Alekseyevich, where they found Nina Leonardovna with Dmitri Dobrolyubov, the bastard son of

Elena Nikolayena Kazakova and either Maxim Lvovich Chichikov or Ivan Konstantinovich Begushkin!

FYODOR   I hear that in America, there are people named Bob. Some people go their entire life being called Bob Smith.

ANYA   America. Isn't that where they believe in life, liberty, and the pursuit of happiness?

FYODOR   I believe so.

ANYA   Amazing such a place has lasted.

[FYODOR *checks his pocket watch.*]

FYODOR   [*Calling to the kitchen.*] Oh, Sasha! Sasha!

SASHA   [*offstage.*] I'll be there in a minute, sir.

FYODOR   It is time for tea.

SASHA   [*offstage.*] I am bringing it now.

[SASHA, *their servant, enters and serves tea.*]

FYODOR   You're three minutes late.

SASHA   I am sorry, sir.

FYODOR   Remember, punctuality is next to godliness.

SASHA   Last week, you told me cleanliness was next to godliness.

FYODOR   Punctuality is on one side of godliness; cleanliness is on the other.

ANYA   Let that be a lesson to you, Sasha.

SASHA   I will, madame. And thank you for your interest in my education.

ANYA   You're welcome.

[SASHA *turns to leave, but then remembers something.*]

SASHA   Oh, sir, madame, excuse me.

FYODOR   Yes, Sasha?

SASHA   Sofya wishes to know what you would like for the evening meal.

ANYA   How should we know? It is not yet time to eat.

SASHA   Could you make a little guess?

FYODOR   Who can predict the future? There are too many imponderables.

SASHA   Please, sir, we need to know.

ANYA   Sasha, go. I am too worn. There is something so tiring about Sundays in January. Already the sky has turned black and blue.

SASHA   Yes, madame.

[SASHA *exits.*]

ANYA   I don't think the servants take as much pride in their work as they once did.

FYODOR   Yes, you're right. I miss feudalism so much.

[*There's a knock on the front door. A pause.* FYODOR *rises.*]

[*Calling to the kitchen.*]

I'll get it, Sasha!

ANYA   You'll get it?!

FYODOR   I need the exercise.

ANYA   It's Sasha's job to open the door.

FYODOR   It's not that important.

ANYA   Mark my words. Today we answer the door; tomorrow they will expect us to dress ourselves.

[FYODOR *opens the door.* NIKOLAI GREGORIEVICH SHUBIN *enters. He looks like he's just heard bad news. He's quite agitated.*]

FYODOR   Nikolai Gregorievich!

NIKOLAI   Good evening, Fyodor Ivanovich, Anna Bogdonovna.*

[**NOTE: He would say the formal "ANNA" here, not "ANYA."*]

ANYA   What a pleasant surprise this visit is.

NIKOLAI   I'm not sure it is.

FYODOR   You don't look well. Are you all right?

NIKOLAI   I have been better.

FYODOR   Would the good doctor like something to drink? A little schnapps, perhaps?

NIKOLAI   No, thank you.

FYODOR   A little vodka then?

NIKOLAI   I'm not thirsty.

FYODOR   Some beet borscht with a little sherry in it?

NIKOLAI   No! Have you heard the news?

FYODOR   What news?

NIKOLAI   The news from St. Petersburg.

ANYA   Has something happened?

NIKOLAI   Yes!

ANYA   Oh, good. So few things actually happen.

NIKOLAI   It is not good.

FYODOR   Why? What happened?

NIKOLAI   You know about all the strikes in the capital, of course.

FYODOR   No.

NIKOLAI   Don't you read the newspaper?

FYODOR   Oh, no. I don't like the way the print rubs off on my fingers.

NIKOLAI   My friends, six days ago a strike started at the Putilov engineering works. All thirteen thousand workers went on strike.

FYODOR   What did the rascals want?

NIKOLAI   Oh, the usual items. An eight-hour day, safe working conditions, decent pay for women, a ban on forced overtime...

ANYA   For that they would go on strike?

FYODOR   Some people turn their desire for progress into an obsession.

NIKOLAI   There's more. Within two days, the strike began spreading to other factories. By Wednesday, the number of people on strike had doubled. By Thursday, doubled again. By yesterday, over one hundred thousand workers were on strike. Not a single chimney remained smoking in any factory in all of St. Petersburg. Not one!

ANYA   I hope someone is taking this opportunity to clean them. They're filthy.

NIKOLAI   You don't understand! Today, there was a demonstration. Two hundred thousand people marched on the Winter Palace.

ANYA   In this weather?! No wonder they're peasants.

NIKOLAI   The police were unable to stop them. They stormed the palace. The Tsar has been deposed!

FYODOR   No!

ANYA   That's impossible.

NIKOLAI   It's revolution! Our entire country is now in the hands of the people!

[*For a moment,* FYODOR *and* ANYA *are stunned. Then* FYODOR *bursts out laughing. Then* ANYA *joins him.*]

FYODOR   What a kidder!

ANYA   What a great joke!

FYODOR   Where did you hear that joke? Did some Jew tell it to you?

NIKOLAI   No.

ANYA   I don't understand Jews. If I were God, I wouldn't have chosen them.

NIKOLAI   There's been a revolution!

ANYA   Who says?

NIKOLAI   I heard it from Yegor Yefimovitch Stankevitch, who heard it from Lyev Alexandrovich Milyukov, who heard it from Sergei Petrovich Purishkevitch.

FYODOR [*To* ANYA.] Sergei Petrovich Purishkevitch cheats at pinochle.

ANYA No!

FYODOR Yes.

NIKOLAI I beg you, listen! Life as you know it is over. If you value your lives, you must flee this country immediately.

ANYA Doctor, please. You are beginning to depress us.

[NIKOLAI *sighs.*]

FYODOR We do appreciate your concern, Doctor. But what you've told us is impossible to believe.

NIKOLAI But it is true, I swear it.

FYODOR Doctor, I am a man of reason, am I not?

NIKOLAI Yes.

FYODOR I can prove to you using the power of logic that there has been no revolution.

ANYA Oh, good. A party game.

[FYODOR *poses, as if in a formal debate.*]

FYODOR Revolution is inconceivable. What is inconceivable is, by definition, inconceivable. Therefore, there has been no revolution.
[*Relaxes, to* NIKOLAI.]
How can you argue with that, Doctor?

NIKOLAI But people saw it, with their own eyes!

FYODOR If I believed everything I saw with my own eyes, I'd never sleep at night. Now then, would you like that drink?

NIKOLAI No! . . . I thought this would be so much easier.

ANYA I have an idea.

FYODOR What?

ANYA Let's ask the servants what happened.

NIKOLAI   The servants?

ANYA   They would certainly know if there's been a revolution. Their class is very closely knit.

FYODOR   Good idea.
[*Calling out.*]
Oh, Sasha! . . . Sasha!

NIKOLAI   [*To* ANYA.] I really am sorry to have to bring you bad news. Both of you have been so kind to me, always developing ailments when I needed the money.

FYODOR   Sasha! . . . Sasha!!!

SASHA   [*Offstage.*] All right, already!!!

[ANYA *and* FYODOR *look at each other.*]

ANYA   That's what happens when you start opening the door.

FYODOR   I don't think that's it.

[SASHA *enters, as drunk as he is very, very happy.*]

SASHA   [*Joyously.*] Hello, my former oppressors!
[*Noticing* NIKOLAI.]
Greetings, Doctor.
[*Bows, then . . .*]
Ooo, I'm a little dizzy.

ANYA   Sasha, what is going on?!

SASHA   We're all having a big party. Would any of you care to join us?

ANYA   No, thank you.

SASHA   Do you know, your champagne tastes as good as we dreamed it would? It's a great way to wash down your caviar.

FYODOR   [*Impatient.*] Sasha, if you don't mind—

SASHA   What can I do for you? I'm here to serve.
[*He breaks out into hysterics. Then . . .*]
Well, I think it's funny.

NIKOLAI   Have you heard the news from St. Petersburg?

SASHA   No, I'm acting this way because I just finished *War and Peace*.

ANYA   Sasha, will you behave yourself?!

SASHA   I shall try, madame.
[*He tries to act sober.*]
How am I doing?

FYODOR   Sasha, what news have you heard?

SASHA   You really want to know?

FYODOR   Yes.

SASHA   You won't like it.

FYODOR   Tell us.

SASHA   Are you sure you want to hear?

FYODOR   Yes.

SASHA   Positive?

FYODOR   What happened?!

SASHA   Okay, you asked for it. Earlier today, Sunday, the 9th of January, 1905, a day that will always be one of my personal favorites, two hundred thousand people, folks just like me, marched on the Winter Palace. Men, women, children, workers, students, two hundred thousand strong, surging through the winter snow. What a picture! Everyone was dressed in their Sunday best, singing hymns, and carrying huge portraits of Our Father, the Tsar...I would have made such a wonderful painter. I begged my parents for some paints, but they were never very encouraging. They said there was more job security in serfdom.

[SASHA *sighs and appears to drift off.*]

FYODOR   Sasha!

SASHA   Yes?

FYODOR   You were telling us about the march.

SASHA Oh, yes. Well, when we reached the Narva Gate, the Cossacks saw this glorious mass of humanity, and they were so moved— you'll love this—they all just laid down their weapons and joined us in our procession. Finally, when we arrived at the palace, Our Father the Tsar saw all of his people united, and he realized he had to surrender to the just demands of his children Russia—or we'd chop him into blintzes. So he abdicated!

FYODOR No.

SASHA Yes!

NIKOLAI I told you.

ANYA Dear God.

SASHA Throughout the country, there is now land and liberty for everyone! All people are free and equal under the law. It's a great day for Russia! It's a great day for human beings everywhere!!!
[*To* FYODOR *and* ANYA.]
Except for maybe folks like you.

ANYA I feel ill.

SASHA It's been nice knowing you.

ANYA What do you mean? Surely, what happened with the Tsar won't change anything here, will it?

SASHA Does the phrase "land reform" mean anything to you?

FYODOR But I own this land.

SASHA Oh, you'll get your share of the land, don't worry. And I'm sure you can borrow the community plow whenever you want.

FYODOR This is too much.

SASHA Come with me to the barn later. I'll show you what a plow looks like.

ANYA Sasha...

SASHA You want to come, too?

ANYA Don't you think you'd be happier working for us?

FYODOR That's right. Maybe we can work out a plan where you'll all gradually take over the land over the next eighty-ninety years, hmmmm?

SASHA I don't think so.

FYODOR The next forty years then.

SASHA Nope.

FYODOR But this isn't fair!

SASHA What can I say? One man's dream; another man's nightmare. Life's kind of crazy, isn't it?

FYODOR But this land is mine. It's been in my family for centuries.

SASHA Sir, I'm sorry, but those were past centuries, not future centuries.

FYODOR But without our land, how will we survive?

[FYODOR *and* ANYA *look at each other, their sad futures becoming real.*]

SASHA Don't you both wish you had died about five minutes ago?

[FYODOR *and* ANYA *don't respond.*]

NIKOLAI Sasha, I think you've said enough.

SASHA I suppose you're right.

[SASHA *begins to leave.*]

ANYA Oh, Sasha, one final question?

SASHA Yes?

ANYA What did Sofya decide to prepare us for the evening meal?

SASHA [*To* ANYA.] You must be kidding. You're doomed!
[*To* FYODOR.]
Doooomed!

[SASHA *exits, as we hear another moo in the distance.*]

ANYA Such impertinence.

FYODOR We are doomed, aren't we?

NIKOLAI Actually, you're doomed. I'm part of the ever-growing middle class.

FYODOR Don't be silly. You're a member of the aristocracy, just like us.

NIKOLAI I'm a doctor. I am not a member of the aristocracy; I just get to dine with them.

ANYA But surely they will need some aristocrats in the new society.

NIKOLAI I'm afraid, as landowners, you'll probably be viewed as an anachronistic leech on the body politic—nothing personal.

FYODOR But we're such nice people. Surely, they can make an exception for us.

NIKOLAI My dear, sweet friends...This might be a good time to take a trip. A long trip. And you might just want to take all your money and valuables with you.

FYODOR But this is my home!

ANYA This is our homeland!

NIKOLAI I promise to write.

FYODOR No!

ANYA There must be something we can do.

FYODOR Maybe there is someone to whom I can write a letter of complaint.

ANYA Yes, that's it!

NIKOLAI My dear, sweet, kind friends, I'm afraid there are social forces at work that cannot be stopped. It is the story of history.

ANYA I never cared for the story of history. There are too many unpleasant people in it.

NIKOLAI I give up. A genius could not convince you of the magnitude of what has happened, and I am not a genius, only a man of above-average intelligence.

FYODOR Would you like to try again after dinner?

NIKOLAI [*Losing his temper.*] NO! No, no, no, no, no!!! Dinner as you know it is over! Over, over, over! My dear, sweet, kind, simple friends, if you remain in Russia, within days you will be eating like peasants. Do you know what that means? . . . Turnips!

FYODOR [*To* ANYA.] I hear Paris is beautiful this time of year.

ANYA I'm not interested.

FYODOR But, darling . . .

ANYA I don't want to go to Paris. I hear the painters there do funny things with light.

FYODOR We shall go, my dear, and we shall triumph.

ANYA What makes you say that?

FYODOR I don't know. It seemed like the right thing to say.

NIKOLAI If you value your lives . . .

FYODOR [*To* ANYA.] My little dumpling . . . Let's go to Paris.

ANYA But I don't know the language.

FYODOR That's okay. They like mimes there.

ANYA Well . . . okay, then.

FYODOR Good. Then it's settled . . . I shall miss this house. Good-bye, old house. Good-bye, my chairs. Good-bye, my darling teacups. Good-bye, my favorite spoon.

NIKOLAI You could take that with you.

FYODOR What good is my spoon without my house! Good-bye, my house. Good-bye, my homeland.
[*From outside, we hear a mournful moo.*]
This is more than I bear.

[FYODOR *breaks into tears.* ANYA *comforts him. After a moment,* SASHA *returns. He is a sobered, humbled man.*]

SASHA Excuse me . . . sir . . . madame.

ANYA Leave us alone, Sasha. Please.

SASHA I have news from St. Petersburg.

ANYA We already know the news from St. Petersburg.

SASHA No, that was a rumor. You know how quickly rumors spread. Much faster than news.

FYODOR Then the rumors aren't true?

SASHA Not exactly. Sofya's second cousin, Pyotr Ilyich Smotritsky, just arrived from St. Petersburg. He told us what really happened.

FYODOR Is he reliable?

SASHA Oh, yes, sir.

ANYA Has he ever embezzled from his own bank?

SASHA I don't think so.

FYODOR Does he cheat at pinochle?

NIKOLAI [*Interrupting.*] What happened?!

SASHA Well, most of what I told you was true. There was a march, people sang, and they were all dressed in their finest clothes. But when our people reached the Narva Gate, we found the road blocked. Suddenly, the Cossacks charged into the crowd, swinging their swords against all they passed. A moment later, army soldiers started shooting into the crowd. By the time it was over, more than a thousand people had been killed.

FYODOR But I thought you said the people were unarmed.

SASHA The Cossacks didn't care.

ANYA How horrible.

NIKOLAI So then the Tsar didn't abdicate?

SASHA That's what's so strange. The Tsar wasn't home. He and his family were at one of his country estates.

NIKOLAI Then why was such drastic action taken?

SASHA Word has it that . . . that the massacre was planned. Our Father the Tsar wanted to show his strength, even if it cost the lives of his children.

ANYA   How awful.

SASHA   Today the snow in St. Petersburg is colored red.

FYODOR   I don't believe it.

SASHA   Well, I don't suppose all the snow is colored red.

FYODOR   Sasha, are you saying that—I don't wish to sound cold but—are you saying that everything is just the way it has always been?

SASHA   Yes, sir.

FYODOR   I see. What a day... Thank you, Sasha, for informing us.

SASHA   You're welcome. By the way, the staff has—how shall I put it—created some losses in the food and drink supply. However, we promise to make it up to you. We figure that if we eat nothing but stale bread and rotten vegetables for the next eight years, we will be even.

FYODOR   I'm sure we can find some other way.

SASHA   Should you desire, sir, you may whip me.

FYODOR   I have never whipped you, Sasha.

SASHA   That's because you don't know how to use a whip. If you'd like, I could teach you.

FYODOR   Can we discuss this later?

SASHA   Thank you, sir.
[*He starts to leave, then remembers.*]
Sofya says the evening meal will be served at its usual time.

ANYA   What has she prepared?

SASHA   She has cooked everything we have, just in case.

[SASHA *exits.*]

FYODOR   Would you like to join us for dinner, Doctor?

NIKOLAI   No, thank you. I must go.

ANYA   Stay and eat. I'm sure we have enough.

NIKOLAI   I am afraid there are a few people to whom I owe an apology. You see, I stopped at seventeen other estates before I stopped here, and so I owe an apology to Andrei Stepanovich Vershinin, Leonid Ivano—

FYODOR   Doctor, please, save your strength for the journey.

NIKOLAI   Good night, my friends.

[NIKOLAI *prepares to leave.*]

FYODOR   Thank you for calling on us, Doctor, even if it was to tell us a false rumor that threw us into the worst panic of our lives.

NIKOLAI   I do feel badly about that.

FYODOR   That's all right. There's nothing like the fear of death to perk up an otherwise drab afternoon.

[FYODOR *opens the front door.*]

ANYA   Good night, Doctor.

NIKOLAI   Good night.

FYODOR   God be with you.

[NIKOLAI *exits.* FYODOR *shuts the door.*]

ANYA   That's the second time today you opened the door.

FYODOR   I shall be more careful in the future.

ANYA   What an intolerable day.

FYODOR   It's all behind us now.

ANYA   I knew the rumors could not be true.

FYODOR   I feel ashamed I ever believed them.

ANYA   There is a reason why the world is the way it is.

FYODOR   God wants it this way, and after all, he is God.

ANYA   What I don't understand is, why did the Tsar feel it was necessary to kill his own people, the people who love him? It is not a rational thing to do.

FYODOR   Perhaps the Tsar is not a rational man.

ANYA   That is a most troubling thought. I do not think I wish to think it.

[ANYA *gives another long, deep, world-weary sigh.* FYODOR *puffs on his pipe, staring into the distance.*]

FYODOR   Tomorrow I think maybe I shall buy a newspaper.

[ANYA *looks at* FYODOR.]

[*The lights fade.*]

• • •

Double Murder

Scott Klavan

Scott Klavan

Scott Klavan appeared on Broadway in 2009 in the role of Roman/The Visitor in Irena's *Vow*, with Tovah Feldshuh, reprising his role from the Off-Broadway run, at Barch Performing Arts Center. Earlier, Klavan played five roles in the stage version of the film hit *The Joy Luck Club*, for Pan Asian Rep. Other Off-Broadway: *Endpapers*, directed by Pamela Berlin, produced by Benjamin Mordecai; *Double Sophia*, The Cherry Lane Theatre; the leading role of Fisby in the revival of the classic comedy *The Teahouse of the August Moon*, as well as the N.Y. premiere of *The Legacy Codes*, also at Pan Asian Rep; *Combustion* at BAM; Treplev in *The Seagull*, directed by Kjetl Bang-Hansen. Klavan has performed regionally in *A Shayna Maidel*, Studio Arena Theatre, Buffalo, N.Y.; *The Common Pursuit*, Studio Theatre, Washington, D.C.; *The Puppetmaster of Lodz*, The Egg, Albany, N.Y. On television in 2009, Klavan performed the title role and did narration for the historical documentary *Mechanic to Millionaire: The Peter Cooper Story*, Gardner Documentary Group. Previously, he has been seen in *Picket Fences* and *As the World Turns*, CBS; films on A&E, NBC, the Sci-Fi Channel, and The Onion News Network. He has done voice-overs and narration for programs, including PBS's *The American Experience* and *Wide Angle*.

Klavan wrote and appeared in *The Double Murder Plays*, a series of one-acts for the 2007 N.Y. International Fringe Festival. He was chosen to participate as a playwright in the 2007 Lincoln Center Theater Directors Lab. A short film he wrote and appears in, *Bad Luck*, was an Official Selection of the 2007 L.A. Shorts Fest. He will appear in his full-length play, *A Child Is in the House*, for Emerging Artists Theatre, 2009–2010.

For many years, Klavan was script and story analyst for legendary actors Paul Newman and Joanne Woodward and also worked in this capacity for companies, including HBO, CAA in Los Angeles, Warner Bros., Viacom, Scott Rudin Prods., Universal Pictures, and Jersey Films. For ten years, he was the dramaturge for Theater Breaking Through Barriers (TBTB), heading a playwriting workshop for visually impaired writers; he wrote the theatrical adaptation of Raymond Carver's classic short story *Cathedral*, produced Off-Broadway by TBTB and reviewed positively in *The New York Times* and *The Village Voice*. His one-act *Unnamed Holocaust Project* was a semi-finalist in the 2006 Strawberry Festival in New York City.

Klavan is a lifetime member of The Actors Studio. He is a graduate of Kenyon College, where he performed in the world premiere of *C.C. Pyle and the Bunion Derby*, by Michael Cristofer, directed by Paul Newman. Klavan is a two-time winner of Kenyon's Paul Newman Acting Trophy.

···production notes···

Double Murder was presented as part of a group of six one-act plays, *The Double Murder Plays*, by Scott Klavan, in the New York International Fringe Festival—Fringe N.Y.C., Aug. 11–25, 2007, at The Independent Studios. A co-production of Theater Breaking Through Barriers (TBTB) and Buddy-Pal Prods.

cast

MAN: Scott Klavan
WOMAN: Harriett Trangucci
Directed by Stephen Jobes
Assistant Director: Ellys R. Abrams

···

[*An upscale apartment. A* MAN *is upstage, dressed in a soft, fashionable sweater. He stands next to a bar: bourbon, vodka, scotch, etc. A* WOMAN *sits in an armchair downstage, her back to him. She is dressed in a hard-edged, stylish business suit and reads a newspaper. At the bar, the* MAN *makes a martini. Then he brings out another bottle: it has a large "poison" symbol on it. He quickly, surreptitiously, mixes the poison into the drink. He garnishes it with a lemon peel. He stirs the drink.*]

[*The* MAN *walks to the* WOMAN, *carrying the drink.*]

MAN   Hello. Here you go.

[*Puts the drink on a table next to her chair. He sits across the table from her, in a smaller, wooden chair.*]

WOMAN   Thanks.
[*Reads paper.*]
What did you do today?

MAN   Oh, work.

WOMAN   Yes? How was that?

[*She picks up drink; he watches her.*]

MAN [*Talking quickly, nervously, self-deprecatingly.*] Well, I'm making copies in the copy room and the thing says: "obstruction tray 4" or whatever it says.

WOMAN [*Chuckles.*] Again?

[*Holds drink in hand.*]

MAN [*Watching her, fast.*] Yeah, and I pulled out all the trays—

WOMAN All of them?

[*Laughs.*]

MAN Which was 4?!

> [*Chuckles nervously.*]

> Then, now, all of the trays are out, and the paper's all over.

WOMAN Ha-ha-ha!

[*Laughing loudly, she puts down drink, without drinking it.*]

MAN [*Seeing her, relaxes.*] I put them all in—and by now, everybody's in the meeting—and press it and the same thing, only now there is an "X" on the screen by all the trays. They took lunch.

WOMAN Ho-ho!

[*Pause. He looks at her hand, near the drink. She picks it up.*]

MAN [*Tenses, fast.*] I went down to get coffee and when I came back, I had to brush by the—what do they call it?—bar, security bar you have to brush by and for some reason—

WOMAN [*Laughing, the drink poised midair.*] What now?

MAN I used the coffee to push the bar and the bag ripped and the coffee spilled all over my pants!

[*Laughs.*]

WOMAN [*Puts the drink down, does not drink.*] Ho-ha-ha-ho!

[*Picks it up again.*]

MAN [*Jumps in.*] But, hey! My pants were dark, so no one could tell the stain! But, later, when I ate lunch, I spilled ketchup and my shirt was yellow!

[WOMAN *cracks up!, puts down drink, without drinking.*]

MAN   [*Relaxes.*] So I had the meeting, which I had messed up all the copies. I ran to the men's store to buy a shirt—$40 for coffee!

[*Chuckles.*]

WOMAN   [*Picks up drink.*] Oh-oh-ha! How was the meeting?

[*About to drink.*]

MAN   [*Explodes.*] My shirt didn't fit, it itched, I forgot my glasses! I'm squinting and couldn't see the proposal, there weren't enough copies...!

WOMAN   [*Does not drink.*] AH-HA-HA! Oh, I hate to laugh but it's so funny! I love your stories! I always have!

MAN   On the bus, I had those bags and it was crowded and I accidentally put my bag on a man's foot!

WOMAN   [*Chortles loudly, bends over from the humor, puts down drink.*] Foot...!

MAN   [*Calms down.*] When he was getting off, he kicked my bag.

WOMAN   Kicked...it!

MAN   In front of everyone. Kicked it hard.

WOMAN   [*Picks up drink, laughing.*] What did you do?

MAN   [*Now, quickly.*] Nothing! I stood there and was humiliated!

WOMAN   Ha-ha-ah! [*Coughs with laughter, puts down drink.*]
        Did you get anything done today?!
        [*Guffaws uproariously.*]
        Have you ever gotten anything done?

MAN   [*Calmly.*] I don't know. I guess not.

WOMAN   [*Picks up drink.*] That's what I love about you!

MAN   [*Panicky.*] And then—then—

WOMAN   [*Puts down drink.*] Yes...?

MAN   [*Stops.*] Oh.

[WOMAN *Picks up drink.*]

MAN   [*Quickly.*] Then, I . . . ! The car! The hood pops up—

WOMAN   [*Laughing.*] I remember!

[*About to drink.*]

MAN   [*Quickly, loudly.*] The latch didn't work and it cracked the windshield!

WOMAN   [*Puts down drink.*] Ha-ha!

MAN   [*Relaxes, laughs, subsides, watches her.*]

[WOMAN *picks up drink.*]

MAN   [*Blurting out.*] I haven't fixed it! I've been—

[WOMAN *puts down drink.*]

[MAN *Stops . . .*]

WOMAN   Hm? Yes?

[*Picks up drink.*]

MAN   A week! Driving with a cracked windshield!

WOMAN   Ha-ha-ha!

[*Puts the drink to her lips.*]

MAN   [*Raising his voice.*] I—I—can't see anything!
          [WOMAN *eats the lemon peel instead of drinking.*]
          [MAN *almost screaming.*]
          AndIgotaticket!

WOMAN   [*Stops, puts drink down; she looks at it. Moves her hand to it.*]

MAN   Fromacop!

[*The* WOMAN *stops, looks at the* MAN. *She pats his arm sympathetically. Then, she rises, leaving her glass on the table.*]

WOMAN   You've had a long day.

[*She goes into the bar area.*]

MAN   Where, where are you . . .

[*In the kitchen, the* WOMAN *makes a drink for him.*]

WOMAN [*Calls.*] In a minute.

MAN Hm?

[*The* WOMAN *finds her own poison bottle; she poisons the drink. She garnishes it with an olive.*]

MAN I have more stories.

WOMAN [*Enters, hands the* MAN *the drink.*] Here you go.

[*Sits again.*]

MAN Oh, thanks.
[*Looks at it; then slowly picks it up.*]
And how was yours?

WOMAN [*Quickly, with great pride and confidence.*] Today, I got the Goldhead grant for tumors.

MAN The Goldhead! Wow!

WOMAN Yes. I did it.

MAN Tumors! All right!
[*Puts down drink, without drinking it, applauds.*]
A job well done! As always!

[*She smiles contentedly, looks at him; he picks up the drink.*]

WOMAN [*Jumping in.*] I told them—they were leaning towards Selma, but I showed them my results, the last, oh, dozen cases. I hired a consultant for the proposal, I went all out!

MAN Huh!

[*His drink wavers in his hand; to the mouth or not?*]

WOMAN [*Fast, boldly.*] I beat her! References. Colleagues, patients. Not a relapse in the bunch. I wasn't going to let it slip by.

MAN Good for you!

[*Then puts down drink without drinking.*]

WOMAN [*Now relaxes.*] There'll be coverage in the *Journal of Medicine* and, certainly, the *Times*, and overseas.

MAN Overseas!

[*Picks up drink.*]

WOMAN [*Quickly.*] It's a joint project with the Norwegian Institute— [*Thinks, then.*]—of Health!

MAN [*Now puts it down.*] Oh, Norway! Hooray!

WOMAN [*Relaxes.*] They're flying me over.
> [*Pause.*]
> To Norway.
> [*He makes a slight motion, with his hand.*]
> Oslo.

MAN [*He picks up the drink.*] Oslo. The capital! Oh-ho-Oslo!

WOMAN [*Quickly.*] It's brain imaging. Diffuse glioma tumors.

MAN Glioma? Ha-hey!

[*Starts to put down drink, thinks better of it.*]

WOMAN [*Fast.*] Yes, and . . . drug delivery. Malignant—and non!

MAN Malig-non. Hmmm.

[*Puts down drink; he looks at her.*]

[*She takes a deep breath; looks at him. He sits still. He eats the olive from his drink. But he doesn't pick up the glass. There is a pause.*]

WOMAN [*Now, with a small, growing doubt.*] I have the highest rating. No one . . .
> [*Pause.*]
> *New York Magazine.* Harvard.
> [*Looks at him; he doesn't move.*]
> Protocols. Double-blind studies.
> [*Pause.*]
> My research, published . . . republished.
> [*He doesn't move.*]

90% survival after five years.

[*Pause.*]

The others—chronic conditions. Mitigating circumstances.

MAN Hmmm.

[*Doesn't move.*]

WOMAN Yet... You know?

[*Pause; a stand-off. Then...*]

MAN Hmmm?

[*Leans toward her.*]

WOMAN [*With a change of tone, sincerely.*] I'm a little nervous about it.

MAN [*Surprised.*] You—are?

[*Pause.*]

WOMAN [*Nods, looks at him, worriedly.*] What if I screw up?

MAN [*Picks up his drink, sympathetically.*] How would you do that?

WOMAN [*Ignoring his drink, speaks genuinely.*] The procedure is virtually untested. The whole world's watching. Seems a great opportunity, but—I talked my way into it. The risks are...

MAN Go on.

[*Holds his drink.*]

WOMAN It fails, all the past, what I've done—forgotten. Just that moment in time. The change ruins everything. I'd be— unrecognizable.

MAN [*Changes his tone, with bravado.*] Look—I told them at the office. I'm doing the job the way I do. It looks silly? I am me.

WOMAN [*Admiringly, her hand moves to her drink.*] Yes?

MAN The results are what counts. How you get there...

[*Shrugs confidently.*]

WOMAN [*Picks it up.*] Right, right. But—

MAN [*Ignoring her drink, with gusto.*] You're only a fool if you believe it!

WOMAN   That's . . . true, I guess. It's true.

MAN   Sure. They get back, see my spreadsheet—they'll forget the coffee, stain—everything.

WOMAN   Yes, they will. Everything. That will change it.

MAN   I'll get my due. Move right up the ladder.

[*They sit, their drinks in their hands.*]

MAN   You'll be fine.
   [*Pause.*]
   The proof of the pudding.

WOMAN   [*Mesmerized, raises her glass.*] Yes. The pudding.

MAN   Do you see?

[*Raises his glass.*]

WOMAN   Yes. Of course. That's smart.
   [*Pause.*]
   That's a good way of looking at it.
   [*Pause.*]
   Darling.

[*They look at each other. Raise their glasses. Simultaneously, as if filled with love and compassion, they intertwine the arms holding the glasses; the time-honored gesture of romance and togetherness.*]

MAN   Here's to us.

[*Pause.*]

WOMAN   [*Smiles warmly.*] Us.

[*He nods, smiles warmly. For the first time, they drink, draining their glasses. They stare out, waiting.*]

[*The lights fade.*]

• • •

Running in Circles Screaming

Jeni Mahoney

Jeni Mahoney

Mahoney's plays, including *The Feast of the Flying Cow . . . and Other Stories of War*, *Mercy Falls*, *Light*, *Come Rain or Come Shine*, *The Martyrdom of Washington Booth*, *Salty*, *Kandahar*, and *Running in Circles Screaming*, have been variously presented at the National Playwrights Conference at the O'Neill Center, InterAct Theater (Philadelphia), Source Theater Festival (Washington, D.C.), L.A. Theater Center, MidWest New Play Festival (Chicago), Lark Theater's Playwrights Week, Rattlestick Productions, NYU's hotINK Festival, Jimmy's No. 43, and London's Greenwich Playhouse, among others.

Her one-acts *Throw of the Moon* and *American Eyes*, commissioned and produced by Gorilla Rep, can be found in *Plays and Playwrights 2001* (NYTheatre Experience). *Light* is featured in *Best Short American Plays 2007–2008* (Applause) and *Great Short Plays: Volume 6* (Playscripts.com) and *Come Rain or Come Shine* can be found in *Best Short American Plays 2005–2006* (Applause). Excerpts from Mahoney's plays can be found in numerous scene and monologue books.

Mahoney is the head of the Playwriting Program at Playwrights Horizons Theater School at New York University's Tisch School for the Arts and the artistic director of id Theater's Seven Devils Playwrights Conference, which has developed more than 80 new American plays since its inception in 2001 and is featured in Michael Wright's 2005 book *Playwriting: At Work and Play*. Mahoney is a member of the Dramatists Guild of America.

···production notes···

Running in Circles Screaming premiered at the Cultural Development Corporation's 2008 Source Festival in Washington, D.C., directed by Paul Douglas Michnewicz with the following cast:

cast

    LOUISE: Maura Suilebhan
    HEATHER: Vanessa Bradchulis
    STAN: Colin Smith

···

[LOUISE (LOU) *sits on a park bench. The sound of children playing. She watches—not focusing on any particular child. Enter* HEATHER, *carrying a large, over-packed tote (toys, snacks). She slumps exhausted onto the bench as she calls out to an unseen child.*]

HEATHER   Jared! Mommy's over here! Stay where Mommy can see you!
     [*To* LOU.]
     Ugh! Boys...

LOU   Huh?

HEATHER   Boys. Right?

LOU   Wouldn't know.

HEATHER   A girl, right? You're so lucky. Which is yours?

LOU   Guess.

HEATHER   Guess?

LOU   Which do you think?

HEATHER   Does she look like you?

LOU   You tell me.

[HEATHER *points out a child.*]

HEATHER   Her?

LOU I'm impressed.

HEATHER Are you kidding? No-brainer. She looks just like you.

LOU Lily.

HEATHER Oh, I just love flower names.

> [*She points to herself.*]
>
> Heather. I would have given my left tit for a girl—excuse my French. But, hey, we each have our crosses to bear, right?

LOU I guess.

HEATHER I told Hank—don't you shoot any'a those boy bullets at me. But what can you do? Right? Guys—

LOU Actually, I think the egg contributes gender.

HEATHER You don't say. You a doctor?

[LOU *shakes her head no.*]

HEATHER So on some subconscious level, I wished this on myself.

LOU Oh, I don't know if intention has anything to do with it . . .

HEATHER Oh, the universe has its reasons.

LOU You get what you deserve—that kind of thing?

HEATHER Yeah, something like that.

LOU Harsh lesson plan.

HEATHER Sometimes that's all that gets me through the day!

LOU Huh. Guess that works when your biggest problem is that you got a boy instead of a girl—

HEATHER But you wanted a girl, though. Am I right?

LOU I wanted a healthy baby.

HEATHER Blah-blah-blah—we're all supposed to say that. All I'm saying is it's easy for you. You got what you wanted.

LOU Well—

HEATHER Girls want girls. Men want boys.

[*To* JARED.]

Jared. What did Mommy tell you about hitting?

LOU   He looks like a great kid.

HEATHER   Really? Trade ya.

LOU   Don't think you'd like that.

HEATHER   [*To* JARED.] *Words, Jared. Use your flippin' words.*
[*Back to* LOU.]
Are you kidding? Look at her. She's an angel.

LOU   Yeah. She's a happy kid.

HEATHER   Happy mom, happy kid. Yeah, I know. Don't say it—

LOU   I didn't—

HEATHER   It's not you. My mother. Get it from her all the time. "Lay off, right?" She doesn't get it.

LOU   I know that feeling.

HEATHER   They couldn't see his . . . his winkie, in the sonograms, so I was all set for a girl. It's like he was hiding it from me.

LOU   I'm sure he wasn't doing it on purpose.

HEATHER   You don't know his father. But we'll get it right this time.

LOU   You're pregnant?

HEATHER   Can't tell? 16 weeks. Not bad, eh?

LOU   No, you look good.

HEATHER   Yeah, pregnancy's the easy part—

LOU   Something to be grateful for.

HEATHER   [*To* JARED.] Jared! What did I just say? No what? That's right. No hitting! I don't care who started it . . .
[*Back to* LOU.]
And Lily playing so nicely over there. So polite. I could just eat her up! I bet you're a good mom too.

LOU   You think?

HEATHER   I don't see you screaming at her to stop hitting, or give back that toy. Some people are just natural mothers—genetically—programmed to mommy.

LOU   Interesting theory.

HEATHER   Wish I was. I mean, it's not his fault that he likes trucks and trains and running in circles screaming.

LOU   Everyone likes running in circles screaming.

HEATHER   I don't. Sometimes I feel like it's all I do.

LOU   If I thought I could get away with it, I'd be running in circles screaming right now.

HEATHER   See? Like that. You get that whole kid thing. It must be nice to have that...

LOU   I could think of a few other things I'd like to have, but—I mean, yeah. I guess. Yeah.

HEATHER   Exactly. You should talk to my friend, Margaret. Can't get pregnant to save her life. I tell her all the time: "Margaret, you have a wonderful life, but you can't have everything." Right? And you should see her husband. Nice guy but he just doesn't look...capable, if you know what I mean.

LOU   Huh.

HEATHER   You can just tell the gene pool wants him outta of the water. But it's sad. Here she is suffering over something that is probably just never meant to be. I mean, come on, take a hint, right?

LOU   Doctors are doing a lot of amazing things with—

HEATHER   Ohmygod, the money she's spent on doctors! "Look," I told her, "get a friggin' dog—you won't have to put it through college." Frankly, if I'd spent more time thinking about it, I might have given the whole thing a second thought myself.

LOU   I'm sure you don't really mean that.

HEATHER Trust me.

LOU You could give Jared to your friend.

HEATHER Don't think I haven't offered.

LOU Seriously.

HEATHER What?

LOU I mean, if he's so terrible and you're so miserable, why don't you give him to someone who really wants him.

[HEATHER *laughs in disbelief.*]

HEATHER Right.
> [*Beat.*]
> You're kidding, right?

LOU No. I'm serious. Why not?

HEATHER He's my son. I mean, would you give up Lily?

LOU I don't feel that way about Lily.

HEATHER I love Jared. Okay? He's my kid. I love him. Geez. I was just kidding.

LOU Oh. You just sounded so unhappy.

HEATHER I was just being friendly. Okay?

LOU Okay.

HEATHER Just letting off steam. That's why I come here, okay?

LOU Oh. I just come here to ... enjoy the kids.

HEATHER Uh-huh. Well, nice for you—nothing to complain about. Lily must be a saint.

LOU Hitting, screaming, running ... that's what kids do.

HEATHER Now you sound like the saint.

LOU Me? Nah. I'm full of envy. Believe it or not, I envy you.

HEATHER Could of fooled me.

[*To* JARED.]

Come on, Jared! Mommy needs a latte and an aspirin. Well...it's been interesting—ah—

LOU   Lou. Louise.

HEATHER   It's been interesting, Louise.

[HEATHER *starts to go. She stops and turns back to* LOU.]

You know, it's none of my business—just some friendly mom-to-mom advice—but if I were as lucky as you, with an angel like that, I would hope I'd handle my good fortune with grace and understanding for those...who's prayers haven't been answered yet.

LOU   Right back at you, Heather.

[HEATHER *starts off, a bit perplexed. She turns to* LOU.]

HEATHER   What are you? One of those women who always has to have the last word?

[LOU *smiles disingenuously and shrugs silently. But as soon as* HEATHER *disappears she mumbles mockingly.*]

LOU   "You one of those people who has to have the last word?"

[LOU *goes back to watching* LILY, *but her encounter with* HEATHER *nags at her.*]

Bitch.

[LOU *checks her watch. Checks on* LILY. *Smiles. Waves. Notices* LILY *standing too close to an edge.*]

Careful, sweetie—

[LOU *starts toward* LILY, *but then sees she is fine.* STAN *enters with two cups of coffee just as* LOU *sits down again.*]

Good girl, Lily. Amazing—

[STAN *hands* LOU *a cup of coffee.*]

Oh, hi. Geez, where'd you go to get this? Paraguay?

STAN   I ran into Mark and Dora. She's due in three weeks.

[LOU *makes a sympathetic face.*]

They had sonograms with them, the whole nine yards.

LOU   You're kidding?

STAN   In her purse. Boy. They showed me the money shot.

LOU   I.U.I.?

STAN   I.V.F.

LOU   First?

STAN   Third.

LOU   Well, I'm proud of you, honey. You took a bullet for the team and even managed to come back with caffeine.
[STAN *changes the subject—he gestures out to* LILY.]
Looks like you've made a new friend.

LOU   Lily.

STAN   Oh, hello, Lily…

LOU   Not really Lily.

STAN   You started without me!

LOU   Sorry, couldn't help myself.
[*They sit and sip their coffee.*]
D'you think it's just some sick joke that God has going where totally ungrateful people get what they want, and people who would be totally grateful get to sit around and listen to the ingrates whine about it?

STAN   I dunno. You'd expect a "cosmic"-sized joke to be funnier.

LOU   He gives and gives to people who do nothing but complain that He gave them blue when they asked for pink. It's pathological. He's pathological. Here we are spending good money on therapy, when He's the one that needs a therapist.

STAN   I think the cosmic joke is that by withholding from people like us, God gets us to enjoy it even more when we're extra grateful later. Ungrateful people? Hey, might as well give them something to occupy themselves with—they'll never appreciate it anyway.

LOU That's not very funny.

STAN Maybe He's not really funny "ha-ha." Maybe He's funny "strange."

LOU Yeah, well, I'm sick of being the butt of some joke I just don't get.

STAN Okay. But I still love you.

LOU Love you too. Hate God. Hate the universe. Hate Mother's Day, diaper commercials, holding the door open for other peoples' strollers. But somehow I still do manage to love you.

STAN As long as your priorities are in order.
[*He notices* LILY *leaving.*]
Oh, look, there she goes. Bye, Lily!

LOU Bye, sweetie.

STAN You wanna pick another?

LOU You pick.

STAN The little brown-haired girl. Red dress.

LOU On the swing?
[STAN *nods.*]
Do you just pick girls to make me happy?

STAN I dunno. I see a kid—boy, girl, black, white, orange—doesn't matter, then I see you, smiling, holding this kid and I think... wow... beautiful. It's like I can see love. And everything else just falls away.

LOU Yeah. What's her name?

STAN Hailey.

LOU Hailey...

STAN Like Hailey's comet.

LOU Right. Hailey: she's bright—

STAN Bright? She's brilliant—

LOU   God, look at her up there!

STAN   She's a comet. Likes to fly.

LOU   You go, Hailey.

STAN   A comet like that doesn't come along every day.

LOU   She's something special all right.

STAN   The light of our lives.

LOU   And millions and millions of light-years away.

• • •

Witness

Peter Maloney

Peter Maloney

Peter Maloney's play *Leash* appeared in *Best American Short Plays 2003–2004* and was also published by Joyce Carol Oates in her quarterly *Ontario Review*. *Witness* (along with *Leash*) is part of Maloney's *Abu Ghraib Triptych*. In it's first production, by Faith Catlin's Signal & Noise Theater, *Abu Ghraib Triptych* was called "a shocking dramatic success as well as a rare example of art confronting our present national dilemma."

His adaptation of Machiavelli's *Mandragola*, commissioned by Washington, D.C.'s Shakespeare Theatre, was recently published by Broadway Play Publishing, Inc. *In The Devil's Bathtub* appeared in the *Kenyon Review*, and three of his plays are published by Samuel French, Inc.

He has performed four autobiographical pieces, *Accident, My Father's Funeral, Accordion Dreams,* and *Kolossal Hero,* at Ensemble Studio Theatre, and *Accident* was published by Faber and Faber in the collection *Marathon 2000.*

Maloney directed Sandra Bullock in Larry Ketron's *No Time Flat*, Kevin Bacon in the American Premiere of John Byrne's *The Slab Boys*, Tommy Lee Jones in Jack Gilhooley's *Time Trial*, Adolph Green and Phyllis Newman in Murray Schisgal's *The New Yorkers*, and Lois Smith and Thomas Gibson in Romulus Linney's *Juliet*.

He recently played "God Who Judges" in Ethan Coen's *Almost an Evening* for the Atlantic Theater. He starred with Estelle Parsons in David Hare's *The Bay at Nice*, and with Brooke Adams in *The Cherry Orchard*. He has been seen on Broadway in *Judgment at Nuremberg*, with Maximilian Schell; *Stanley*, with Antony Sher; Pavel Kohout's *Poor Murderer*, with Maria Schell; Eugene O'Neill's *Hughie*, with Ben Gazzara; and in the Lincoln Center Theater productions *Dinner at Eight, Arcadia, Carousel, Six Degrees of Separation, Abe Lincoln in Illinois,* and *Our Town*. He has appeared in 47 films, including *K-Pax, Boiler Room, Requiem for a Dream, The Crucible, Washington Square, JFK, Desperately Seeking Susan,* and John Carpenter's *The Thing!*

A member of Ensemble Studio Theatre, the Actors Studio, and an alumnus of the New Dramatists, Maloney is a Fox Foundation fellow.

character

KASIM

place

Abu Ghraib Prison, Iraq

time

April 2004

• • •

[*Sound of metal door slamming very loudly. At same time lights bump up. Shouts of prisoners, dogs barking somewhere.*]

[KASIM *sits on the lower bunk of an iron bed. There is no mattress, only a plywood board.* KASIM *wears an orange jumpsuit. He holds a baseball in one hand and regards it. He opens his mouth wide, as if he wants to take a bite of the baseball. He looks up at us.*]

KASIM   It occurs to me...perhaps they thought we *eat* these things. That they thought it is some kind of fruit, and that we eat it. I could have told them that *this* is not indigenous to Iraq, that baseballs do not grow on trees here. And that, in any case, it is not a fruit. But they do not speak my language. And the translator was not there when they tried to feed it to me.

[KASIM *looks at the baseball. He opens his mouth as wide as possible. He closes his mouth, looks at us.*]

It barely fit into my mouth. They had to break two teeth to get it in.

[*He opens his mouth wide again, points with a finger to broken teeth in back.*]

I tried to spit the baseball out, to push it out with my tongue, but they tied a scarf around my head to hold it in.

With the baseball in my mouth, I could only breathe through my nose. It was fortunate for me that it was not the season of my asthma, or I might have suffocated. I was frightened, and I wanted to tell them about my asthma, but the baseball in my mouth made it impossible for me to speak.

And, in any case, they would not have understood me. And the translator was not there.

I had expected that they would understand my language, or, in fact, *any* language that I might have spoken. Frankly, I was surprised that language even came into it. I imagined that, in an encounter of this kind, words would be unnecessary.

I have never seen a baseball game. Except in the movies.

I have a video store. Mostly bootlegs my cousin Nouri brings in from Syria. I've got all the latest, man. On Rashid Street, near the copperware market. Perhaps you know it, KVCD Video? No? Perhaps if you are in the neighborhood you can look in on my shop and if I see you again you can tell me if it is still there.

[*He looks at the baseball, remembers, smiling.*]

Field of Dreams. Starring Mr. . . . Kevin . . .

[*He brings his arm back, mimes throwing the ball.*]

Costner.

[*Pain in his right shoulder. He sets the baseball down on the bunk bed.*]

I cannot speak about what has happened to me here. Because . . . I will soon be leaving and . . . they asked me not to talk about certain things. They said you would not understand. Certain things you would understand and other things you wouldn't. I myself am confused.

I was abducted on the day the Americans captured Saddam. I was with my friend Ameen. The news of Saddam's capture had just come over the TV. I closed up my shop and we ran out into the street. The TV in the window we left on so that people outside could watch the events as they unfolded. I had loaned Ameen my video camera. He was making a film about the situation here. At the time of the invasion, he had filmed the falling statues, and now he wanted to film the people's reaction to the fall of the man himself. The reaction of the man in the street. We were hurrying along the river in the direction of the Al-Salam Palace. There were so many people, all of them shouting, dancing in the streets. American soldiers sitting atop their Humvees, grinning, smoking cigarettes. I was so happy to see Saddam go away. You know he destroyed our country. He humiliated us. I thank you, President Bush.

There was one tank on the street. Ameen laughs and says, "Hey, it's Clint Eastwood's tank." I look, and even with my bad English I can make out, stenciled on the barrel of the big gun: "GO AHEAD, MAKE MY DAY." I am standing right by the tank. Ameen was taking pictures of all the action when somebody behind us starts shooting at the Americans. Fucking Fedayeen. Stupid guys. I hear the firing and the bullets hitting the tank and I ducked down. It becomes a kind of instinct. I know those fuckers are likely to fire grenades next, so I drop to the ground and I thought, I will roll under the tank. The tank will protect me. But it's not that easy to roll under a tank. In fact you can't do it. The . . . things that go around and around the wheels . . . treads. And anyway now an American soldier has his foot on my back and his rifle pushing hard behind my ear and he is screaming at me in English. The tank is shaking and I hear explosions, and sure enough Clint is firing the big gun in the direction the shots came from, he doesn't realize that the Fedayeen are gone. They were there and now they're gone. But that doesn't stop Clint from firing on the place they were. I am lying on my stomach with this boot on my back and the barrel of the gun pushing my head into the pavement and then my video camera joins me there on the ground, all the pieces of it clattering into the gutter. Before I know it my hands are tied together behind my back with the plastic laces and I am being pulled up onto my feet. Ameen is up against the tank, another soldier's got him covered. His hands are tied, too, and he has a sandbag over his head. And just before the bag goes over *my* head I see that not only the Fedayeen are gone, so is the building they were firing from. In fact, the whole neighborhood isn't there anymore, just piles of concrete and clouds of dust. Stupid fucking Fedayeen.

They took us in a Humvee, with other guys they rounded up. To Camp Cropper, out near the airport. They put us in a tent. I didn't see Ameen again.

[*He is quiet for a moment, then, suddenly agitated, he stands and, looking up as if to the upper tier of cells, cries out in a loud voice.*]

AMEEN! . . . DON'T WORRY ABOUT THE FUCKING CAMERA, MAN! I CAN ALWAYS GET ANOTHER CAMERA!

[*He is quiet again.*]

We were in the tent for eight days. Bagged and cuffed. They gave us a can to piss in, but if you had to piss and it wasn't the *time* to piss and there was no one around to cut the cuffs off you . . . There were some stinking fucking dishdashas in that tent after eight days, I'll tell you. Eight days of pissing yourself and a clean jumpsuit looks pretty good.

That was in December. It was cold. No one in the tent knew why we were there. Somebody in the tent knew some English and he asked the soldiers why we were there. They told us we knew why. But we didn't know. They said they were the ones who ask the questions and if they didn't like the answers they'd send us all to Guantanamo. They kept saying we were going to Guantanamo, that once we were there we'd be wishing we were back here. I didn't like hearing this shit. I got tired of hearing about Guantanamo. On the day they moved us out of Cropper one of the soldiers said we were going to Guantanamo. I said he could shove Guantanamo up his ass, it was just another fucking prison where they lock up Afghanis and Al Qaeda guys, and what am I doing here, I run a video store!

I didn't say it in English, I don't speak English. But this other stupid guy, the one of us who knew a little English, he *translates* for the fucking American! So when they are loading us into the truck to move us out, this soldier who I told to shove Guantanamo up his ass pulls me aside, holds me back. Everybody is in the back of the truck but me, they're packed in, cuffed and bagged, and the soldier is ready to put a bag on my head. But before he does he takes out his wallet and flips through some pictures he keeps in there. There's his mother and his wife or his girlfriend and his kid or his little brother, I don't know, and he finds the picture he's looking for. He puts his hand on my shoulder like we are buddies and he holds out the wallet with the picture for me to see. It's a picture of him in a red and black checked cap. He's holding a rifle, (an ordinary rifle, not the big gun he's carrying now), and tied across the front of his truck is a deer. He's holding on to the horn of this big deer and looking proud of himself.

[*Change of tone, more intimate. It is important to* KASIM *that we know what he thinks about this.*]

Which reminds me. We can't talk about the art of acting without speaking of Mr. . . . Robert . . . De Niro.

[*He waits, as if to check if we agree, his eyes darting left and right. He mimes lifting a rifle, sighting down the barrel.*]

The next thing I know I'm in the dark again and being lifted up, and they throw me across the front of the truck and tie me down. The soldiers are laughing and at first I'm not minding being tied down because the truck has been idling for a while and I am suddenly warmer than I have been in over a week. But by the time we are halfway to Abu Ghraib the hood is red fucking hot and the metal is burning me right through my shirt and my pants.

[*He touches his jumpsuit very gingerly with his fingertips around his middle, his thighs.*]

Can you do something for me? Maybe you can get in touch with my family? Tell my wife where I am. That I'm OK.

Do you know the Backstreet Boys? My daughter likes the Backstreet Boys. She *loves* them. Especially Nick. She sent away for a picture, but it never came. That's all she wants in this life, she says, is a picture of this Backstreet Boy signed, "To Layla, love Nick."

Maybe it came while I'm in here. Five months, man. Five fucking months, and I still don't know what they want from me.

The Deer Hunter. Yeah.

In the middle of the trip here, a sandstorm hit, and I was really glad for the sandbag on my head, which protected me somewhat. When we got here, they untied me, took the bag off, and this . . . unearthly . . . unearthly light was everywhere, because of the dust. Everything was . . . *ghamidh*. You know this word? Mysterious. Ambiguous. Yeah.

When we got here we finally could take a shower. They took our clothes away. They took everything away. My watch. The thing is, I wonder if it's really five months, or does it just seem that way? They can do crazy things with time, you know. Stop it, practically. What if it's only been five *hours*? What if they haven't even noticed I'm gone?

I'm not supposed to tell what happened here. They say you wouldn't understand. But it's not right to do these things to people! Without permission, and without explaining anything! It's inhuman.

Of course they aren't human, that's the thing. They can disguise themselves. As anything. John Carpenter got that part right. That was a good film, but it was too negative. *The Thing*, starring Mr. Kurt Russell. And Kurt had to be a macho guy, naturally, and so naturally all the creatures are bad. Which is not right. Some of them are good, I can tell you. In fact, I would say that most of them are good. Not the big white guy in the clear glasses who works nights. Not Roper. And there are other bad ones, but most of them are good.

I've seen things you wouldn't believe. That's why we aren't supposed to tell you. Because you wouldn't believe it. It's not the time for you to begin believing. I don't know why they picked me. I guess they think it's time for me.

Their ships are sometimes disguised as helicopters. You can tell by the light. It is the brightest light you've ever seen. You can't look into it without it hurting.

I don't think they *want* to hurt us. They forced me to lie down. In a cubicle. It was cool and damp and it smelled bad. They put the bright light on me and looked me over. All over. They seemed quite concerned, about my burns from the truck. They checked me all over to see if I was hurt. Because I *was* hurt. It was like I was paralyzed. There was never just one of them. They were always with another one, or in a group. They *looked* human, most of them. Humanoid, I guess is what they are. They just touch you with their hand or an instrument and you go numb. At first it hurts a lot, for an instant, but then it doesn't hurt at all. You can't feel anything, and you can't move. You just lie there. You can't believe that you are just lying there, not saying anything, not protesting, but you can't. You just can't. Sometimes there are computers there and the beings are putting data into the computers while they do these things to you. And they are always taking pictures. There are balconies, and sometimes there are other beings watching from above. There isn't much furniture. You can't always tell by looking at them whether they are male or female, but somehow, you just...know. The shorter ones are the helpers. The taller ones are in charge. That is definite. The small ones especially stare at you. It is dangerous to look at them. Somehow you know that, so you try not to look in their eyes.

Listen, I'm worried about Ameen. Saddam put his brother in here and he never came out. He did something, I don't know what, and one night the Mukhabarat came and got him and brought him here and he was never seen again. That's why Ameen hates Saddam so much. And he said if he ever was put in here he would kill himself. Somebody here *did* kill himself. Maybe you can find out if Ameen is here. There must be a list. Maybe he escaped.

[*He picks up the baseball, throws it to the floor so that it bounces up and back into his hand.*]

Like Mr....

[*He throws the ball against the floor again.*]

Steve...

[*He throws the ball against the floor again, smiles.*]

McQueen. *The Cooler King.* Yeah, man. Go to Rashid Street, to my shop. Ameen might be there, keeping an eye on things for me. He is my best friend.

[*He sets the baseball on the bunk bed.*]

I can't talk about the situation here. I am personally of the opinion that they want to take over. I think where they come from is...running out of energy, whatever sustains them, and they have to leave that place. And so they need to take over here. This is the preparation. They are exploring, to see if this is a good place for them to come and live.

They show us pictures, wide-screen, 360 degrees. In 3-D, no special glasses required. Pictures of things we see all the time, but stopped noticing. The gutters running like sewers; the marshlands disappeared; the pipelines burning in Kuwait; the sky black with smoke. We tried to tell them that it isn't all our fault. That Saddam did a lot of this shit. That the sanctions did a lot of it. Then the Americans, and in reaction to the

Americans, the fucking Fedayeen. But they didn't want to hear any
excuses. They know the Garden of Eden, the original *Janat Adn* was *just a
few miles from here!* From where we are standing, did you know that? Oh,
yes, they know what they are doing by coming here. And they want us to
realize what we are doing to the earth. If they are going to come here and
take over, well, there has to be something left, after all. Something they
can use. To sustain their race. Enable them to go on, to continue.

When they make us strip, I think it has something to do with reproduction.
So they come here in disguise, and their ships are disguised. And they
make us strip and they do these experiments so they can learn about us. I
think that when they make us lie down naked on top of one another it is
all a misunderstanding. And when they make us touch ourselves...
masturbate... it is only to find out how the penis works, something like
that.

[*He struggles with what he is feeling.*]

I do not think I can go back to the life I had before. I don't want to go back.
I think I will never see my wife again. I don't think I could be with her
anymore. Not now. And Layla will be fine in the care of her mother, who
was always much more strict with her than I was. I spoil her, I admit it.

I don't have much time left, but I will tell you what I think.

I think that these beings may be... angels. I think they are beings between
us and God. It is not always easy to recognize them. In John Carpenter's
film, for example, when Norris has a heart attack and they get him up on
the gurney and the doctor climbs up with the defibrillator to try to shock
him back to life and Norris's chest suddenly *opens up*, then *closes quick* on
the doctor's arms, cutting them off at the elbows, then *opens up again* and
another head, smaller, uglier, with sharper teeth but recognizably Norris,
rises up out of his chest on a writhing neck, well, it is horrible, no question.
And of course Kurt Russell immediately turns his flame-thrower on it and
kills it.

But who is to say that the monster was not an really an angel. In disguise.
Or just angry. We will never know, because Kurt Russell killed it. Maybe
he just didn't recognize it for what it was. Or maybe he did. I don't know.

Would that we knew what the nightly visitant is.

Last night the visitant was E.T. Right here in my cell. I knew there was going to be another examination when they brought out the sheets and blankets and hung them over the bars so that no one could see in. I appreciate that. Privacy is good. They made me strip, which I hate to do, but I have gotten somewhat used to it. They needed to take another sample of some kind, I suppose. They never say. Four of them held me down, facedown on the bunk here. Then E.T. was there. I recognized him, even though he was wearing fatigues like the others. He is short and ugly and his head is too big for his body and his eyes are huge. He looked at me. I tried not to look at him. He held up his finger and waved it back and forth in front of my face until I looked up. He was smiling, and his finger was glowing because he was E.T.

Then he put the glowing finger up my ass.

[*He struggles with what he is feeling.*]

It hurt and I cried out for God's help. He put it in my ass, the others were all laughing, and then he took it out again.

[*He looks at the floor for a moment, then looks back up at us.*]

I believe I am leaving here tonight. They have examined me. All tests have been done, and the results are in. I've been inoculated against smallpox and diphtheria. There is no history of liver disease in my family. I have assured them of my complete cooperation. Tonight the impossible light will come down at the proper angle to form a ramp of energy from here to there. A guide will float us up the ramp straight...through...the bars.

AMEEN!...YOUR FRIEND IS NOT MAD!

Straight through the bars to the ship, which is waiting for us. It will be...as if...I am a full bucket, pulled up from the well's darkness, then lifted out and up into the light.

AMEEN!...GOD HAS GIVEN HIS ANGELS CHARGE OVER US!

We live in the night ocean, wondering, "What are these lights?" The ship...The ship is a wheel of light, turning in the firmament.

[*A very bright* LIGHT *comes on above the cell, shines down through a grill in the ceiling.*]

A secret, turning in us, makes the universe turn.

[*The light is moved back and forth by someone above the cell.*]

I have my jumpsuit. I am ready. I'm ready to go into the ship. I'm ready to go.

[*We hear the sound of heavy boots on the metal grill. Lights fade, leaving just the overhead light shining down on the man in the orange jumpsuit.*]

[*Blackout.*]

• • •

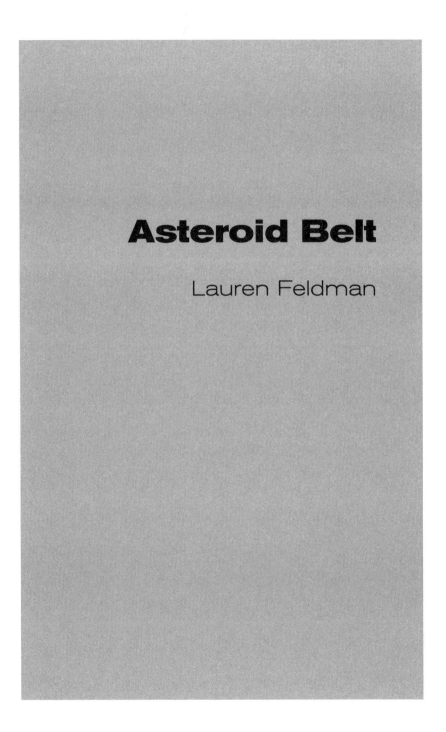

Asteroid Belt

Lauren Feldman

Lauren Feldman

Lauren Feldman's full-length plays include: *A People*; *The Egg-Layers*; *Grace, or the Art of Climbing*; and *Fill Our Mouths* [a play in English and American Sign Language]. One-acts include: *The Coupling Heuristic: A Minuet*; *Hecuba: A Bitch's Lament*; *When It Rains*; *Asteroid Belt*; *The Kissing Play*; and others—as well as the short solo play *Funny Story* and the collaborative/devised plays *The Apocryphal Project*; *Phaedra's Dilemma*; and *Grey Gone*.

Her plays have been produced throughout the U.S. and in London, Canada, and Australia. She was a U.S. playwright delegate with the Royal Court Theatre and with World Interplay Australia, and has been an artist in residence at The Missoula Colony (Montana Rep), Sewanee University of the South, and Theater Emory's Brave New Works Festival.

Education: The Shakespeare Programme, British-American Drama Academy; B.A. in English, Cornell University; M.F.A. in playwriting, Yale School of Drama. She writes, performs, and teaches playwriting. She also rock-climbs.

characters

CARLY, 20 years old, any ethnicity

SUE, 40s–50s, any ethnicity

JAY, 40s–50s, any ethnicity

• • •

[*At rise:* SUE *and* JAY *in bed.* SUE *is holding a book, trying to read.* JAY *is channel surfing. On the other side of the stage is the kitchen. Throughout,* CARLY *should be integrated in the space—moving through it, living in it, interacting. Note:* CARLY's *height/size should be changed to fit the actor.*]

CARLY   I'm sailing down Sunset Drive, I'm about to take a left into my neighborhood, about to pull into our driveway, check on the mail, drag my feet up the terra-cotta path to the front door, wheedle my key into the hole, and welcome myself back home after a long day and longer night at the theater. I'm about to shed my shirt, peel off my jeans, and crawl unwashed, unfed, unclothed, unkempt into my two-foot-high childhood bed that Mom still dresses in a Winnie-the-Pooh bedsheet ensemble. It's 11:36 p.m., it's pouring, I'm tired, I'm hungry, I'm twenty years old, a college senior home for the summer, an English major, a Shakespeare lover, a nonsmoker but a smirker, an aspiring actor, an aspiring writer, an aspiring wife and mother, a five-foot-four* aspiring adult, a size-6 dress, a size-6 shoes, a size 34-B, a girl, a girl, a girl sailing down Sunset Drive about to be struck by an oncoming car.

[SUE *smacks* JAY *with her book.*]

JAY   What?

SUE   Move over.

JAY   Why?

SUE   I'm cramped.

[JAY *is already on the far side of the bed, but he scoots over more.*]

JAY   I see that.

CARLY   I can see it coming clear as day, clear as a sleek white Pontiac Grand Am streaking sixty miles an hour down Sunset like a comet, like an asteroid, like an entire asteroid *belt* blazing across a night-black road, about to explode into my car. I can see it. It's heading right toward me, about to crater the front of my car, and there's not a damn thing I can do about it but watch.

SUE   What could you possibly be watching at this hour?

JAY   What? This is good stuff.

[*A phone rings.* JAY *picks up.* SUE *expects the caller to be* CARLY. *When* JAY *hears that it isn't, he shakes his head to* SUE.]

JAY   [*Into phone.*] Hello? Oh, hi, Jeff. Sure, hold on.
      [*Calling off.*]
      Ashley, phone call.

SUE   She's in bed already.

JAY   At ten? She's a teenager.

SUE   It's past eleven. She's sleeping, Jay. She has camp in the morning.

JAY   This is Ashley. She is not sleeping.

CARLY   Of course she's not sleeping.

JAY   [*Into phone.*] You got it, Ash? All right. G'night, Jeff.

[JAY *hangs up, gives* SUE *the what-did-I-tell-you look.*]

CARLY   Ashley's on her bed watching *Sex and the City*, the volume turned all the way down, though, because it's past her bedtime and there's camp tomorrow, she's a counselor—good kid, my sister. Mom's watching the red digits change steadily, slowly, on the clock by the bed as they creep closer and closer to midnight; the minutes seem long, the seconds themselves interminable, as they always do when either of her children are not yet safely tucked into their Winnie-the-Pooh bedsheet ensembles. Dad's watching his weight this week, but right now he's watching Mom watching the clock as he watches *Iron Chef*—on mute, of course, so as not to irk Mom. And I'm watching them watching, all in my mind's eye, while my own eye watches a Pontiac meteor blazing and my

Chevy Tahoe plowing toward the same intersection in space and time. And I'm watching, and I'm sweating, and I'm thinking, Oh My Good God Lord Almighty Christ in Heaven Jesus Mary and Joseph Three Kings of Bethlehem How Still We See Thee Lie Leviticus Spartacus Abacus Adonai Elohaynu Old and New Testaments Thou Shalt Not Swear Fuck Torah Talmud Kabbalah Koran Conjugal Cardinal Father Rabbi Deacon Priest Pope Holy Jesus Holy Mary Holy Christ Holy Cow Holy Sonnets Holy Shit—I'm gonna die.

SUE I can't concentrate. Would you please, please turn it down?

JAY It's on mute. If you want to get yourself all bent out of shape, that's fine. But don't push your hysterics to my side of the bed.

SUE I'm not in hysterics. I am concerned, yes. Don't exaggerate.

JAY I never exaggerate.

CARLY I'm probably exaggerating. I've got an air bag, a seat belt, a brake pedal that's worked so far, and I'm in a vehicle the size of the Goodyear Blimp, so I should be okay, right? If I just swerve best I can and let the ass of the car absorb most of the crash, I should be all right, right? (No answer.) Right. And if I start honking now, that'll buy me some time, or at least a bit of warning. But time—time!—that's what I need. I can't do spontaneity! If I were good under pressure, I'd have gone into firefighting or waitressing or improv. There's a reason I'm a read-books-and-write-essays-at-your-own-pace-and-no-one's-life-is-on-the-line-anyhow English major. I have, what, a smidgen of seconds to figure out what to do, and I can't do it to save my life. And that's not even hyperbole!

[JAY *gets up.*]

SUE Where are you going?

JAY Kitchen.

SUE How can you eat?

JAY Just getting water.

SUE So now you're angry.

JAY Angry? Jesus, Sue, don't come down on me when it's you who—

SUE Why can't you understand that I'm worried sick that it's the middle of the night and I have a child who's still not home? I'm a wreck, and you're watching TV.

JAY You're reading a book.

SUE I'm holding a book. I can't—

JAY All right. All right.

[JAY *starts toward the kitchen.*]

SUE Where are you going?!

JAY To the kitchen. I'm thirsty. Sue. My love. I am not angry. And I know you better than you give me credit for. I'll be back.

SUE I'm sorry.

JAY I'll be right back.

[JAY *goes to the kitchen. Throughout the following he drinks a glass of milk and prepares a cup of water for* SUE.]

CARLY Oh Dad'll be pissed when he finds out. Angry with himself, with me, with God probably. And Mom'll be angry with Dad, and Dad with her, and Ashley with them, and everyone with Ashley, and she'll be soooo angry with me. Yes, anger will seize the world tonight, and all because I should not have driven—tonight or ever. I am a dark, stark danger to society. I am the venom to order and harmony. I am the venomous nemesis to safety on the road. I am HAZARD INCARNATE!

[JAY *returns to the bedroom with the water.*]

JAY Careful, don't spill. I made it just the way you like it. From the bottle, not the tap, one small ice cube, plastic cup, no straw, filled to the two-thirds line.

SUE It's delicious.

JAY And I spiked it with Nyquil. You'll thank me for it later.

[*Beat.*]

SUE It's almost twelve.

JAY   Eleven-thirty.

SUE   Rehearsal ends at ten. Every night it ends at ten.

JAY   She's twenty years old, hon. Big girl. She's old enough to cut her own meat.

CARLY   But I'm just a kid, Dad.

SUE   That's not the issue.

CARLY   I'm just a girl.

JAY   Then what is the issue?

CARLY   I'm just a twenty-year-old girl.

SUE   The issue is she's still not home.

CARLY   And I can be so stupid sometimes.

JAY   Rehearsal must've run late.

CARLY   Do you know what I was doing?

JAY   And she just forgot to call.

CARLY   I wasn't drinking before this.

SUE   I want to know where she is, Jay.

CARLY   I wasn't smoking.

JAY   It's raining. There's traffic.

CARLY   I don't smoke, remember?

JAY   She's a good kid.

CARLY   I wasn't even texting.

JAY   She's fine.

CARLY   I'm *not* fine! Do you know what I was doing? I w...
[*Embarrassed to confess this...*]
I was watching the rain...flitter...into puddles on the road. I was watching it titter against the windshield. I watched it streaking like sunrays across the windows, imagined it running in rivulets along the sides of the Tahoe, tickling its flanks. I was drinking in the rose-colored wash of watercolor stoplights spilled

along the road and the squiggles of streetlamps reflected in the wet of the gravel. I was captivated by this quiet wash of beauty shining through our city. All this beauty absorbed in an instant of thought, in a single, singular glance.... But that instant, that's all it took to thrust me into THIS. HERE. NOW. SHIT!

SUE   [*Simultaneously with* CARLY.] Shit!

JAY   What?

SUE   It spilled.

JAY   It's okay.

SUE   Dammit.

JAY   It's fine. Honey, it's only water.

[JAY *looks at the clock.* SUE *sees this, lays her hand on his.*]

CARLY   I don't know why I'm telling you this. I guess I figure that maybe, maybe if I tell you, tell it all, talk it through, maybe I can change it, something will come to me and I can change the ending, or Fate, if that's what it is. Or that maybe something will change on its own, just because, because maybe I can rack up enough sympathy points—oh, God—to earn myself a miracle. The meteor is streaming, I can see it streaking, blazing, scorching white before me, right before me, white, right before my eyes— but I don't want to stop talking, because the moment I stop talking it will have happened. But I'm okay now. Now I'm okay, and if I just keep talking, oh, as long as I'm talking, as long as you can still hear me talking, I'm okay, I'm okay, I'm okay, I'm okay, I'm here and I'm okay, I'm okay, I'm okay, I am okay.

[*A brilliant flash of lights.*]

[SUE *and* JAY *look up.*]

[*Blackout.*]

• • •

Glass Knives

Liliana Almendarez

Liliana Almendarez

Liliana Almendarez was born and raised in Brooklyn, New York. She received her B.A. in English, creative writing from State University of New York, Oswego, and will graduate with an M.F.A. in poetry and playwriting from Long Island University, Brooklyn, in December 2009. Liliana's plays have had staged readings at Queen's Theater in the Park and St. Clement's Theater.

Almendarez co-developed and co-facilitated Our Expressions Theater Program with Kerri Mesner to train children and teens (ages eight–seventeen) to write and perform original theater works in a Saturday intensive program. She co-wrote, directed, and co-produced *Truth Be Told*, a digital-video lesbian soap opera aired on cable access in Canada and New York. She works in a variety of mediums and media platforms.

Almendarez would like to thank her family, Antony Galbraith, Katt Lissard, Mark Cole, Rob Urbinati, Barbara Kahn, Janis Astor del Valle, Kerri Mesner, Lewis Warsh, Jessica Hagedorn, Marilyn Boutwell, and Christine Francavilla.

characters

JULISSA COLON, 19-year-old Mexican American from Brooklyn. She is in college studying finance. The first in her family to go to college.

JUAN COLON, 40-year-old Mexican man. Father to JULISSA and ANA. Civil servant for New York City for the past ten years.

BLANCA COLON, 39-year-old Mexican woman. Mother to JULISSA and ANA. Housewife. Has started to secretly read articles that JULISSA has been sending her .

ANA COLON, 15-year-old teen. An honor student in high school, she is smart and sassy. Taking dance classes as extra-curricular.

MARK ANDREWS, 19-year old-African American who grew up in the same neighborhood but met JULISSA in college. He is prelaw. Very driven and ambitious.

ROBERT GARCIA, 20-year-old Colombian. Smart in a very practical way. Went to high school with JULISSA, where they dated for three years. He works at a body-shop auto place.

setting

The living room and kitchen area of a two-bedroom apartment in Brooklyn, N.Y. Apartment is immaculate, everything in place. Lace doilies on coffee table and couch. Downstage could be used as the hallway segment.

time

Present day: The day starts on the Wednesday evening before Thanksgiving and the story arcs across the weekend.

scene 1

[*Stage is parted into two areas, living room and kitchen.*]

[*Lights dim. BLANCA sits on the sofa, opens up a magazine, and slowly starts to read aloud. She has a heavy Spanish accent when she speaks English. Lights up.*]

BLANCA　 . . . her co . . . mit . . . ment to dis . . . mant . . . leeing.

[BLANCA *stops and takes up a pocket dictionary and looks up the word.*]

BLANCA dis…mant…ling dismantling…dismantling [*Beat.*] to take apart.

[BLANCA *goes back to reading the magazine more softly.* JULISSA *and* MARK *walk across downstage along "hallway" so audience can hear* MARK *complain.* MARK *is lugging a big bag.* JULISSA *carries her backpack.*]

MARK What do you have in this bag? Rocks?

JULISSA We're almost there. It's the last door of this hallway.

MARK You should have told me your place was a walk-up.

JULISSA It's only three flights.

[BLANCA *hears voices and hides the articles between the sofa cushions. She straightens out the sofa.* JULISSA *and* MARK *enter living area.*]

JULISSA I'm home.

BLANCA Julissa.

JULISSA Ay, Mami, you're always cleaning.

BLANCA Yo pense que papi te iba a recojer?

JULISSA Papi didn't go to the bus station already, did he?

BLANCA Fue a recojer a Ana.

JULISSA Mami, te presento un amigo, Mark Andrews. Mark, this is my mother, Blanca.

[BLANCA *doesn't look pleased but shakes his hand limply.*]

BLANCA Ni-eece to meet joo.

MARK Nice to meet you, Mrs. Colon.

JULISSA We took an earlier bus and Mark's parents gave us a ride home. He lives close by.

BLANCA Really? How nice.

MARK My dad's waiting downstairs for me, I should go. It was nice meeting you Mrs. Colon. Julie, I'll give you a call tomorrow.

[JULISSA *and* MARK *hug briefly.* BLANCA *sits on the sofa and pinches* JULISSA *on the leg.* JULISSA *reacts but continues the conversation with* MARK.]

JULISSA   Stop by tomorrow if you can. I'll treat you to some rice and beans.

MARK   I'll be sure to do that.

BLANCA   Julissa, nos vamos a la casa de tu tio. No hagas planes.

JULISSA   Pero, Mami, we always get back early.
[*To* MARK.]
We have plans to visit family in Jersey.

MARK   We'll work it out later, I really have to go.

[MARK *gives her a quick peck on the cheek and exits.* JULISSA *turns to* BLANCA.]

JULISSA   Why'd you pinch me?

BLANCA   Vas a ver. Waaaait til jour papi gets home.

JULISSA   What?

BLANCA   Ya te olvidastes tus propia costumbres?

JULISSA   How was I being rude?
[*BLANCA pretends she is cleaning lint from the pillows of the sofa.*]
No seas haci . . . I just got home. Did you read any of the articles I sent you?

BLANCA   No tengo tiempo.

JULISSA   [*Starts to unpack, taking several bags of laundry out of her suitcase.*]
When are you going to make the time?
[*Beat.*]
Papi didn't say something to you, did he?

BLANCA   Tengo mucho que hacer. And I know eeenuf Eenglesh.

JULISSA   Okay, if you know enough, then this whole weekend you are only going to talk to me in English.

BLANCA   Pa'que?

JULISSA So you can practice. Maybe take some classes or something? Don't you want to go out there, do something for yourself?

BLANCA La carne esta cara, siempre hay biles que pagar, y mis hijas estan en la escuela. Que mas nessecito saber?

JULISSA Pero hay mas, Mami.

[JULISSA *takes the suitcase and exits to "her room." JULISSA enters again, talking the whole time.*]

Someday very soon me and Ana are going to leave the house. Papi will be working and there will be no one to make a mess for you to clean up. Then what are you going to do?

[BLANCA *picks up the laundry* JULISSA *left on the sofa and hands it to* JULISSA.]

BLANCA I'm going to finish cooking. Hice tu favorito, arroz amarillo con pollo guizado.

[JULISSA *exits, then enters, following* BLANCA *into the kitchen.* JULISSA *begins to prepare lemonade.* JULISSA *lets* BLANCA *tastes the lemonade, and* BLANCA *nods her approval. They sit at the kitchen table to talk.*]

BLANCA Que crees que le paso a Alicia?

JULISSA Tell me in English.

BLANCA Uhm...she found Mauricio AGAIN with another woman.

JULISSA Again? Did she kick him out this time?

BLANCA She tried to shoot dem.

JULISSA Oh my God, did anyone get hurt?

BLANCA She went to jail for one night, but Mauricio got her out. She goes to court next month.

[BLANCA *laughs softly.*]

JULISSA Poor Alicia. It's not funny.

BLANCA She tried to shoot him *down there*, but she missed.

JULISSA You're terrible.

BLANCA Se lo merece.

JULISSA Y Ana?

BLANCA Dance class. No te dijo? She just got on the honor roll.

JULISSA Y Papi?

BLANCA He's okay. He's not drinking como antes and he's taking classes for his job.

JULISSA No more fights?

BLANCA Some.

JULISSA Money?

BLANCA Como siempre.

JULISSA At least he's not drinking.

BLANCA Gracias a Dios.

[ANA *enters living room area.* JUAN *enters right behind.*]

ANA Julissa? . . . JULISSA.

JULISSA In the kitchen.

ANA JULIE! I've got so much to tell you. When did you get here? Guess what. I made it to the honor roll. It means more work but at least I'm in a higher track. And I can take AP classes next year. Which of course means I can try out for Cornell or Barnard. What do you think? This is so cool that you're here this week . . . you can come to my recital this Saturday. I've been practicing every night. Do you know David's not even talking to me anymore and I didn't even do anything to him. Guess who's been asking for you. Robert. He came around before I went to class, and he said he wanted to see you. Are you getting back together with him?

JUAN Breathe, breath . . .

[JULISSA *kisses* JUAN *on the cheek.*]

[*Mimicking* ANA, *very affected way and as fast as he can.*]

I've been so busy at work . . . I'm taking night classes, so you've gotta help me with my English homework. I came home early thinking I was going to pick you up but now you're here so I don't have to. What time did you get here? And what day are you going back?

ANA Papi, stop!

JUAN That's how you sound.

ANA I do not.

JUAN You can say, why, hello, dear sister? How are things with you?

ANA Ah, come on! I don't talk like that.

JULISSA I didn't know you guys missed me so much.

JUAN You're here early.

JULISSA I took an earlier bus and Mark's parents drove me home.

JUAN Who's Mark?

BLANCA Un prieto.

[BLANCA *brings a tablecloth to start setting the table.* ANA *helps.*]

JULISSA No prieto. African American.

BLANCA [BLANCA *brings over plates.*] Mas feo.

JULISSA He's cute.

[BLANCA *brings a pan of food to the table.*]

BLANCA I don't think so.

JULISSA Good thing I think so.

BLANCA Don't be fresh.

JUAN How serious are you two?

JULISSA We're just friends.

JUAN Good. Dejalo haci.

JULISSA You haven't even met him.

JUAN I don't want any hoodlums in my house.

JULISSA   He's in college, not some gang banger.

JUAN   How do you know?

JULISSA   Because he grew up in right here, just like me and the last time I checked there were no vatos around.

JUAN   You never know. Are we taking you back to school?

JULISSA   Mark is bringing back his car, so he's going to give me a ride back. I'm not here even five minutes and you are already trying to get rid of me.

JUAN   Ask Ana, she's the one that wants you out of here so she can have the room all to herself.

[ANA *looks shocked as she brings* JUAN *a beer and pours a glass for him.*]

ANA   Don't believe him, Julissa

JULISSA   Since when do you *do* things for Papi?

ANA   Well, you weren't around, so it's not like I had a choice. Guess what, I even do dishes.

JULISSA   You actually have her doing housework. I should stay away more often.

[BLANCA *brings more food to the table. A bowl of yellow rice.*]

BLANCA   Dejala quieta!

[JULISSA *and* ANA *both pick up* JUAN's *plate, and they struggle with it for a couple of seconds.*]

JUAN   How are classes?

[*Plate slips and falls.*]

BLANCA   What are you two doing?

JULISSA   I'll clean it up.

JUAN   Ana, get the salsa from the fridge.

ANA   I can't find it.

JULISSA   I'll get it.

[ANA *closes the fridge door on* JULISSA.]

ANA Robert came by the other day. He was asking for you. He wanted to know when you were coming home.

JULISSA Did you tell him?

[*Beat.*]

Of course you did.

JUAN Before you start hanging out with your friends, first make sure you do what you have to around the house.

JULISSA Papi, I know.

[*Beat.*]

I thought you liked Robert.

JUAN He reminds me of me when I was his age.

ANA What about Mark?

JUAN What *about* him? One has nothing to do with the other. Robert... now he will make a good husband...some day.

JULISSA *Husband?* Please! Let me finish my first semester of school before you start making wedding plans.

JUAN What is your friend studying?

JULISSA Philosophy and—

JUAN He's studying to think?

JULISSA He's prelaw. Philosophy will help.

[*Beat.*]

I've been meaning to tell you about something. I want to change my major. I've been talking it over with some friends and...and I just don't really like the business classes that I'm taking.

JUAN You just started, how do you know if it's for you?

BLANCA Are you talking about quitting school?

JULISSA I'm thinking of changing my major to English.

JUAN You know English just fine.

BLANCA   Que vas hacer con Ingles?

JUAN   Wind up being a teacher or something? Business...finance... that's where you can have a *real* career...with real money.

JULISSA   I wouldn't exactly get paid with Monopoly money if I teach.

JUAN   But what teachers get paid...you won't make enough. And what about those shoot-outs at schools. Is that really where you want to work?

JULISSA   Papi, I can make this decision by myself.

JUAN   But you haven't. You and *your friends* made a decision.

[JULISSA *gets up from the table.*]

JULISSA   That's not fair.

JUAN   Stop acting like a brat. We'll talk about this when you're not so emotional.

BLANCA   Julissa, sit down. Finish your dinner. This is family.

JULISSA   I'm not hungry. I'm going out.

[JULISSA *exits.*]

BLANCA   Ya es mujer.

JUAN   What about her dreams? I thought she was going to college so she can be something. But teaching?

ANA   Her dreams, Papi? Or yours?

JUAN   Are you in this conversation?

ANA   At least she's staying in school. She didn't say she was going to quit.

JUAN   It's just not good enough.

ANA   She's in college, makes good grades, works to pay for tuition. She does everything you want her to do. Give her a break.

JUAN   You are too young to be talking back to me.

ANA   Who's going to tell you the truth? Julissa loses her temper to quick. And Mami...

[BLANCA *glares.*]

Forget it. I'm going to my room.

[ANA *gets up to leave.*]

BLANCA You haven't finished.

[BLANCA *points to the chair. ANA sits.*]

JUAN I'm going to watch the news. Tell me when she gets in. I don't want her coming in and out whenever she pleases. This is still my house.

[JUAN *exits.* BLANCA *and* ANA *start to clear the table.*]

[*Lights dim.* ANA *exits.*]

[BLANCA *moves into the living room, where she sits on the sofa, reading.* JULISSA *enters. Lights up.*]

BLANCA Sabes que hora es? It's 2:45 in the morning.

JULISSA I was hanging out with Mark. Is Papi awake?

BLANCA He fell asleep. I don't want you walking out like that again, entiendes?

JULISSA But he doesn't listen.

[BLANCA *moves in and cups* JULISSA'*s face in her hands.*]

BLANCA I don't like you staying out so late. It's not safe and I worry.

JULISSA I was with Mark.

BLANCA You never know.

JULISSA He wouldn't hurt me. I wish you and Papi would start treating me like an adult. I'm nineteen years old.

BLANCA Vaja la voz. Just because you're a big college student doesn't mean that you can come and go when you like. You are still living in this house and we still pay your bills.

JULISSA Me and Papi pay the bills. *My* summer job paid for some of *my* tuition. *My* job at school is paying for *my* expenses. I'm paying my own damn bills. All you do is clean the house and act dumb so you don't even have to try.

[BLANCA *slaps* JULISSA *across the face.*]

Mami, I'm sorry.

[*Beat.*]

I...I didn't mean it.

BLANCA   [BLANCA *turns away from* JULISSA.] Go to bed.

[JULISSA *exits.* BLANCA *takes up the magazine she was reading and starts to tear it apart and dumps it in a wastebasket.* BLANCA *exits.*]

[*Lights out.*]

[*End scene.*]

scene 2

[JULISSA *is in the kitchen, taking pies out of the oven. She has a flower bundle that she separates into two bundles.* BLANCA *rushes into the kitchen, and she doesn't know what to do first.*]

BLANCA   Por que no me levantastes?

JULISSA   I was up, I made the pies for dinner so you can sleep in a little.

[BLANCA *stops. Slowly tastes one of the pies with her finger. Makes a face of disgust.*]

BLANCA   Falta azucar.

[BLANCA *exits kitchen, enters living room.* JULISSA *follows close behind with flowers.*]

JULISSA   Happy Thanksgiving

[BLANCA *looks at the flowers with disdain.* JULISSA *hands them to her.* BLANCA *puts the flowers in a vase.* BLANCA *exits.*]

[JULISSA *goes back to the kitchen, where she picks up the rest of the flowers.* JUAN *enters living room, adjusting his tie, as* JULISSA *passes* JUAN *to the front door.*]

JULISSA   Don't you look nice.

JUAN   Thank you, thank you. And where are you going?

JULISSA   Over to Mark's. I just wanted to give these flowers to his mother. I'll be back quick. He lives close by.

JUAN   We're leaving as soon as Mami finishes getting dressed, so—

JULISSA   Now I'm on a time limit?

JUAN   Julissa!

JULISSA   I said I'll be right back!

JUAN   Since when do you come and go as you please in this house?

JULISSA   Pa, that's how it is for me at school. I go whenever I want. I didn't have to tell anyone.

JUAN   This is not school. This is home. Your home. You should know better.

JULISSA   I'm not a little girl anymore.

JUAN   But you're still under my roof. The same rules still apply here.

JULISSA   What about bending one or two?

JUAN   You're only 18.

JULISSA   When you were 16 you were out in the world working. Didn't you tell me that?

JUAN   That's different. I had to do it for my family. It was necessary. You out at all hours of the night is not.

JULISSA   I didn't say it was necessary. I'm just saying that at 19 I'm too old for a curfew.

JUAN   Anything can happen to you. I stay up waiting until you get home … only when I know you're safe can I sleep.

JULISSA   Anything can happen to me at anytime. At school I stay out until 3 or 4 o'clock in the morning.

JUAN   But I don't see that … not like when you're here.

JULISSA   Then I won't stay out past 1, okay?

JUAN   Midnight.

JULISSA   Geeze, now I'm Cinderella. You know I won't change into a pumpkin.

JUAN   Julissa—

JULISSA   Okay, okay, midnight it is then. And no nagging about it either, you have to trust that I will come back on time.

JUAN   That one you'll have to talk to your mother about.

JULISSA   I don't think she wants to hear anything I have to say.

JUAN   Why?

JULISSA   Never mind. Midnight it is.

JUAN   Done.

[JULISSA *starts to leave but turns back.*]

JULISSA   I don't have it in me to be a business major anymore, Papi—

JUAN   Not this again—

JULISSA   The classes are so hard and the more I learn the less I want to do it for the rest of my life.

JUAN   But teaching? They don't get any respect in this country.

JULISSA   I've been working as a tutor in the writing center and I'm really good at it. You know how I am whenever you have questions with your papers. I like it.

JUAN   But you'll never make enough money that way. Don't you want to buy a house someday?

JULISSA   Someday but—

JUAN   On that kind of salary it will never happen.

JULISSA   Would it be a big deal if it doesn't happen?

JUAN   We wanted to give you girls all the best opportunities so you can have a better life. Do better. Be better. We didn't sacrifice the way we did so you can become a teacher. We expected more from you.

JULISSA   I never asked you to do this for me.

JUAN   You went away to school because that's what you wanted, no?

JULISSA   Then this decision to go into English is mine to make too.

JUAN   Can't business be the backup plan? English is a subject, not a career.

JULISSA   College is about finding yourself.

JUAN   Are you lost? It's a mistake to go through school without a focus.

JULISSA   Then it'll be my mistake . . . I just know that I won't be able to last in school if I keep taking these classes.

JUAN   It will cost you time and money. Both of which you'll never get back.

JULISSA   Just trust me.

JUAN   When do you have to decide for sure?

JULISSA   The sooner the better.

JUAN   Do me a favor, finish out the rest of the semester and let's talk about it when you come back in December. Bring me some information about the major and the classes and then we'll talk. I'm not saying no, but I'm not saying yes either. What happens if you decide that English classes are too hard? I just want to make sure you are not jumping from one thing to another, okay?

JULISSA   I can do that.

JUAN   Anything else?

JULISSA   Mark is coming over later today. I want you to get to know him better.

JUAN   Why?

JULISSA   Mark is more than a friend.

JUAN   But you said—

JULISSA   I know what I said but I wanted to give you both a chance to get to know him first before—

JUAN   Before we say no.

JULISSA   Before I told you. Even if you both said no, it wouldn't change my mind about him. At least talk to him.

JUAN You know how your mother is about them.

JULISSA Then you don't mind that he's black?

JUAN I didn't say that.

JULISSA You don't even know him yet. He's a good guy. Very smart. Smarter than me.

JUAN I don't think that's possible.

JULISSA Well … just don't call the police on him if he knocks on the door, okay?

JUAN [*Visibly offended.*] I would never do that!

JULISSA I'm just kidding. I'm going to run these over to his mother and I'll be right back.

JUAN Don't tell your mother about Mark yet … she'll be—

JULISSA Disappointed?

JUAN Let's just say she'll need time to adjust.

JULISSA There goes her dreams for little white babies.

JUAN Please, Julissa … don't even joke about getting pregnant. I can't handle that right now.

JULISSA Let's just end this conversation now before we start arguing.

JUAN I expect you to behave in college, young lady.

JULISSA I know, Papi. I know.

JUAN Go … hurry back. It's getting late.

JULISSA I won't be long.

[JULISSA *exits.*]

[*Lights out.*]

[*End scene.*]

scene 3

[JULISSA *and* ANA *are sitting on the sofa.* ANA *is leaning on* JULISSA.]

ANA I am soooo full.

JULISSA Tia Luisa always makes too much rice.

ANA And she always heaps big spoonfuls onto my plate.

JULISSA I can't believe we ate so much. I feel sick.

ANA Shut up, you're making me sick.

JULISSA No one forced you to eat so much.

ANA Julie, is Mami mad at you because you walked out on Papi last night?

JULISSA Nah, I said something I shouldn't have said when I walked in last night.

ANA She ignored you all day.

JULISSA Really? I didn't notice.

ANA I mean, what did you say to her? The last time she was *that* mad she kicked Pa out of the house.

[*Doorbell rings.* ANA *crosses to answer the door, but before she opens the door...*]

I almost forgot. Robert said he'd be over in a little while.

[ANA *opens the door.* MARK *is standing in the doorway.*]

MARK Hi, I'm Mark. You must be Ana.

[ANA *waves.* JULISSA *walks over to the door.* ANA *stands between them, watching one and the other as they talk.*]

JULISSA I thought you were going to call before you came by.

MARK Is this a bad time?

JULISSA You should have called.

MARK You didn't call when you stopped by this morning. Do you want me to leave?

JULISSA I didn't say that.

MARK Do you want me to come in or not?

JULISSA You're already in.

MARK Are you mad at me about something?

JULISSA Just a long hard day with my family.

MARK And?

JULISSA And I just found out—[*Gives* ANA *a deadly look.*]—that an old friend might drop by.

MARK So that's why I'm still standing in the doorway.

JULISSA I'm sorry, Mark. Come in. This is my little sister, Ana. Ana, this is Mark.

[ANA *waves but remains standing between them as she rocks back and forth. She just stands there, and* JULISSA *gives her a nod to get lost.* ANA *stays put, and she looks from* JULISSA *to* MARK. *They both stare at* ANA.]

ANA Ah...I'm...going to go make a phone call.

JULISSA Thank you.

ANA [*Stage whisper to* JULISSA.] El no es feo.

[JULISSA *shoos her away.* ANA *exits.*]

MARK Who thinks I'm ugly?

JULISSA Don't listen to her...she's fifteen.

[JULISSA *and* MARK *move to the sofa and sit down.*]

MARK She's good at it.
    [*Beat.*]
    What time is Robert coming over?

JULISSA Any minute now.

MARK Are you going to tell him about us?

JULISSA Eventually.

MARK   Eventually? You're not having second thoughts, are you?

JULISSA   I just don't know how to explain it to him.

MARK   You keep putting it off, which makes me think that you're not over him yet.

JULISSA   [*Stage whisper.*] Mark, you know my history with him. You don't "get over" that in a couple of weeks.

MARK   Two months, Julissa. It's time you come clean to him about us. Otherwise—

JULISSA   Don't start with the ultimatums.

MARK   Otherwise you are telling me that *he* is more important than I am to you.

JULISSA   I haven't seen him in three months and—

MARK   And?

JULISSA   I'm just not sure—

MARK   Of?

JULISSA   —seeing him. Can't you understand that?

[MARK *gets up, exasperated.*]

MARK   Of course I understand . . . but I don't have to like it.

JULISSA   Awww, baby, don't you know you're the one for me?
[*Gives* MARK *a kiss on the lips.*]
Trust me.

MARK   Famous last words.

JULISSA   That's not fair. When you were breaking up with Shana I didn't give you a hard time, did I?

MARK   Just a little.

JULISSA   [*Lightly punches him on the shoulder.*] You are such a liar.

MARK   All right, you were the epitome of a trusting friend.

JULISSA   I think we were more than friends by then.

[JULISSA *and* MARK *kiss.*]

JULISSA   My parents might come out any minute.

MARK   So that's why you're kisses are more exciting.

[JULISSA *and* MARK *kiss again.*]

[*Doorbell rings.* JULISSA *and* MARK *both stand up.* JULISSA *puts her hand on his chest.*]

JULISSA   Let me handle this, please. Promise me you'll behave.
          [JULISSA *crosses to door before she opens.*]
          Promise?

MARK   Scout's honor.

[JULISSA *opens the door.* ROBERT *takes* JULISSA *in a whirling hug.*]

ROBERT   Julie! God, I've missed you.

[ROBERT *takes* JULISSA's *face and he is about to kiss her full on the lips.* MARK *crosses to* JULISSA *and* ROBERT.]

MARK   Julissa! Want to introduce?

JULISSA   Roberto, this is... [*Forgetting* MARK's *name.*]...Mark!...Mark Andrews. Mark, this is Robert.

MARK   [*Sarcasm to* JULISSA.] Nice.

[MARK *puts his hand out to shake* ROBERT's *hand.* ROBERT *looks at* MARK's *extended hand and turns to* JULISSA.]

ROBERT   Who's this?

JULISSA   A friend from school.

MARK   Friend?

ROBERT   What?

JULISSA   [*To* MARK.] You promised.

ROBERT   Julissa, what's going on?

JULISSA   I'm sorry I didn't tell you but we've been going out up at school.

ROBERT   Since when?

[MARK *moves in behind* JULISSA, *where he pulls her closer to him. Very possessive move.*]

MARK   She's with me now.

[ROBERT *takes* JULISSA *by her upper arms and whirls her away from* MARK *so that* ROBERT *is talking solely to* JULISSA.]

ROBERT   Why didn't you tell me? I've been waiting for you for months and you come back with . . . *him?*

[MARK *reaches over and puts a hand on* ROBERT'*s shoulder.*]

MARK   Get your hands off her—

ROBERT   [ROBERT *turns around and grabs* MARK *by the shirt and pushes* MARK *away.*] Get the hell off of me.

JULISSA   [*Screechy.*] Stop it!
           [MARK *is flung back and he knocks over the vase of flowers. Vase crashes to the floor.*]
           Mark!
           [MARK *rushes* ROBERT.]
           Robert!

[JUAN *enters and pulls* MARK *and* ROBERT *apart.*]

[BLANCA *enters.* ANA *enters.*]

JUAN   What the hell is going on? Julissa?
           [*To* MARK *and* ROBERT.]
           You don't come to *my* house with this garbage!

ROBERT   Disculpe, senor. I don't want any trouble.

BLANCA   Juan, que'sta pasando?
           [*Notices broken vase and gets down to pick up pieces.*]
           Aye my florero.

MARK   [*To* BLANCA.] I'm sorry about the vase.

[BLANCA *gives him a stern look.* MARK *gets down and starts to pick up broken glass too.*]

BLANCA   Don't! You'll cut yourself.

[MARK *gets up to face* JUAN.]

JUAN   What's this about?

ROBERT   [*Points to* MARK.] He started it.

JUAN   Julissa?

JULISSA   Pa, we were just talking—

JUAN   Tomorrow you talk. Tonight I want you out of my house.
[*To* MARK.]
Both of you.

MARK   Good night, sir. I'm really sorry about the vase.
[*To* JULISSA.]
I'll call you tomorrow.

[MARK *reaches out to kiss her and* JULISSA *turns away from him.* MARK *exits.*]

ROBERT   [*To* JUAN.] I'm sorry about this mess but I'd really like a chance to talk to Julissa tonight.

JUAN   Mañana.

ROBERT   [*To* JULISSA.] This isn't over, Julie ... I still love you.

[ROBERT *exits. As soon as* ROBERT *exits,* ANA *jumps up and crosses to* JULISSA.]

ANA   This is so great! Guys fighting over you.

JUAN   So this is the Mark that you wanted me to get to know. I'm not impressed.

JULISSA   He didn't start this.
[JULISSA *sees* JUAN'*s stern look.*]
I don't know where to start.

JUAN   I don't want them back tonight.

JULISSA   I hear you, Pa.

JUAN [*To* BLANCA.] Let Julissa and Ana finish cleaning up this mess, Mami.

[JUAN *exits*. BLANCA *follows*.]

BLANCA Don't cut yourselves.

[JULISSA *crosses to pick up the rest of the mess.* ANA *checks to make sure* JUAN *and* BLANCA *are gone.*]

ANA Why were they fighting?

JULISSA It's complicated, Ana.

ANA [*Pointing to herself.*] Hello, honor student. I think I can keep up.

JULISSA Mark's more than a friend.

ANA Well, duh, that's obvious.

JULISSA We've been dating for the past couple of months...and I didn't tell Robert...I didn't know how...and you know how Mami and Papi are about black guys.

[JULISSA *takes the broken glass to the kitchen.* ANA *follows.*]

ANA Oh my God! Are you *ashamed* of Mark? How could you be like that? He's such a cute guy.

JULISSA I'm not ashamed of Mark. I just didn't know how to break the news to them. You know how they can be. Very protective.

ANA How did you two meet? Was it love at first sight? Are you *sleeping* with him?

JULISSA Shut up before Papi hears you.

ANA Well, I'm not a baby anymore. I'm sixteen and I've been seeing David, so I know stuff. And he been wanting to...you know... take our relationship to the next step.

JULISSA Ana! You're only fifteen. Please tell me you haven't slept with him yet.

ANA Fifteen and seven months. Did you sleep with him?

JULISSA First answer my question.

ANA   You always told me to save it for love.

JULISSA   When did I ever tell *you* that?

ANA   Okay, you didn't tell *me* exactly but you always said that to Janet and Lucy.

JULISSA   You little sneak. Maybe eavesdropping has its advantages.

ANA   Sooooo...tell me, I want details. Don't leave anything out.

JULISSA   It was the first couple of days at school and it was all very new and scary. I meet so many people but not anyone I really want to hang out with. At least not right away. Do you know what I mean?

[ANA *shakes her head no.*]

Everybody is saying the same thing, hi my name is Jane or John from Hicksville, USA, and I tell them I'm from Brooklyn, New York. They asked me stuff like, "Did you ever see someone get shot? Or mugged? Did you ever have to carry a knife? Were you ever in a gang? Did you go to clubs? Did you hang out in *the Village?*" They acted like it was a whole different country or something. When I told them that I would ride the subway home...they would act weird.

[*Prissy.*]

"Like oh my gawd, I could never live in the city, it's so dangerous." It made me feel like I was an alien. Anyway, one night these people invite me to hang out in Kevin's room to watch *Saturday Night Live*...

ANA   Euuuugh.

JULISSA   I thought, what the hell I've got nothing better else to do. So they're all laughing at the stupidest jokes and I sit there thinking it's not that funny. They see that I'm not laughing, so they explain the jokes to me like I'm retarded. I start to get up to leave 'cause I'm just not having any fun. Mark pulls me aside and tells me to ignore them. We start talking and I find out he's from the neighborhood and it's an instant connection. It was so strange... I never thought black guys were cute. You know...

[*Imitating* BLANCA *with a strong Spanish accent.*]

Big nose, big lips... lighter is better para mejorarse la Raza. That night it was different. Here I am coming from the city, I just broke up with Robert, I'm a little too loud, clothes a little too tight, hanging out with a bunch of blanquitos with their J-Crew T-shirts and boxer shorts. It was scary and then there was Mark.

ANA   You know you are starting to sound more and more like a blanquita.

JULISSA   He was also going through a breakup with his girlfriend back home. And so we talked a lot. We would go to the movies, hang out at the local bars, he even got me listening to reggae. Then one day we were watching the sunset by the lake...

ANA   Aaaaah, how romantic.

JULISSA   Can I finish?

ANA   So he kissed you, right? And then what?

JULISSA   Actually he picked me up and threw me into the lake. We went back to my room soaking wet and...

[JULISSA *slowly walks out from the kitchen into the living room. She sits on the couch.*]

ANA   And?! And? Tell me! Details! Details. I want juicy details.

JUAN   [*From offstage.*] Ana, keep it down!

ANA   [*To* JUAN.] Sorry...
      [*To* JULISSA.]
      And?

JULISSA   And the walls have ears and it's none of your business.

ANA   Awww, come on. I'd tell you if anything happened with David.

JULISSA   Like what?

ANA   Not much. We've been talking for about a month. He's seventeen and he's so good-looking. He's gotten a lot of play from older sluts. He's kind of a troublemaker at school and Papi hates him.

JULISSA   Papi hates everybody.

ANA   He came by one day with some serious hyped-up clothes but Papi thought he looked like a hood. He is, kind of, but I don't care. He likes me.

JULISSA   Does Mami know?

ANA   Yeah.

JULISSA   No way! I had to wait until I was seventeen before I could even talk to a guy. That's so unfair.

ANA   [*Valley girl accent.*] Like way! So like David now wants to do the nasty and like I don't know what to do.

JULISSA   Are you finished making fun of me?
[*Beat.*]
Are you ready?

ANA   Heck no! I like him a lot but I don't know if I like him that much. He's so cool but [*Shrugs.*] I just want to be sure that he's "the one" first.

JULISSA   My little sis is growing up.

ANA   God, don't! I'm going to go call him.

JULISSA   Careful, Papi's still up.

ANA   So should I call you senora now?

JULISSA   Senorita until I'm married.

ANA   Or until you lose it.
[ANA *exits.* ANA *enters with a little piece of paper.*]
I guess you won't be needing Robert's new phone number.

[ANA *flaunts the paper in front of* JULISSA *and throws it out in a paper wastebasket near the sofa.* JULISSA *gets up from the sofa goes over to* ANA *and gives her a little push.*]

JULISSA   Isn't it past your bedtime?

[ANA *exits.* JULISSA *goes to the wastepaper basket and checks over her shoulder before she grabs the paper.* ANA *enters and sees* JULISSA. ANA *smiles and covers her mouth and exits to her bedroom.* JULISSA *sees the torn magazine and takes them out of the basket.* BLANCA *enters.* JULISSA *turns around with the scraps of magazine in hand.*]

JULISSA   Why didn't you tell me?

BLANCA   No importa.

[BLANCA *walks over and takes the basket away from* JULISSA.]

JULISSA   I didn't know.

[BLANCA *continues to ignore* JULISSA *as she crosses to the kitchen area to dump the garbage.* JULISSA *follows.*]

JULISSA   Please don't stop because of something stupid I said.

BLANCA   [*Thick Spanish accent.*] Sometimes . . . I listen to Ana . . . and I can't talk . . . to her. She's growing up so fast . . . and my English is . . . slow. So I sit . . . every night . . . just to read . . . a little bit. Yo quiero que mi hija confia conmigo de sus deseos y problemas. You are in college . . . so I'm here with Ana . . . but she talks to you . . . before she talks to me. So I worry . . . that Ana thinks she can't talk to me.
[*Beat.*]
I want to go to school but I think I'm too old to start now after all this time. I don't want to do it if I'm just going to fail.

JULISSA   I didn't know.

[JULISSA *and* BLANCA *hug.*]

JULISSA   Listen, if you want to go back to school, I'll help you. And so will Ana. Maybe this'll get you two closer.

[BLANCA *nods, and she reaches into a drawer and pulls out another magazine.*]

BLANCA   Help me with this one.

JULISSA   *Ms.* magazine. I didn't send you this one.

BLANCA   I bought it last week because it has an essay on teen girls and pregnancy in the Latino community.
[BLANCA *opens the magazine.*]
Explain this part . . .

[*Lights fade without being a total blackout.* BLANCA *and* JULISSA *mock a conversation in the dimming light for a few beats.*]

[*Lights out.*]

[*End scene.*]

scene 4

[*Living room.*]

[BLANCA *on sofa reading a magazine.* JUAN *enters.*]

BLANCA   Porque tan temprano?

JUAN   I've got to study for the test I have on Monday. Is Julissa around? I really need her to help me with something.

BLANCA   Quieres ayuda o quieres que ella te lo haga?

JUAN   I'll do it but she can help me, can't she?

   [JUAN *goes to desk, where there is a pile of books stacked. He takes a couple of them and heads for the kitchen.*]

   Where did she go?

BLANCA   Las muchachas fueron a comprar ropa.

JUAN   What were you doing?

BLANCA   A little reading.

JUAN   Oh.

[JUAN *enters kitchen.* BLANCA *follows with a pamphlet in hand.*]

BLANCA   Juan...

   [*Beat.*]

   I've been thinking. I...I want to take some classes too.

JUAN   Pa'que?

BLANCA   No tengo nada que hacer.

JUAN   Who's going to clean the house? Who's going to cook?

BLANCA   Ana can help with the cleaning. Julissa could clean the apartment by the time she was twelve all by herself. And we can take turns with the cooking.

JUAN   Let me think about it.

BLANCA   Think about what?

JUAN   Don't I give you everything you need?

BLANCA   A little extra money would help us . . . get a little ahead.

JUAN   With Julissa in college and me taking night classes, I don't know how we can afford it, Blanca.

BLANCA   [*Hands* JUAN *the pamphlet.*] Dice aqui que hay financial aid para mujers who want to do job training to go into office work.

JUAN   What about Ana?

BLANCA   Ana is not like Julissa. Ella no me necessita como Julissa. She comes home, does her homework, goes to dance classes . . . and I see her at dinner. She's old enough now.

JUAN   I don't think now is a good time.

BLANCA   Cuando? When Ana finishes high school? College? When?

JUAN   Mas al rato.

BLANCA   No so joven, Juan.

JUAN   I know you're not young anymore.

[BLANCA *sits down.*]

BLANCA   I can do it. It will give me a chance to practice my English . . . and read more. I think I can do it. Okay?

JUAN   Y si fallas?

BLANCA   Ana will help me. When I was in I school I was a good student. All A's.

JUAN   That was a long time ago.

BLANCA   I could've done anything but . . .

JUAN   Where are we going to get the money?

BLANCA   No se.

JUAN   I have to study.

[JUAN *starts to read.*]

BLANCA   No. We never talk about what . . . I want. Hablamos de los billes, Ana, Julissa, tu trabajo, tu tareja, pero nunca de mi.

JUAN   Must it be right this second?

BLANCA   Cuando, Juan?

JUAN   Not now!

BLANCA   Don't do that. I'm not one of your daughters ... I'm your wife.

JUAN   Are you going to start dinner soon?

[BLANCA *furiously turns away and heads for the stove, where she begins to slam pots and pans.* JULISSA *and* ANA *enter living room.* JUAN *exits kitchen area and heads for bedroom.*]

ANA   Did anybody call?

JULISSA   I'm just going out for a little while.

JUAN   Que mucho joden la paciencia ustedes.

[JUAN *exits.*]

ANA   They must be at it again.

JULISSA   I wonder what it is this time?

[JULISSA *enters kitchen area.*]

ANA   I'm not going in there. I might get punished for breathing wrong.

[ANA *exits.*]

BLANCA   [*To herself.*] Yo no soy una pinche esclava. Que cre que le voy a cuidar solamente la casa ... necessito mas ...

JULISSA   What happened?

BLANCA   Dejame quieta niña.

JULISSA   Let me help.

[JULISSA *helps her mother get a plate from the cupboard, and the plate slips and falls.*]

JULISSA   I'm sorry, Mami, I'll pick it up.

BLANCA   Dejalo! ... Aaayeee!

[JUAN *and* ANA *rush in when they hear* BLANCA *scream.*]

JULISSA   [*To* BLANCA.] It'll be okay.

JUAN   Que paso?

JULISSA   Mami cut herself on the broken dish.

[JUAN *gently pushes* JULISSA *aside to get to* BLANCA. JUAN *soothes her in a low tone.* JULISSA *guides* ANA *out of the kitchen.*]

ANA   What happened?

JULISSA   Beats me. If they ask, tell them I went out.

ANA   You're going to just leave me here?

JULISSA   Come on then.

[JULISSA *and* ANA *exit.*]

[*Lights out.*]

[*End scene.*]

scene 5

[*Living room.*]

[*Doorbell rings.* JULISSA *crosses from kitchen to open door.* ROBERT *enters.*]

ROBERT   Hey, can I come in?

JULISSA   I was going to call you.

ROBERT   [*Beat.*] I'm sorry about what happened the other day. I just wasn't expecting...

JULISSA   I should've told you sooner. I just kept losing my nerve.

ROBERT   You should have told me.

JULISSA   I met Mark up at school and—

ROBERT   I figured that part out already. What I want to know is what about us?

JULISSA   Robert, we broke up months ago—

ROBERT   Because you broke it off.

JULISSA   Because you kept cheating me.

ROBERT   I haven't been with anyone since you left.

JULISSA   [*Stands.*] It was not *one* mistake but many, many mistakes. Then you wait to be faithful to me *after* we break up?

ROBERT   I've missed you.

JULISSA   You didn't call me. How would I know that?

ROBERT   You know I don't like staying on the phone. Come on, Julissa . . . I'm trying here.

JULISSA   You just didn't try hard enough. It's too late.

ROBERT   Is that why you're with Mark? To get back at me?

JULISSA   I've changed.

ROBERT   I've changed too . . . for you. So that we could be better . . . together. And now your new friends are more important? What about the friends you left behind? What about me?

JULISSA   We were never just friends, Rob. I wanted more from you but you always let me down.

ROBERT   Can't we just start fresh? Move on to something new and better between us.

JULISSA   If I told you I slept with Mark, could you forget the past?

ROBERT   Could I just hold it against you every time we fight, just like you did with me?

JULISSA   That's not funny.

ROBERT   Come on, that was a little funny.
[*Beat.*]
Julie, I still love you. I know you think you've changed but I really want things to work out between us.

JULISSA   I can't, not anymore.

ROBERT   You've only known this guy for three months. We've been together for three years. Could you really just throw all that away for some college geek that you barely know?

JULISSA This has nothing to do with him. It's me. I mean, I still love you—

ROBERT If you love me the way you say you do . . . then why are you with this guy?

JULISSA But I don't trust you anymore. You've just hurt me so much, Rob. How do I know that you won't do it again?

ROBERT You just don't know how to forgive me. Worse still is, you won't ever let me forget it.

I've changed too. These last couple of months without you were really hard for me. I guess I needed time to really appreciate what I had with you. All I'm asking for is another chance.

JULISSA Really?

ROBERT Yes, really. Come on, mamita, just give me one more chance. You know how much I love you. You know how good we are together.

[ROBERT *closes in and kisses her.* JULISSA *kisses him back for a beat, then pushes against him to stop.*]

[JULISSA *puts a hand to her lips, turns away, and smiles to herself. She turns back to* ROBERT.]

JULISSA That was a mistake.

ROBERT It felt right to me.

JULISSA You should really leave.

ROBERT I don't get it. What's wrong?

JULISSA It was in the kiss, Rob.

ROBERT Would you just tell me what the hell you're talking about?

JULISSA I'm just not *in love* with you anymore. That kiss finally made me realize it.

ROBERT Are you playing with me? This isn't funny, Julissa.

JULISSA I really thought I was still in love with you. All this time, holding Mark off because I needed to resolve whatever was left between us. And now... and now I really know for sure that I'm over you.

ROBERT   That's it! That's all I get after three years? I'm-not-in-love-with-you bullshit after one stupid kiss?

JULISSA   It's more than you gave me in the whole time we were together. One woman is as good as another with you and now after three months I'm supposed to trust you again like it never happened.

[*Doorbell rings.*]

ROBERT   You could never just let it go... you had to hold on to every single mistake like it meant something.

JULISSA   It really doesn't mean anything to me anymore. I'm finally letting you go.

ROBERT   So now you think you're all that. Miss College Thang. Too good for your own kind.

[*Doorbell rings.*]

That's okay, though, it's not like I'll be lonely tonight.

[*Doorbell rings.* JULISSA *crosses and opens the door.* MARK *enters.*]

I can replace you with just one phone call.

[*To* MARK.]

You can have the slut!

JULISSA   Who you calling a slut?!

[JULISSA *starts to go after* ROBERT.]

MARK   [*Holds* JULISSA *back.*] Let him go.

[BLANCA *and* JUAN *enter cross downstage "hallway". Pass* ROBERT, *who does not speak to them.*]

What the hell is going on?

JULISSA   He actually called *me* a slut. He's the man-whore but he calls me a slut. He sleeps with anything with a pulse and we break up because of it but I'm the slut.

MARK   Calm down and talk to me.

JULISSA   It's over.

MARK   Really?

JULISSA   Finally.

[BLANCA *and* JUAN *enter living room.*]

BLANCA   Que le paso a Roberto?

[BLANCA *looks accusingly to* MARK. MARK *looks very uncomfortable and steps back.*]

JULISSA   I broke up with him again.

BLANCA   Again?

JULISSA   [*Takes* MARK *by the arm.*] I'm dating Mark now.

BLANCA   Oh, really?

JUAN   What about yesterday? You think that's the way to act in someone's home?

MARK   I'm really sorry about that. There was no excuse for my behavior. It will never happen again.

JULISSA   Papi, Robert started that whole thing. Mark was only trying to help me.
[*Beat.*]
I would have said something sooner but everything was just too crazy.

MARK   You were pissed off at me? What did I do?

JULISSA   Not now.

BLANCA   So it's really over between you and Roberto?

JULISSA   Yes.

BLANCA   But I liked him.

JULISSA   Mami, I like Mark more.

JUAN   [*To* MARK.] As long as you don't hurt my little girl, we won't have a problem, will we?

MARK   No, sir. She'll be safe with me.

[JUAN *extends his hand, and* MARK *shakes it gratefully.*]

JULISSA   We're going out for a little while. We should be back by dinner. Is it okay if Mark has dinner with us tonight?

BLANCA   Is okay.

JUAN   [*To* JULISSA.] Before you go, I need help with one thing.

JULISSA   [*To* MARK.] Do you mind? It'll only take a couple of minutes. I promised.

MARK   I can wait.

[JUAN *and* JULISSA *cross to kitchen.* BLANCA *and* MARK *are left standing in the living room. Very uncomfortable.*]

BLANCA   Do you want anything to drink?

MARK   No, I'm fine, thank you.

[BLANCA *motions him to sit down on the couch as she sits.*]

BLANCA   So, Mark, who is your mother?

MARK   Rose! . . . Rose Andrews.

BLANCA   I don't know her.
     [*Beat.*]
     What does she do?

MARK   She's a nurse at Cumberland Hospital.

BLANCA   That's nice. Ana was born there.

MARK   Really?

BLANCA   What about your father?

MARK   What about him?

BLANCA   What does he do?

MARK   He owns a grocery store on 5th avenue and 9th street.

BLANCA   They charge too much for rice there.

MARK Really?

[MARK *places head in hands and shakes his head. Lights dim in living room. Lights up in kitchen.*]

JULISSA So do you get it now?

JUAN Maybe you should take this test for me.

JULISSA Sorry, you're on your own. I have my own logics test to study for.

JUAN Did your mother tell you she's thinking about taking classes?

JULISSA She mentioned it. I think it's a great idea. She would learn so much.

JUAN You don't think she's too old.

JULISSA Only as old as you are and you're taking classes.

JUAN But I have to for my job. She doesn't have to do anything.

JULISSA But she wants to.

JUAN And I shouldn't stop her?

JULISSA Not unless you want her making your life miserable.

JUAN No, we don't want that. One day of her ignoring you was enough for me.

JULISSA Thanks. All right, Papi. Mark is waiting for me.

JUAN About that boy.

JULISSA He's not a boy—

JUAN Your friend.

JULISSA Boyfriend.

JUAN You could have told us sooner. You don't have to keep secrets from us. I know you are growing up and you are trying to make a way for yourself... but it would mean a lot to me if you kept us in the loop. I don't want you to ever feel like you can't tell us something.

JULISSA Does that mean you've changed your mind about Mark?

JUAN I didn't say I hated him.

JULISSA But you don't want me dating him.

JUAN I didn't say that either... I'm not automatically going to dislike every guy you bring into this house.

JULISSA Except David...

JUAN That one I don't like. And he's just a friend if I have anything to do with it.

JULISSA So does this mean you're okay with Mark?

JUAN I will be. Just give me time.

JULISSA All right then, just don't take too much time, please.

JUAN Then we'll see you two tonight? I'm sure that we will get a chance to talk then.

JULISSA Thanks, Pa.

[JULISSA *crosses kitchen into living room and grabs up a very relieved* MARK.]

[JULISSA *and* MARK *cross downstage "hallway."*]

JULISSA Did you make any headway with my mom?

MARK I think she officially hates me now.

JULISSA Aww, baby, good thing I love you.

MARK Now tell me why you were pissed off at me?

[JULISSA *and* MARK *exit.*]

[*Lights out.*]

[*End scene.*]

scene 6

[*Living room.*]

[JUAN *and* BLANCA *are in kitchen.*]

[JULISSA *enters. She pulls a bag into the living room.*]

JULISSA [*Shouts across room.*] Mark just called. He's picking me up in a couple of minutes.

BLANCA Do you have everything?

JULISSA Everything I need.

BLANCA I'm just finishing making some sandwiches for you two.

[BLANCA *crosses from living room to kitchen.* ANA *enters. Drags a heavier bag into the living room.*]

ANA I thought you'd never leave. Now I can get my room back.

JULISSA Listen, before I go, make sure you talk to Mami a little. She wants to know what's going on with you. You make her worry.

ANA I know, I know.

JULISSA And don't let David push you anything you're not ready for. And if you cross that threshold, use condoms.

ANA I'm not stupid.

JULISSA Boys make us stupid sometimes. Promise me.

ANA I promise.

JULISSA And call me if you need to chat, vent, whenever you want, okay?

ANA Okay, okay.

[JULISSA *and* ANA *hug. Doorbell rings.*]

JULISSA [*To* ANA.] Get the door.

[ANA *opens door.* MARK *enters and waves hello to* ANA. ANA *points to* JULISSA'*s bag.*]

JULISSA I'm leaving.

[BLANCA *comes out with a paper bag of sandwiches.* JUAN *enters living room and pulls money out of his wallet and hands to* JULISSA. JUAN *kisses* JULISSA *on the cheek.*]

JUAN Call us when you get there.

JULISSA I will.

BLANCA [*Hands* JULISSA *the bag.*] Be very careful on the way up.
　　　　　[*To* MARK.]
　　　　　Please don't drive too fast.

JULISSA Yes, yes.

[BLANCA *and* JULISSA *hug quickly.*]

ANA Okay, okay. Bye, bye, bye.

[ANA *guides/pushes* JULISSA *out the door.* JULISSA *and* MARK *cross "hallway."*]

MARK Geeze, Julie, what did you pack in here?

JULISSA Stop your whining and put some muscle into it.

MARK Nice.

JULISSA Besides, I still have to tell you about the kiss.

MARK Kiss? What kiss? With Robert? Who kissed who? Julissa! You better be kidding, otherwise you're going to be hitchhiking back to campus.

[MARK *picks up speed behind* JULISSA.]

[BLANCA *stands slightly out the door, listening to them leave. Everything is quiet for a beat.* BLANCA *closes door and sits on the couch.*]

ANA Mami, is it okay if I go out with David tonight? He wants to take me to the movies.

JUAN [*From kitchen.*] Not tonight.

ANA [*Shouts in the direction of the kitchen.*] Awww, why not?

JUAN [*From kitchen.*] You have school tomorrow.

ANA   I go back on Wednesday, Papi.

BLANCA   Me and you have to have a long talk after you help me around the house. I'm going to start taking classes very soon. I won't be here as much. You are going to have to help out a little bit more.

ANA   Really?

JUAN   [*Crosses from kitchen to bedroom.*] You heard your mother.
[*To* BLANCA.]
I'm going go watch a little TV and then I'll study some more.

[JUAN *exits.*]

BLANCA   [*To* ANA.] We should talk first.

ANA   About what?

BLANCA   [*Pause . . . then slowly.*] Do you know anything about sex?

ANA   Awwww, Maaaa.

[ANA *covers her face in embarrassment.*]

[*Light out.*]

• • •

Hearts and Minds

Adam Kraar

Adam Kraar

Adam Kraar's plays include *New World Rhapsody* (Manhattan Theatre Club commission), *The Spirit House* (premiered at Performance Network of Ann Arbor), *The Abandoned El* (premiered at Illinois Theatre Center), *Storm in the Iron Box* (National Play Award runner-up), and *Freedom High* (Queens Theatre in the Park). His work has been produced and developed by Primary Stages, N.Y. Stage and Film, N.Y. Shakespeare Festival, Ensemble Studio, Theatreworks U.S.A., Rude Mechanicals, Urban Stages, Lark Theatre, H. B. Playwrights Theatre, LaMama ETC, Geva Theatre, Inge Center for the Arts, and others. Awards: Sewanee Writers' Conference, Bloomington Playwrights Project, Virtual Theatre Project, Southeastern Theatre Conference, New River Dramatists fellowship, Byrdcliffe's Handel Fellowship, and the Millay Colony Berilla Kerr fellowship. Plays published by: Dramatic Publishing, Smith & Kraus, and Applause Books. Kraar grew up in India, Thailand, Singapore, and the U.S., earned an M.F.A. from Columbia University, and lives in Brooklyn with his wife, Karen.

characters

    REBECCA LEVINE, 35, a college teacher
    RUDI SOROKIN, 24, a student, originally from Russia
    MONA MAZOUD, 22, from Lebanon

place

New York City

time

The present

character descriptions

REBECCA LEVINE, 35

Dizzily soulful, she's channeled all her passion into teaching. The college has become the center of her world and, because she's losing her position there, she desperately, irrationally, tries to overcome the impending loss by connecting with the students. She came to teaching late, after being adrift as a mediocre poet and overcoming mild substance addiction and failed romances. But she's not pathetic—even though she is still developing her social skills, in teaching she has found her calling. She's comically over-earnest: wants to solve all the problems of the world (including her own) in the classroom. She's not originally from New York City.

RUDI SOROKIN, 24

A student, originally from Russia, who immigrated to Israel when he was a teen, and came to the United States several years ago. Manic intensity, fierce ambition, bright and perceptive, but with moral and intellectual clumsiness. He's excitable and can turn on a dime. His passion and his appetites spill over the boundaries of his common sense. Still, he has a rough-hewn charm. He believes that he believes in the American Dream and his ability to get ahead. But he's not nearly as confident as he thinks.

And, in spite of himself, he has a conscience—he's a mensch. Almost fluent in English, he has a light Russian accent.

MONA MAZOUD, 22

A student, from Lebanon, but fairly Americanized; no accent. Mona is an introvert, and a young widow. Beneath her quiet, sweet surface, brightness and sadness. While she's not a wimp, she avoids confrontation.

• • •

[*The stage represents a section of a college classroom, lit by fluorescent lights. Some rows of chairs with little desks attached. At the front of the classroom—which is probably close to downstage—is the teacher's desk. On the desk are papers, books, and a glass candy bowl. Behind and near the desk are a couple of office chairs with wheels. The room has one door, which is open. The room should make it clear that this is not a well-endowed college: perhaps a fluorescent light occasionally flickers, or the walls need a paint job. It is night, after the last evening class of the fall semester. Very few people are left on campus.*]

[*At rise,* REBECCA LEVINE *stands behind the teacher's desk, sorting through messy stacks of papers.* REBECCA *is 35, wears thick glasses and an oddly colorful dress. After eight seconds,* REBECCA *stops to read one of the papers and suddenly lets out a quick anguished sob. She then looks at the door of the classroom, quickly collects herself, and resumes stacking papers.*]

[RUDI SOROKIN, *24, sticks his head in the doorway, then knocks.* RUDI *wears a long black wool coat, good slacks, a tailored shirt, and a tie. He is handsome, boyish, and somewhat manic.*]

RUDI   Professor?

REBECCA   Rudi! Come in, come in.

[RUDI *closes the door and enters the classroom.*]

RUDI   I know you have many things to—

REBECCA   [*Overeager.*] No, no, no, this is perfect. Let's . . .
　　　[*Sits down.*]

[RUDI *pulls a chair up to the desk.* REBECCA *moves her chair around to the front of the desk so that she'll be closer to* RUDI. *After she sits,* RUDI *does too.*]

Would you like some chocolate?

RUDI   No thanks.

REBECCA   How 'bout the last root beer barrel?

[RUDI *gestures "no thanks."*]

[*Wistfully.*]

Nobody wants my candy.

[*Beat.*]

RUDI   That is a most colorful dress. Very voluminous.

REBECCA   Thank you. Uh, I think you mean—

RUDI   Of course. What did I say?

REBECCA   Well, voluminous means big.

RUDI   Oh my God. My English, ah! Huge? Ha-ha. Of course not!

REBECCA   If you're talking about colors, they might be luminous . . . except these are really almost pastel—

RUDI   I only started speaking English when I was 15; at the time, I was studying Hebrew. But my brain functions in Russian, so . . .

REBECCA   Your English is fine, Rudi. Basically.

[*Beat.*]

So, your family left Russia for Israel when you were . . . ?

RUDI   Fourteen.

REBECCA   That must have been quite . . .

RUDI   You don't have a cell phone, do you? I can set you up—

REBECCA   No thanks.

RUDI   Free minutes—

REBECCA   Thank you, but—

RUDI Why not?

REBECCA I don't like cell phones.

RUDI That's like saying you don't like bathrooms. —Of course, I don't mean . . . I'm sure you like bathrooms—

REBECCA Let's . . .

RUDI Yes. Please. Please.

[*Pause.*]

REBECCA [*Getting down to business.*] How did you feel about it?

RUDI A few errors in grammar were made, but overall, I think, very good. Strong.

REBECCA Well—

RUDI Absolutely. Therefore, I don't understand how I should get such a grade.

REBECCA First—

RUDI Please remember I am full-time student with full-time job. In spite of this, my speech was most effective.

REBECCA You really [believe that]—?

RUDI You said persuasive speech should use emotion, no? I used emotion.

REBECCA You did—

RUDI [*Getting excited.*] You see? This grade makes no sense.

REBECCA I think we need to take a step back, take a deep breath—

RUDI Did I not speak with resonance?

REBECCA Yes . . .

RUDI [*Exaggerating his consonants.*] My consonants, all exaggerated?

REBECCA Rudi. This is not a judgment on you—

RUDI Then who?

REBECCA   The real—the real question is, did you persuade—?

RUDI   [*Gearing up for a fierce defense.*] Avi said my speech was the most persuasive. Others, too, agreed, though they are afraid to say so.

[*Trying to center,* REBECCA, *lips pursed, does a slow yogic release of her breath.* RUDI *stares at her.*]

...What? Please.

REBECCA   Rudi...it...it was a verbal bomb.

RUDI   My speech was a bomb?!

REBECCA   Not—

RUDI   Did my speech go off in a crowded cafe, killing eight people? Did it injure twenty-four, cause damage of a million dollars?

REBECCA   Maybe "bomb" was the wrong...

[*Nervously trying to defuse the tension.*]

Sure you don't want the root beer barrel?...Then I guess it's mine. I'll end up voluminous after all....Rudi:...What was the purpose of your speech?

RUDI   To persuade that the Palestinians—and all Arabs—will never allow Israel to exist.

[*Beat.* REBECCA *is tempted to challenge this belief, but decides to turn it into a teaching opportunity.*]

REBECCA   What audience were you trying to reach?

RUDI   Anybody.

REBECCA   As I've explained—

RUDI   The class, I was talking to the class; of course.

REBECCA   You were screaming—

RUDI   Emotion!

REBECCA   Yes—good, potentially—but! Even the edgiest, dopest hip-hop artists work within a—

RUDI   I am not proposing that my speech is perfect. But this grade, ha!...

REBECCA Rudi...What would you like to do with your life?

RUDI There is not much I can do with a D.

REBECCA I mean, after you graduate. What's your life goal?

RUDI I plan to be chief executive of international telecommunications corporation.

REBECCA Why?

RUDI I like to manage many men to make competitive business.

REBECCA And women?

RUDI I want a wife of course. Why do you ask?

REBECCA What I meant was, you only want to manage men?

RUDI Women too, of course.

REBECCA What about the people who might come from, say, the Middle East? Like Mona?

RUDI Ah...What grade did Mona get for her speech?

REBECCA That's not—

RUDI Half the time I can't even hear what she's saying. Is that a way to make a speech?
[*Pause.* REBECCA *takes off her glasses and rubs her eyes.*]
Professor, you are Jewish, yes?

REBECCA That's really not—

RUDI In America, maybe you can forget. But—

REBECCA Rudi, I think you have a lot going for you. Your passion, your appetite for justice, your charm—

RUDI [*Putting on modesty.*] Well...

REBECCA —have the potential...

RUDI Thank you. Thank you, professor. May I shake your hand?

[*Slight pause.* REBECCA *shakes his hand, but then pulls her hand away.*]

REBECCA   But: You are a better man than the guy who gave that speech.

RUDI   I know, I should've practiced—

REBECCA   You're not listening to me!

RUDI   [*"Go on."*] ...Please.

REBECCA   You get so caught up ...in your...But if you become blind to other human beings—

RUDI   Blind? Me?

REBECCA   You were really insensitive to some people in this class.

RUDI   Like Mona.

REBECCA   Not just Mona.

RUDI   Does this have something to do with the fact that your department chairman was observing our class?

REBECCA   [*This touches a nerve, but she hides it.*] No.

RUDI   She's your boss. Does her opinion not matter?

REBECCA   Today it doesn't, okay?

RUDI   During my speech, I thought she had eaten some bad fish.
[*Making a joke.*]
Maybe some bad clams, no?

REBECCA   Rudi...

RUDI   [*Genuinely concerned.*] ...Did you get in trouble because—?

REBECCA   You keep [interrupting]—

RUDI   If I did anything that—

REBECCA   [*A contained, uncharacteristic explosion.*] Rudi!! For God's sake—!
[*Pause. They look at each other. Then REBECCA looks away from RUDI, takes out a tissue, and quickly blows her nose.*]
Excuse me.

[*She blows her nose some more, then puts away tissue.*]

RUDI ...So.

[*Beat. She takes out tissue, blows one last time, then puts it away.*]

REBECCA If you could try to see that your grade is connected...to larger issues.

RUDI Such as the state of my soul, yes?

REBECCA Do you believe that you have a soul?

RUDI Professor, it is one of those questions for which I have not had much time.

[*Beat.*]

And you? Are you believing in the soul?

REBECCA Yes. *Yes.* You know, the word "enthusiasm" comes from the Greek. It means "the god within."

RUDI The god within. I like that...I think you have the god within.

REBECCA Thank you, Rudi. You're a very enthusiastic person yourself.

[*Slight pause. There is a knock on the door.*]

I'm sorry. Come in.

[*The door opens and* MONA MAZOUD *sticks her head into the classroom.*]

MONA Oh...I'm sorry, professor.

REBECCA That's okay, Mona. Did you...?

RUDI [*Standing up; falsely polite.*] If it's a quick question, please.

[*He gestures, "Go ahead."*]

MONA I can wait, for a little bit.

RUDI No, no, no; go ahead.

MONA My ride is coming at eight, so I could...

REBECCA Rudi, would you mind, just for—?

RUDI Outside? I made an appointment.

MONA I only need five minutes.

RUDI   I know your "five minutes." More like twenty-five.

[*A tense pause.*]

REBECCA   ...Hey: What's going on here?...What do you mean "your five minutes"?...Come in, Mona. Come in.

> [MONA, *22, comes into the classroom, hesitantly. She is Lebanese. Dressed plainly in dark slacks, a gray blouse, and an inexpensive winter coat with a hood, she has a knapsack slung over her shoulder.*]
>
> Sit down, please.

RUDI   Professor—

MONA   It's all right; I can—

REBECCA   Sit.

[MONA *sits, very tentatively.*]

REBECCA   [*To* MONA.] Want the last root beer barrel?

MONA   Oh, I love those! Thank you.

REBECCA   Thank you.

[REBECCA *brings the candy bowl over to* MONA, *who takes the root beer barrel.*]

RUDI   Tomorrow evening, I have engineering final. Six a.m., I must get up for work.

REBECCA   Then we'll keep this brief. Please.

> [RUDI *reluctantly sits down.* REBECCA *remains standing.*]
>
> Before this class, did you know Mona at all?

RUDI   Why...why do you take her side?

REBECCA   There's no sides here. Remember when I talked about the Greek polis, the body politic? We're all of us like arms and legs on the same—

> [RUDI, *clearly exasperated, shakes his head; and mutters something in Russian.*]
>
> I want you both to close your eyes....Just trust me and close your eyes.

RUDI   Another game which has no point. I am not in this school to stuff my face with root beer barrels. And, and, I do not have time for some fantasy about...

REBECCA   About what?

RUDI   ... This is not fair.

REBECCA   Fantasy about what? Tell me.

RUDI   No. I will file a complaint, a formal complaint—

MONA   [*Standing up.*] I'll leave.

RUDI   Yes, leave.

REBECCA   Mona—

MONA   I just came to find out what classes you'll be teaching next semester—

RUDI   She can get this online. But she is so—

MONA   [*Suddenly assertive.*] I am not lazy!

RUDI   [*Standing up.*] Oh yes? Our informative speech project? You were only one on team who showed up without research. She just sat there, eating candy.

REBECCA   Will you—will you please sit down, both of you?

RUDI   [*Emphatically.*] No.

REBECCA   Rudi—

RUDI   I am filing grievance with Dr. Peters and the dean—

MONA   [*To* REBECCA.] I'll send you an e-mail, okay? I have to catch my ride...I'll e-mail you.

[MONA *exits. Pause.*]

RUDI   Professor: please understand—

REBECCA   Do you have any idea...!?

RUDI   I am inside a pressure cooker.

REBECCA   We all are.

RUDI She doesn't work.

REBECCA She...writes poetry. When she was nineteen years old, she was married. To a horticulturalist—a man who made things grow. She showed me his picture. His eyes were...like dark honey.... Two weeks after they were married, on their honeymoon—in the Mediterranean—he drowned. He was swimming, and the undercurrent...

RUDI ...I apologize.

REBECCA Will you apologize to her?

RUDI For what exactly?

REBECCA I can't talk to you.

RUDI I'm just asking—

REBECCA Just...get out of here.

RUDI Professor...

REBECCA I'm not professor. And I don't have to talk to you.

RUDI Dr. Peters fired you....Because of my speech?

REBECCA ...No, that was just...

RUDI The straw on the camel's back?

REBECCA [*Nods.*] ...Peters felt I mishandled the whole thing. And I did—letting you slip by all semester, letting you present that speech. And then, the uproar afterwards...

RUDI I'm sorry.

[REBECCA *gathers up her papers and puts them in her bag.*]

RUDI You have the potential to be very good teacher.

REBECCA You think so?

RUDI You will improve.

REBECCA Rudi, I hope you try to keep the god inside...alive...

RUDI What will you do now?

REBECCA   I have no idea.

RUDI   I will apologize to Mona.... Sincerely. I will.
[*Beat.*]
Professor... There must be something—*something*—I can do, for extra credit.

REBECCA   ... If you write me a solid outline—supporting each of your points... we might be able to raise you half a grade.

RUDI   Half a...?! Half a grade? Then what have we been talking about?!

REBECCA   Your speech. Which I think needed to be discussed.

RUDI   Please understand. I don't... I don't earn enough from my job.... So... my father is assisting. My GPA goes below a B, he will cut me off.

REBECCA   I'm sure if you sit down with your father—

RUDI   He never wanted me to have education. He will be happy if I have to leave America and work in his office as clerk.

[*Beat.*]

REBECCA   I'm sorry. I can't just—

RUDI   Why not?

REBECCA   Because it wouldn't be fair to you.

RUDI   I don't mind!

REBECCA   I'm not going to—

RUDI   But...! Is this your final offer?

REBECCA   It's not a negotiation.

RUDI   Is there something else? Perhaps...?

REBECCA   What?

RUDI   I do you a favor. And—

REBECCA   What kind of favor?

RUDI   Maybe you want to go on a trip.

REBECCA   You would send me on a trip...?

RUDI   I could go with you.

REBECCA   Rudi, I'm really disappointed you'd—

RUDI   Or you could go on your own. That's fine. Let's be realistic. You're leaving this school. There's nothing unethical about this.

REBECCA   Yes, there is.

RUDI   All this learning, all these beautiful words, means nothing if it doesn't put bread on your table. Am I right?

REBECCA   I hope not.

[*Beat.*]

RUDI   Because you want to teach me something? Don't you understand, all I will be learning is to suffocate on dust of obsolete invoices.

REBECCA   I'm sure [that's not your only option]—

RUDI   You're leaving. What difference does it make? I ask you, what difference?

REBECCA   I think you already know.

   [*Beat. Then* RUDI *bounds up to* REBECCA, *getting much too close, and glares at her menacingly. After several seconds, he crosses away from her.*]
   ...I think our conference is over.

[*After a moment,* RUDI *takes out a cigarette and lights it.*]

REBECCA   You can't smoke in here.

RUDI   What can they do? Expel me?

[*Slight pause.* REBECCA *picks up her stuff and starts for the door.* RUDI *quickly intercepts her, blocking her way.*]

REBECCA   Would you please get out of my way?

RUDI   You are blocking my way.

REBECCA   This isn't you, Rudi Sorokin.

RUDI Oh yes?

REBECCA Will you put out that damn cigarette?

[RUDI *takes a drag.*]

RUDI My grandfather was like you. Always looking for the good in everyone, even men in Moscow who spit on him every day. Never smoked a cigarette in his life, he died of heart attack at age 52.

[REBECCA *tries to grab the cigarette away from* RUDI, *but he holds it out of her reach.*]

REBECCA You're making me sick, okay? I can't deal with this! I can't deal with this! What do you want from my life? Want me to give you an A?

RUDI Give me a B—

REBECCA For what? For what?

RUDI Because—

REBECCA "What difference does it make"?

RUDI Yes!

REBECCA Nothing, nothing gets in there, does it? What happens, Rudi? Next, *you'll* be spitting—You're practically spitting on me right now. Spraying your...

RUDI My what?

REBECCA Just—*GET OUT*! Get out of my life, before I, I...!

[RUDI *puts the cigarette out on the floor with his heel. Pause.*]

RUDI All that is left to me is cigarettes, vodka, and filing. I am finished.

REBECCA ...That's ridiculous.

RUDI No; that is my future.

[RUDI *sits down at a desk and rests his head on his hand, genuinely beaten, yet also histrionically laying on his despair. Pause.*]

REBECCA   I know how you feel, but...I felt that way tonight, knowing
         that this is my last class, possibly ever....I came to teaching late;
         and I'm still catching up. The opportunities...
         [*Pause.*]
         But you know something, Rudi? If you can find a way to help
         someone—really touch them, maybe where they've never been
         touched before—then nothing else matters.

[*Pause.*]

RUDI   What if, instead of learning something, we just fail?
       [*They look at each other for a long time.*]
       Professor, your eyes are exquisite.

REBECCA   ...You never give up, do you?

RUDI   Will you deny it?...Why don't we forget all this, and go get a
       drink together?

[REBECCA *shakes her head.*]

REBECCA   [*Firmly.*] ...Goodnight, Rudi.

[RUDI *gets up.*]

RUDI   So...there is no possibility—?

REBECCA   You can always take the course again.

RUDI   Professor...!

REBECCA   You need to stop...*hondling*, and take an honest look at—

[*"Hondling" is Yiddish for haggling.*]

RUDI   Fuck you; okay? Fuck you.

[*Pause.* RUDI *leaves. Pause.*]

REBECCA   [*She calls after him.*] Rudi...

[*She looks around, then slowly walks around the classroom, looking down at some of the
desks as if she is looking at students. She gets to the desk where* RUDI *was sitting and
stops. She reaches out and imagines touching his head. She sighs desolately, then looks
around some more. She goes quickly to the front of the room, trying not to lose it. She
pretends to address the class:*]

REBECCA   Okay, class. Listen up. We need to focus. I want you all to close your eyes. Just do it. Now take a series of deep, deep breaths.

[*As if getting him into line.*]

...Rudi. Take the breath all the way down and slowly let it out....Keep breathing....Somewhere inside your body is a tight ball. I've got one right now in my stomach. I want you to send the breath to wherever that tight ball is, let the breath dissolve that hard little ball...and then breathe out the molecules that came off of the ball....Do it again. Rudi, I want you to really see the ball....All right, Rudi, then see the bialy. Just keep breathing.

[RUDI *appears in the doorway, upstage. He apparently overheard her talking to herself, and now leans in to see what's going on.* REBECCA *does not see him.*]

...Now the ball—or the bialy—has disappeared, and the only thing is your breath, coming in, slowly, and going out, slowly...and the molecules of your breath are swirling around this classroom, mixing together with the molecules of other students and teachers, who teach and learn, and pour out ideas and passions. Imagine if you will molecules of people who lived and died, and spoke and wrote long before us—those particles are here too. The molecules are all mixing together, connecting in new ways, actually creating something unprecedented. With each breath, what you're breathing in is different than what you just breathed out. And that altered air is filtering into your bloodstream, going into your brain, pumping into your heart.

...Take a moment and listen to the new air, surging through you. It's not just your breath or my breath. It's the oxygen we all have to share in order to survive. And if we really let it in, it can change everything....Now, open your eyes. And please turn your chairs so you can face each other.

[*Addressing the empty desk where she had imagined* RUDI, *as if he is resisting the suggestion.*]

...Rudi, please. Please....Please!

[*Silence.* REBECCA *looks at the empty classroom, tears filling her eyes.* RUDI, *who's been watching all this from the doorway, pretends he just arrived.*]

RUDI   Excuse me: professor?

REBECCA   Rudi! Did you [hear] . . . ?

RUDI   Please allow me to apologize . . .

REBECCA   It's been a long semester. Were you [*Standing there before.*] . . . ?

RUDI   Second, is there any possibility you will reconsider the grade for my speech?

[REBECCA *answers him "no" with a look.*]

RUDI   Then I would like to do the extra credit. . . . Even if it only raises me half a grade.

REBECCA   What about your father?

[*Pause.* RUDI *hasn't thought through his plan. Then* . . .]

RUDI   I am not getting my education for him. I will find a way. And maybe even persuade you to buy a cell phone. When you get new job. May I write you this outline?

REBECCA   Yes. But you must get it to me by Thursday.

RUDI   *Thursday*?

REBECCA   E-mailed to me by noon.

[RUDI *looks at her, trying to gauge if there's any possibility of negotiating an extension.* REBECCA *looks back at him, making it clear she's standing firm. The lights quickly fade to black.*]

• • •

In Conclusive Woman

Julie Rae (Pratt)
Mollenkamp

Julie Rae (Pratt) Mollenkamp

Dr. Julie Rae (Pratt) Mollenkamp is an associate professor and graduate coordinator of theatre at the University of Central Missouri.

Recent artistic projects include: directing *Thoroughly Modern Millie*, *Shadow Gets a Black Eye: A Korogoz Tale* (world premiere), *Fat Pig*, and *Anna in the Tropics*; performing as Medea in *Medea Medium*, Ma in *The Grapes of Wrath*, Mme. Ranevskaya in *The Cherry Orchard* onstage; Julia in *Another Woman*, Dr. David in *Classroom Safety*, and Woman in *disengaged* on film; and writing and recording *The Vagina Song*, *Them Elmer and Geraldine Blues*, and *YOU*, available on iTunes.

Her work has garnered thirty-three Kennedy Center American College Theatre Festival Regional awards and five National KCACTF commendations. She has published eleven articles on theatre pedagogy and history, theatre for social change, feminist theatre, and performance studies. She is the immediate past Vice President for Membership and Marketing of the Association for Theatre in Higher Education and a past chair of the National Communication Association Theatre Division.

She is the recipient of the Outstanding Teaching and Service Award from the National Communication Association Theatre Division, the Excellence in Teaching Award and the Faculty Achievement Award at UCM, the Kennedy Center American College Theatre Inaugural Road Warrior Award, the Vagina Warrior Award for her work on The V Day Initiative, as well as numerous acclamations for her acting and directing work.

A Multi-Media Play originally performed with the Ryan Repertory Company, Brooklyn, New York.

time and place

Here and now

stage setting

Two projection screens, a bench, a vanity with chair, and a bench

text key

Regular text: Spoken lines
Italics: Voice-Over
SNAP: Finger Snap
Bold: On Screen

• • •

VIDEO: *The Teacher* [on Screen One]; *Academic Strip Tease* [on Screen two]

When we were naked for first time, he looked down at me and said, "Ok, tell me everything." I love it when people talk dirty.

• • •

Good evening, scholars. My name is Doctor Julie Rae Pratt. Hold a bachelor's degree, a master's degree, and a Ph.D. Have 25 years teaching experience in secondary and post-secondary venues. Published papers in prestigious scholarly journals and have been invited to speak at major national and international conferences.

As a teacher, I strive to provide students with a comprehensive experience involving intellectual, emotional, physical, and spiritual facets, which contribute to their personal, social, and political development.

These are some of the words and phrases used while teaching:

Do the work.
Wet.
Open.
Dripping.
Erect.
Hard.
Delicious.
Pink and puckered.
Open the lips wider.
Hair can get it the way but its part of the fun.
Look toward the differences that's what's compelling.
Butts are funny.

• • •

From a Midwestern matriarchal family, which the world saw as patriarchal, but we all knew who was really in charge. I was often saddened, even as a little girl, about the lack of equality in my parents' relationship. I can't remember a moment where they kissed, where they cuddled on the couch, where their passion was evident, where they praised each other, where they shared moments of silence; where they fought furiously; where conjoined in any emotional or intimate way. They were not partners, they each refused to give, they each lived out their lives together at odds.

My father would fuck up and bring Mom roses and she would be furious because we couldn't afford them, she felt he did it to make HIM feel better—not to give her a gift.

She didn't like *Flowers* too frivolous *Jewelry* too expensive *clothes* not permanent *Household Items* relegating.

That always stayed with me cuz I wondered what the hell she did want? I bet he did too.

So why were they married? What did he see in her? A take-charge woman who paid attention to him. He was an only child. His parents were so in love with each other that he got left out.

What did she see in him?
Security, security, security.
Her dad left. She was daddy's little girl. He just left her.
He had 21 other kids with seven other women.

Her relations with men—you know what she told me? *Never trust them.*
Never trust them. Never trust them. They will fuck you over at every
chance they can get, they will, they will, they will, they will fuck me over.
Forgivers need not apply
She taught me to find strength in myself, and security in others.

• • •

These are excerpts from student evaluations received at the end of
stupendously long, painful, glorious, bloody, exhilarating semesters: SNAP
Julie has a way of pushing students to reach their fullest potential. From the very
beginning she requires/demands student participation.
"*She brought energy to the classroom and made us feel like we were learning with*
her and that what we had to say mattered."
"*Students felt comfortable taking risks in something they have never done*
before."
"*She creates a relaxed environment in which to learn, perform, and experiment.*"
"*She applied her knowledge in creative, interesting ways. The variety of projects*
and exercises is very good."

Excerpts from student evaluations received at the end of frighteningly
quick, wonderful, tumultuous, enlightening, horrifying goddamn
semesters: SNAP
"*Dr. Julie makes us work too hard, her classes are too intense.*"
"*She grades too harshly, she's too demanding.*"
"*The methods used to elicit answers were too forceful.*"
"*The professor seems scattered and unprepared.*"
"*Her classes give me way too much stress. Too much material, too little time.*"
"*She tries to cram too much in.*"
Part of my self-definition is teacher. It's something I have trouble turning
off, cuz I like the trip too much and because I can usually see . . . SNAP

• • •

The drain hole from my radical hysterectomy was above my pubis. It would have been obscured if I had a decent bush, but I'm blond—the tube stayed in me too long and caused an abrasion when it was taken out. Lost 9 lbs. in blood and water from the hole the day it was removed. SEXY!

But that's nothing. The gastric bypass surgery—they made me a brand-new stomach by creating a small pouch at the top of the old, fat, never-full stomach. The new, improved, smaller stomach is connected directly to the middle portion of the small intestine (jejunum), bypassing the rest of the stomach and the upper portion of the small intestine (duodenum). Feel full more quickly than when my stomach was its original size, which reduces the amount of food I can eat. Bypassing part of the intestine also results in fewer calories being absorbed. This leads to weight loss. Truly. When your stomach is only the size of a circus peanut, the pounds just fly away like Dumbo. Try 120 lbs! I lost nearly half my body weight. It's as if there were two Julies inside, and one just silently melted away.

Sometimes I wonder where she went . . . probably to an all-night diner.

Told only 5 people about this surgery. Because I was ashamed? Embarrassed? Conflicted? Scared? Or figured it wasn't anyone's fucking business.

Funny how things change . . .

Of course, losing nearly one-half of me did some fucked-up things to my skin. Half of Julie was gone, but all of the smooth, creamy, pink skin that covered her was still there. And there. And there. And there. You've seen Shar-Peis, the Chinese wrinkled dogs?

I felt worlds better, but I looked like a villain from that Dick Tracy movie—and I don't mean Madonna! Something would have to be done. Back to the knife!

"Tummy Tuck" time. "Okay, class, we're going to do Head, shoulders, knees, and toes and then Tummy tuck!

Audience Sing-Along

They removed a 7-inch smiley face of skin from my belly. They took the smile, the many pounds of flesh of my gut, pulled the top part down to the bottom, and sewed them together, leaving a flat belly, something I've never had in my life. The vertical scars above and below the fake belly button, unique for its pleasing heart shape, are from the bypass. As an added bonus, most of the hysterectomy scar was removed.

I've been 268 lbs and 140 lbs—140 lbs is better.
But maybe not for the reasons you think.

Sixth grade, so I'd had my period for a year, and was fairly well developed. At eleven I had my tonsils and my adenoids out. Unspeakably ill, had to go back, hemorrhaged twice, had to be cauterized in the emergency room, it was horrendous and awful, and at the end of it, a month later, I had lost 25 lbs. and was actually too skinny. To make me feel better, my mom took me to the mall. This was the most frightening public experience I'd ever had in my life. The men would not leave me alone; it scared the living piss out of me. It was predatory—the male gaze and attention was so uncomfortable, so vicious, so obvious, and out of control that even my mom noticed my fear. She ran me out of there. Knew I'd just become the prey. For the first time, the prime target.

This was the same year he said, "Ew, I don't want to do that any more, what's wrong with you?" All that converged at the same time. At the peak of my adolescent beauty, rejected by the only thing I had known as normal, all this other pain appeared.

But I knew how to fix that.
I began feeding that fear right away.
Sneaking cheese sandwiches,
Spending 3 hours in intense ballet class and then
Furtively eating a 1/2 gallon of ice cream.
Sneaking food.
Always Always Always
Hiding it in my room, in the basement, in the car, in the backyard.

No longer wanted to be the prime target. I wanted back the power I felt before.

Purposefully became a fat chick and used and enjoyed all the power of my size until that size threatened my life. That's what it took. SNAP

• • •

My junior high teacher—he loved me, expanded me, inspired me, sought and nurtured my gifts. He praised me, told me when I fucked up, laughed with me, held me when I cried, helped me learn and grow. Finally knew what it meant to be daddy's girl.
Hugged him at graduation, he pressed his stiffy against me.
What the fuck?

• • •

My influence rarely extends to women anymore, when they used to be my strongest allies—before I was wise and jolly and best of all fat—they could take advice from me because they could lord over me based on my size— that's huge with women—
"I love you but make sure there is something I have that is better than you."
I'm *Thinner*
Prettier
Smarter
Funnier
Happier
Healthier
Fertile
For some reason, thinner and prettier is best. But maybe not for the reasons you think.

• • •

I lay in bed with my mom.
She still loves to cuddle.
And she wakes up, looks at me, smiles, and says, "You really must meet my daughter Julie. She got a Ph.D., you know. You'd love her."

These are the little gifts that cut
And cut
And cut the pain.

These are more of the words and phrases used while teaching:
Satisfying.
Climax.
A good build is always pleasurable.
When you do it well, you'll be happily exhausted at the end
Afterglow.
Don't cut off the dynamite before it explodes.
Playing with others is more fun than playing alone.
But playing alone doesn't suck.
Get your ducks in a row.
Get your poop in a group.
Codify.
Silence is power.
When you hate you love and when you love you hate.

• • •

He and I would seek every opportunity to be naked together.
It was guised as:
Playing doctor,
Lessons he could teach me,
Giving each other a bath,
Sometimes with pee.

The ONE time I remember rejecting his advances was when I awoke in the middle of the night on the toilet, legs spread, he was kneeling in front of me, his penis in between the lips of my vagina. He was peeing. It suddenly didn't feel good anymore. It felt cold and wet. Was tired, groggy to the point of unawareness. Began to cry. He quickly swept me up in his arms, took me to bed, and held me safely for a long time. Suddenly, wasn't alone, so not afraid. Felt connected and even bad for not doing what he wanted.

He drilled a hole in the stairwell so we could watch each other in the shower. That's when I first saw him cum. He was in the shower. Sat furtively on the stairwell with a book in my hand. It was so exciting. And it made me feel special.

Still like to watch. Used to feel guilty about it but decided not to. What turns us on first is what continues to turn on us. The faces may change but the act remains the same. Like to watch and be furtive and give fully. Just as when I first became sexual.
And THAT'S OK.

• • •

My name is Dr. J. I have been observed kneeling at 1:30 in the morning on a kitchen floor surrounded by chanting students as I sucked down a beer bong. *Doc J.*, *Doc J.*, *Doc J.!* Are you familiar with beer bongs? A large funnel connected to a hose connected to a mouth?
It helps if one has done various things over the course of one's life to diminish the gag reflex... Spit up the first time. It had been nearly fifteen years since I last bonged a beer. Which, by the way, was also in front of students... and my mother.

I have fed students, individually, in pairs and in groups. Danced with them, cried with them, laughed with them. Helped them get jobs, have babies, go to court, get medicine and abortions. Paid their electric bills, car insurance, and tuition. Created some good and some not so good art with them.

And taught them a few things about acting, directing, theater history and management, teaching theater, collaboration, and being an artist with vision. Sometimes the learning happened on purpose, sometimes it happened by mistake. But it happened.

They've cleaned, repaired, and decorated my house, maintained my lawn and gardens, introduced me to those they love, and come back to tell me of their lives. I'm their mentor, their teacher, their friend, and one time, a lover.

Students need to see that teachers are human and that they learn, too. Especially, teachers learn from their students.

It begins when I THOUGHT I was 5 or 6. When my mom and I talked about it later, she told me I was closer to 2 years old. My babysitter was the 17-year-old from across the street. He let me eat popcorn, paint on the wall with pudding, tucked me in with music playing. Awoke to him pulling my underpants down. The smell of laundry bleach was in the air and had wet sticky stuff on my back. Rolled over. He flew up, pants around his ankles, and left the room. Didn't know why he wouldn't play with me any more. It hurt my feelings, so told my mom about it the next day. He never sat for us again.

At 6, walking home from first grade, a man in a car asked me for help. He wanted me to come closer to the car. Knew I shouldn't but couldn't resist the attention—he picked me. I must be smart. Or pretty. As I approached, realized he was playing with something in his lap. Surprise! Watched him cum as I stepped up to his car window. It was scary and awesome and frightening and horrific and fascinating. Walked quickly back to school rather than home. Albert Einstein Elementary was closer and wanted to be safe.

• • •

Unsolicited Advice
If you ever decide that you want to stay with her for the rest of your life, or at least for the next 2 weeks, these are some things you should think about:
You don't have to understand her, just recognize her
Little gifts are a blast
Do what you want and let her do what she wants
Collaboration is fun, it's great to play by yourself, even better to play with others
Stroke her when you don't want to but she needs it
Give oral pleasure
Help her grow in the least mean way you can muster
Don't be too lazy
BE HONEST and KIND to each other, its the greatest way to care
Become that united front against all forces, it's really cool
Grow into a good daddy

Go on adventures—grocery store, lingerie shops, hardware hatches, pick
pumpkins and collect leaves and look at stars and take vacations and
SHARE SHARE SHARE SHARE SHARE
That's what partners do.

If you ever decide that you want to stay with him for the rest of your life,
or at least for the next 2 weeks, you should do the exact same things. Plus
learn how to milk the prostate. He'll like it.
SNAP

Mom has always been the Force in my life.
Mom has always been the Source that I draw from. Mom has always been
the Course that I cannot seem to chart.

My mom's biggest fear was not being able to take care of herself. She
often did it as a child, when her mother worked and her father was gone.
It was a great source of pride to her that when my father left, she not only
survived, she thrived. She is PHENOMENAL WOMAN!

Year 1—When she began to fumble, I notice. At 52, she got a major long-
term disability insurance policy. That's when I knew she knew.

Watched her for 5 years before mentioning things to my brothers. They
retreated into total denial, the little fuckers—men in my life often have
the luxury of not dealing and that exhausts me—they know women in our
family will deal with the shit and of course we do.

My sister-in-law picked up on it and we began the conversation—stories
repeated, people misnamed, taking too long to shop, working 9 hours a
day, then 10, 11, then in the office on weekends to get the job she could
no longer do well done. Not done well, but done.

Year 7—Finally mention it, she's horrified, remind her that I promised I
would take care of her, would tell her what I saw, did that when I was in
my 20s, at the same time we agreed to take care of the other's pets if
something happened to either of us.

So, mentioned it—denial anger paranoia frustration—She hated me and
loved me more for it.

Let's get help, perhaps it's nothing, but we need to know.

Was there in the room with her when the words came out—Alzheimer's. But we knew it for a long time before.

Anger, denial, bargaining, depression, acceptance—these were a whole lot of fun.

Year 11—She called the police at 4:00 a.m., claiming there was someone in her house, they had been there for years but they now were threatening her—Arabs and Negroes and Mexicans, oh my.

She was obsessed with everyone getting her. We kept her in her condo as long as we could. Belligerent and tricky, she had been hiding the disease for so long, she knew how to play it. It's a manic thing and so horrifying to watch.

Then it's too late, she can no longer maintain after maintaining for more than 12 years—

Keeping the secret—hiding the disability—not showing the weakness. All lessons learned.

• • •

I am Inconclusive Woman, woman, woman . . .
Able to hide pain in a single bound.
Performs herself powerfully.
Laugh even though her heart is breaking.
Pretends all is normal when her baby just died.
Publish two papers as her husband fucks around.
Makes others feel good when she is dead on the inside.

Acts like she's confident and she becomes confident.

• • •

Also a MILF. A mother you'd like to fuck but NOT spend your life with? Every relationship destined to change profoundly as he or she dances out the door as all the little ones do? That ultimate goal of teachers and parents—to prepare them to leave and be free, not gone but not here.

I will NOT be the consummate mother.
Won't get to raise my own biological children—*Mommy, Mommy, Mommy!*
But do have the privilege of editing the kids of others. And the best part of that is we get to play and they go home. And the worst part of that is we get to play and they go home. SNAP

At twelve, we decided to stay home sick from school. We wanted to play. Unfortunately or fortunately, my mom really was sick that day and stayed home with us. While my mom slept in her bed, on the couch I attempted with all my 12-year-old wiles to seduce him. Finally, after looking up my nightgown for the longest time, he threw my legs back together, pulled my nightgown down, picked me up, and yelled at me. "Cover yourself up! What's wrong with you?"

I knew our family affair was over.

Our last sexual time together happened about a month earlier. We were listening to records in his room, lying on the floor. He pulled my shirt up and massaged my breasts. "This is all you can have guys do to you. If they do more, you could get pregnant. Be careful. Don't let that happen." He made the right choice not to fuck his sister. But the pain of that rejection stayed with me for a long time. And led to the desperate search for and tremendous fear of— relationships with men.

I know how much he loves me still. Know that he would walk through fire for me—know this.
Just wish I didn't have to always ask him—wish he was just there.

• • •

Don't think my mom consciously knew about anything that was going on with me and my brother, but when there's that level of dysfunction in the family, you know something's wrong. Human beings can just tell stuff like that, and women are especially good at it. Except my mom. She loved, she nurtured, she cared endlessly—she just didn't see.
I knew she knew something was wrong, she just didn't know what.
She never asked.
I never told.

And now it's too late.
SNAP

I sometimes make points with knives so men will listen. Are you listening?

Used to have trouble getting men to listen to me because I was small.
Then had trouble getting men to listen to me because I was fat.
Now have trouble getting men to listen to me because I'm a threat.

• • •

Unsolicited Advice
Becoming an object gets you attention—you become subject for a while.
Girls seek to be subject—we are taught that it's all that is worthy.
Yet, we're all both. And it's OK to be both—being an object is FUN, hard,
scary, being a subject is FUN, hard, scary.

They're just different. Balance is key here.

The idea is we're supposed to accept is this—girls are supposed to show
restraint, politeness, make logical safer choices. Bad behavior = See You
Next Tuesday, and we can't have that! Boys can do awful things and it's not
their fault; they can't help themselves.

Well, FUCK THAT! When do I get to be out of control? Take what I
want? Push the envelope? Destroy some shit? And be totally unaccountable
for my actions?

Boys will be boys? Fine!
But girls will be girls and we'd all better be prepared for the consequences!
SNAP
VIDEO: *Them Elmer and Geraldine Blues*

• • •

Men exposing themselves—at the store, at work, at school.
Obscene phone calls—where they asked for me before engaging.
Accidental sodomy from a one-night stand.
Being thrown up against a wall by a student.

Being felt up in public.
Gay men reveling in my body because THEY WERE GAY and I didn't exist as a sex object—their erections proved otherwise.

Proud happy feminist, proactive, accomplished, loving, joyous, smart, funny, caring, giving, giving, giving, giving, giving, giving, giving!

Not taking, not taking too much, not feeling worthy.
Unafraid to ask for what I wanted but desperate for no one to find out what I needed.
Unable to fully take care of me—but no one knows that.
Generous and loving to a fault.

In Conclusive Wo—fuck it.

• • •

 My female students are so much smarter than I was at their age, and I'm so pleased. They still suffer the same shit—oppression, being dismissed, mixed messages—but they evolve faster.

They are amazing and I love to hear what they are thinking.

Want them to understand that they are NOT the weaker sex. They are NOT the stronger sex. They are only and always who they are—and the potential in that is infinite. And that loving each other, not competing, not hurting, not undermining, not attacking, will ultimately bring them their greatest satisfaction.
Women are women's BEST allies.

• • •

14-year-old high school freshman—fainting and have migraines—1-week hospital stay with every scary test one can imagine—a borderline epileptic, they say. "There are two fuzzy shadows on your brain scan that we'll keep our eye on."
Inconclusive.
SNAP

• • •

J.—first life-altering emotional love—gay: *140 lbs*
R.—second love—celibate: *+20 lbs*
N.—lose virginity AND broken engagement: *–10 lbs*
A 3-person affair with N. and A.: *–6 lbs*
F.—gay: *+20 lbs*
B.—black and beautiful: *weight stayed the same*

I'm a 19-year-old college student—have a lump removed from my left breast.
Tell NO ONE. Drive myself to the hospital, lie to drive myself home. Not
cancer but they're not sure what it is.
Inconclusive.
SNAP
D.—engaged—my first orgasm with my first vibrator: *+30 lbs*
I've since given over 30 vibrators away to my girlfriends—my mother
LOVED the rabbit I got her!

21-year-old college graduate—summer—get pregnant.
Six weeks on when I have an abortion.
Safe.
Clean.
Expensive.
Painful.
Legal.

• • •

22-year-old high school teacher—winter—slip, fall on the ice, and rupture
5 discs in my back—thus continues the magical journey of surgical
enhancement—spent 4 days hanging from the ceiling. Doesn't work.
Inconclusive.

• • •

Play happily through my 20s with increasing amounts of delicious fatness
in my body and a back that is tricky.

Sleep with a variety of people—who the fuck knows my weight? Dieting and gaining all the time. My back goes in and out—I relegate pain to another part of the brain.

Sexual survivors are good at that. SNAP

• • •

G.—engaged—dumps me while putting the down payment on our house: *+30 lbs*
P.—a best friend—furtive sexual encounters he tells no one: *weight stays the same*
M.—it was healing—she suffered a loss and I lost my father: *+30 lbs*

Mostly happy—truly happy in ways others aren't because enjoy the ride— find great joy in sensual pleasures—looking, tasting, touching, smelling, hearing everything.
SNAP
Michael—engaged—we marry.
As I walk down the isle, I think, "Till divorce us do part."

• • •

33-year-old college professor—one week back from the honeymoon when I begin to hemorrhage vaginally—find out I'm pregnant in the emergency room but the baby is in big-time trouble—wait it out for 5 more weeks before I go into labor and miscarry it—while teaching a class—expel into the toilet, put it in my pocket and go back and teach for another 2 hours. *Inconclusive.*

34.

35.

36—various "procedures" to help with fertility.
Scrape my uterus.
Blow out my fallopian tubes.
Laparoscopy my ovaries to remove cysts.
Undergo all these Kodak moments at teaching hospitals, so there are tons watching the fun.

Fertility drugs, artificial insemination, in vitro fertilization—10s of thousands of dollars.

The results are many miscarriages very early in pregnancy.

Inconclusive

One of the perks of infertility is never having to worry about birth control.

37-year old wife—260 lbs—can't maintain a pregnancy. My back is in trouble again—can hardly walk and am losing the ability to do so as the nerves are slowly being severed by the disks.

Direct three successful productions, publish two articles, and am elected the leader of a national organization.

37-year-old-hospital patient—back surgery. *The procedure has been 95% effective* It doesn't work. *Inconclusive.*

37-year-old-hospital impatient—second back surgery. *The procedure has been 96% effective.* It doesn't work. *Inconclusive.*

At 268 lbs— can't walk and am literally going insane from the pain.

My doctor cries, "You're so young and beautiful," so I hold and comfort him.

Receive a teaching award and receive a major research grant.

37-year-old basket case—insurance pays for gastric bypass surgery.

This was the most painful surgery of my life

but it's elective, so the drugs are fantastic.

Tell 5 people.

Hide the disability. Keep the secret.

38.

39.

40—Getting stronger and looking good BUT learning new eating habits sucked. Having large friends and family treat me like a traitor hurt. Having a student accuse me of playing to the beauty myth made me feel ashamed.

Husband has an affair with one of his yoga students. Tell no one because he won't admit it to me—he breaks the rules of our communion by lying about it—mostly because he can't handle my new body and the overt power that comes with it—power I've always wielded but now—it's more threatening because of the way I look. I forgive because the history of the relationship is worth more.

FEEL BETTER and BETTER and BETTER
And get pregnant!!!
With twins

• • •

I was going to have two babies. One for each of us.
Came home from school, laid out my grading, put on my pj's, went to the bathroom, peed, and wiped blood.
Put my hand down there and smear blood and tissue and know it's over—holding a dead fetus in my hand and my wiping has destroyed it.
Run and dress and drive to the hospital.
All the while keeping my hand sacred, sacred, sacred, sacred, sacred, sacred, sacred.
Am able to walk into the emergency room and calmly tell them I'm 12 weeks pregnant, which is when you're supposed to be safe.
You've made it to three months!
Show the receptionist my hand. They rush me to my doctor's office and sit and wait and examine what's in my sacred hand. The doctors appear and they run tests. And more tests. And more tests. Never stop looking into my hand. According to the ultra-sound, one baby is gone but the other is still OK. Woweowoweowowowowowowowoweeeeeeee.
They keep my hand sacred until it's time for me to go home.*
Then the nurse says she needs to take what's in my hand.
I make sounds I've never heard before or since, growl and scream and bite and cry and lash out and don't watch as they take it from my hand.
My potential child, the one I'd worked so hard for.
My husband is finally there and he alone can calm me enough to leave.*
Got to calm down because there's still a baby growing inside me.*
But don't have a good feeling about it.
Within 96 hours, lose the other. Labor for 5 days—in CONSTANT PAIN but continue to teach and direct and deliver it on the toilet—put it in a velvet box and we say good-bye and it's over.

The autopsy showed both fetuses developing normally. The doctors had no idea why I miscarried.

It's (fall) SNAP

VIDEO: *The Vagina Song*

• • •

LOVED my big squishy body. It was fun and giggly and sweet and FAT. Jell-O has made millions off those qualities. When I was alone, always naked. Touched myself everywhere all the time. Was soft and cuddly and large. In public, my Jell-O was raspberry with anchovies, pleasure with pain. It was sweet taking up space, and a lot of fun. Space is power.

But it was also EMBARRASSING. People were cruel—*"Fat cow." "Fat pig." "You're gross." "How disgusting!" "You smell bad."* Even though I didn't—but that doesn't matter.

Outward appearance changes what comes to you in life. There are rare exceptions to that, but exceptions are not the rule. The way we look on the outside is the way we are perceived by others. Had a certain amount of success when weighed 268 lbs. At 140 lbs, my success doubled, trebled. The way I look opens doors for me. Lived on both sides of that big fat coin.

And you know the craziest thing is I am the average size of the American woman. Size 14 and I'm still a fat chick.

• • •

After 4 miscarriages and an unacknowledged affair—begin again, Julie Rae. A new job with a promotion and a new family plan—adopt Ananda Rae from India—we wait for her until 9/11 takes her from our arms too—no international adoption.

Get pregnant the old-fashioned way—by celebrating a new house in every room—make it to 3 months and 3 weeks before announce it to colleagues at a conference.

Miscarry her on the toilet after 5 hours of agonizing labor—all by myself. She was beautiful and lifeless and perfect and not there.

Begin using birth control for the first time in 10 years.

41-year-old. I have a major infection. They can't identify what it is. "Doctor, can you come here? I've never seen anything like this." Drugs make it worse—the infection actually eats the antibiotic and grows. *Inconclusive.*

• • •

We await the birth of our biracial son—coming to us from a woman in Louisiana. Two days before I open a show, the Louisiana mom has her baby and runs away with him and a huge chunk of our money. Can understand why she wouldn't want to give him up. I GIVE UP. DONE. Never going to be the mother of a newborn.

The heart takes longer to admit it. Leave the nursery set up for 8 months after the fact, then donate it all to a women's shelter.

• • •

Amazed at the amount of profound life experiences that happen to women in the most unglamorous of places—while seated on the toilet.

When men pee, they get to hold their genitalia in their hand. That familiarity breeds all kinds of power.

For women, it's a much greater challenge. You really have to work to see what's down there, you...oh, hell, you've all seen *The Vagina Monologues* and know it's worth it to have a gander. And it often happens the first time while on the toilet.

We *pee there;*
poop there;
masturbate there;
bleed there;
exchange information there;
find out we're pregnant there;
find out we're not pregnant there.

It's really a sacred place, beyond just being where one can take a truly satisfying shit.
SNAP

• • •

She who used to provide 3 hot meals a day, sew all our clothes, run a daycare, sing in a barbershop chorus, manage a one-woman office arrived at our house with a suitcase containing 4 sweaters, 2 pairs of pants, 10,000,000 pairs of socks, no winter jackets, 25 cans of cat food, and a can of frosting.

And we helped her, she got better, we trained her like a newborn—to focus, to listen, put on make-up, to dress, to do laundry, and she felt good and useful and resentful and angry.

She's so pissed about the situation and we deal with that, she's so sad and we deal with that, she's so embarrassed and we deal with that. The worst thing for her is the recognition that at some point it won't matter to her but that I will always know and be in pain about it.
STOP!

More words and phrases used while teaching:
Suck it out.
Cowboy up.
Ovum to the wall.
Risk being naked—it's exhilarating.
Challenge authority.
Don't think like me—get educated and THINK FOR YOURSELF so you can engage with me.
Actions have consequences—be prepared.
Waves and layers are evocative—add more and more and more and more and more and more and more and MORE AND MORE AND MORE!
Push the envelope.
TAKE THE RISK!

I occasionally take my own advice. SNAP.

• • •

"Assisted" living, what a comfortable euphemism—a bed, a bureau, a couch, a table, a TV center, we shopped and I picked it all out but gave the illusion it was her choice. It made it easier—practice fire drills, and locking the door, put the key around her neck, see her at breakfast or lunch and again after work so she can stay at this level of independence for as long as possible.

She lives the non-life of assisted living and is unhappy. Begin taking her for walks as the weather warms up because I know she needs more care than assisted living but in order to move facilities with her insurance in tact, she has to PROVE it by wondering off. Get her chipped and on the dementia patient hotline in case her walk gets her lost, she wears three pieces of ID jewelry because it's coming and want her safe.

Give her the code to the door in song form—"1354, that's the way we open door." We laugh because "the" door doesn't fit in the rhythm.

She finally does it, she walks out the door and to the lake we always go to and waits for them to find her, it takes under an hour.

She gives me her watch—knowing that it will stop—I'm one of those people that fucks up electronic equipment—because it's time and she tells me to always know it was time and I did the right thing.

• • •

My mother is in a lockdown Alzheimer's unit, my mother is in a bib, my mother is in a merry walker, my mother is unable to walk, my mother is drooling, crying, laughing, sleeping most of the time, surrounded by glorious women and men who love her, make her safe, and take care of her, it's so lovely and awful, such a relief and such guilt.

It's odd to hope your mom has a fatal disease so she can die, but sometimes I did. It meant her freedom and mine.

[*Look at screen.*]

41-year-old experiment—told there is an 80% change of advanced uterine and/or ovarian cancer—a potential side effect of years of fertility treatments.

Have a radical hysterectomy, not cancer—still almost die because the urinary infection left so much scar tissue that it began to meld my insides together—it wasn't a problem until it involved the kidney and the diaphragm and the bowels—all of the reproductive stuff just allowed itself to congeal into one mass—how profound—how *Inconclusive*.

I'm supposed to be flat on my back for three months—can't—have a job, a mother with dementia and a husband who is having yet another affair. With a secretary. And he won't admit it—even after I find out. I ask him to wait, wait, wait and help me.

Consult a lawyer and write my own divorce—served him the papers in black leather from head to toe on Valentine's Day—still have a drainage ball coming out of my gut from surgery, so put it in my bra to make my tits look bigger.

Two weeks after my fourth minor surgery in three months, Go to court in a gorgeous blue suit and scarf, plead my own case, and win EVERYTHING!

But lose one of my greatest teachers.

Live through it—the darkness gives way to the tiny pinprick of light. I know I'll soon be dancing in it.

• • •

NEVER ONCE met a woman who hadn't experienced some kind of sexual assault—not ONCE. EVERY SINGLE WOMAN I KNOW, EVERY ONE, and MOST MEN.

Can I have a show of hands?
Let's see if we can be a community.

Any questions?
Unsolicited Advice
We've got to stop telling our boys they can take what they want. We must balance the privilege of boys and girls better, celebrate the gifts of each, cherish them, and help them learn respect and honor for self, for others. And to be kind.

• • •

44-year-old Barbie doll. What does one do when she is not going to have the family she planned, is divorced, and is taking care of her mother who has Alzheimer's? She becomes an adolescent boy. She takes those first baby steps into the hormones, she pretends she can live forever, she worries not, she takes major risks, she does things like drink too much, smoke too much, enjoy pot too much. She shirks as many responsibilities as she can. She messes with her career by taking risks, such as partying, among other things, with her students. She indiscriminately has sex with many, many, many people, and it's really fun. For about a year and a half. And then it starts to ring a little bit hollow.

• • •

Turn to a women in the audience.
"You're worth it. You're number one!"
Women are not told that enough.

Turn to the man nearest her.
You're told that, aren't you? Have whatever you want. Expect whatever you want! Oh, don't shrink away from me. I'm not going to stab you.

[*Wink*.]

But I'm gonna think long and hard about it.

• • •

I AM the Surgically Enhanced Feminist.
My body is so damaged from all the surgeries that the insurance company pays for a tummy tuck and a breast lift with augmentation. It's really rather surreal to see your nipples sitting in a tray waiting to be put back on. 36D. I was supposed to be a C cup but
Inconclusive.
And as the body gets healthier, the vanity kicks in. What I learned in my 40s is that the person I really need to be honest with is—(TA-DA)—ME!

It is not better to look good than to feel good.
It is better to feel good because you like how you look.

• • •

You think I would have learned that by now. I teach actors, for Christ's sake. Theirs is a profession where 99% of the reason they get a job is because of the way they look. And 99% of them have to follow a very specific standard of beauty in order to work in most arenas. It's just the facts of life. It isn't right, so I battle to change the system from within.

SNAP

• • •

46-year-old content. Really happy. I learn that worrying is praying for what you don't want, so I meditate on what I do want. I receive the most intriguing message.
SNAP

Subject: Sincerely
I am 27 years old. I am a virgin. I feel you may be the one to teach me, goddess.
I e-mail back.
SNAP
I am a good teacher, Daniel. Tell me more.

• • •

Things said as a director:

Welcome to the circle
I make the frame for the work and give the other artists the brushes to paint
withhelp their hands along
Best idea wins
Always know that I'm the queen
And we create beautiful works together
Bring three new things to every rehearsal

Push push push push push push push
Eat well—fruits, veggies, protein, and carbs
Get sleep and water
Plan academics and life well
Work BEFORE you play—the playing is that much sweeter and burden free

• • •

And Daniel tells me more—romantic, creative, emotional intellectual, hilarious, hot e-mails—like a civil war letter-writing courtship. And God knows I feel like I've been to battle.

We write—we meet—the first meeting is public with no talking. Just furtive, knowing glances and passionate forbidden kisses behind a closed door. He picks me up. I'm flying.

My body is my art. It is the landscape that tells my story. And Daniel loves it as much as I do.
We connect is profound ways.
I am more me in his presence. I desire to be my best self , willingly shift with joy because it makes us BOTH happy. We're not perfect—but, man, do we have laugh!

Soon, Daniel is no longer a virgin in a physical sense—and I'm no longer a virgin to partnership. He tells me he is the reward at the end of my journey. He is right.

We marry. As I walk down the isle, I know "till death so us part."

Our family.

And the dream that never dies, the wound that never heals, the ache that never left, finds peace. We begin the process of EXPANDING our family.
(surrogacy) (Begin again)
We're currently in the two-week wait. Hope . . . it's a beautiful thing.

[*Cross both hands and feet.*]

I still don't know where I'm going. I just know I'm not going there alone.
Gained 30 lbs
VIDEO: *YOU*

• • •

It's not the shit that happens to us, it's what we choose to do with it. ME?
I work to stay open to the possibilities, be here now, laugh as much as
possible, and enjoy the ride.

Unsolicited Advice:
Thank all of your teachers—from your family to your friends to
ANYONE who touched you and pissed you off, laughed with you
and hurt you.

Love everyone and they'll love you, OR NOT. Either way, you grow.

CONCLUSIVE

VIDEO: Sunset.

• • •

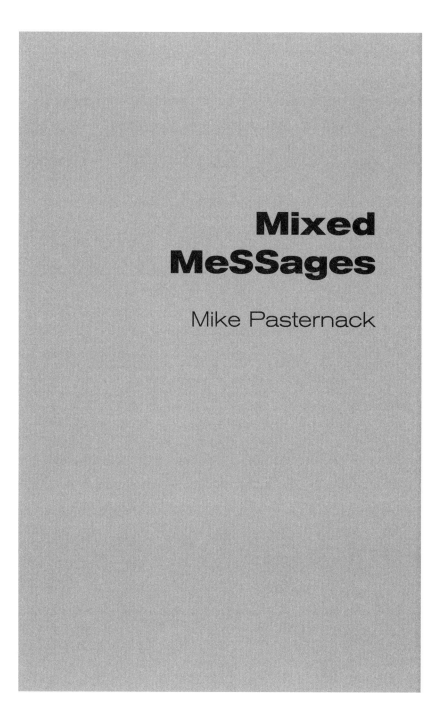

Mixed MeSSages

Mike Pasternack

Mike Pasternack

Mike Pasternack was lucky to have been born to artistic parents, and has been involved in theatre, film and music for almost all of his life. He has been both a performer and a technician on various projects, ranging from student films to Equity showcases, and has gained renown as a character actor as well as having handled most aspects of technical theatre. Pasternack is also an historian and has traveled to Germany, where he had the opportunity to do research and interview World War II veterans in person. He holds a master's degree in media arts (film theory), and when not working on artistic projects he is employed as an associate professor of communication studies and theatre.

characters

(*in order of appearance*)

> **MATTHEW LORACK**, 20, an American GI
>
> **ATTENDANT**, an American GI
>
> **FIRST MP**, an American military policeman, a sergeant
>
> **SECOND MP**, an American military policeman
>
> **LIEUTENANT FITZGERALD**, an American officer
>
> **PAULIE**, 20s, an American GI
>
> **FIRST SS MAN**
>
> **SECOND SS MAN**
>
> **FIRST US SOLDIER**
>
> **SECOND US SOLDIER**
>
> **WERNER GRAF**, late 20s, a medic in the Waffen-SS rank of SS-Untersturmführer
>
> **SS LT. COLONEL**, a decorated officer, rank of SS-Obersturmbannführer
>
> **SS ADJUTANT**, rank of SS-Untersturmführer
>
> Various **EXTRAS**, American prisoners, SS soldiers

time

December, 1944

place

The Ardennes Forest, Belgium

··· production note ···

The sets should be kept minimal, representative of each scene. The costumes and props need to be as authentic as possible. Projections in black and white are to be used to depict settings and scenes. Newsreel footage is preferable for the combat scenes.

Projection 1: "Belgium, December 1944"
Projection 2 (still): The forest: trees and snow
Sound: Battle. Gunfire, tanks, artillery

scene 1

(A forest in Belgium, 1944)

[*In the darkness, we hear footsteps and breathing. The ground is covered with heavy snow, and this hinders the runner. The sound of the breathing becomes louder as the footsteps become faster and faster, and then suddenly dead-stop. A lone figure becomes visible as the lights slowly come up onstage. MATTHEW LORACK, 20, an American GI, stands alone in the forest. He is tall, with blonde hair and blue eyes. Were it not for the American uniform, he would be the Aryan ideal. He wears the insignia of a private, Seventh Armored Division. He is obviously lost and disoriented, and appears exhausted, making him seem older than his years. LORACK stands motionless and out of breath as he realizes he is directly in front of a German tank.*]

Projection 3 (still): The German tank.
Projection 4 (stock footage): The Panzer has become aware of LORACK and its front-mounted machine gun begins to rotate in LORACK's direction.

[LORACK *reaches for a grenade as he leaps to the side.*]

Sound: The Panzer's machine gun fires.

[*Blackout.*]

scene 2

[*Sometime later.*]

Projection 5 (still): A US army medical tent. A white flag with a cross flies above the tent identifying it as a field hospital, although its present use is as a hastily constructed field morgue.

[*The darkness becomes a pure white light, and the sound of heavy breathing is heard once again. Slowly, the white light reveals the interior of a US Army medical tent, with sheet-covered bodies on cots. The only light comes from an incandescent bulb strung from a wire overhead, casting a ghostly luminescence. An ATTENDANT is seated at a desk deeply caught up in his work, typing letters of regret to the dead men's families. On the center cot an exposed foot with a tag tied to its toe protrudes from beneath the sheet. The foot slowly begins to move; it is LORACK beneath the sheet.*]

LORACK   [*Suddenly sitting up.*] What the hell is going on?

[*The* ATTENDANT, *seeing the corpse sit up, screams and runs from the tent.*]

Sound: A truck engine starting and screeching away.

[LORACK *is now alone in a roomful of sheet-covered corpses and has a large, recently-sewn wound on his chest. He composes himself and gets off the cot. Wearing nothing but his dog tags, he takes a uniform from a pile of clothing and gets dressed. He leaves the tent, grabbing a heavy overcoat and rifle on his way out.*]

[*Blackout.*]

scene 3

[*The forest, a few moments later.*]

Projection 6 (still): The forest, same as Projection 1.

Sound: Occasional bursts of gunfire at a distance.

Projection 7 (footage): LORACK's legs walking through deep snow.

Projection 8 (still): The snow-covered forest.

[*Lights up on* LORACK, *lost, making his way through the heavy snow, using the rifle as a walking stick. He stops center stage as he notices something downstage left. The lights come up downstage left, revealing two American military policemen (MPs) standing beside a Jeep, guarding a road checkpoint.* LORACK, *happy to see them, approaches the Jeep waving.*]

LORACK   Hey! Over here!

[*The* FIRST MP *raises his machine gun.*]

FIRST MP   Hold it right there, you!

LORACK   Wait...I'm American...

SECOND MP   Freeze right where you are or I'll split you in half!

LORACK   But...

FIRST MP   Hey, they did a real good job with this one, Murphy. Look: our "own" walking wounded!

SECOND MP   Get your hands in the air, Kraut!

LORACK   I'm an American soldier, Seventh Armored...

SECOND MP   Get 'em up!

FIRST MP   We know all about you guys—same SS unit that rescued Mussolini. Now you're runnin' around dressed like us. Who is your commanding officer?

LORACK   Captain Wahlberg...

FIRST MP   Oh, they did a great job with you, you Nazi prick. He bought it last week!

LORACK   Look, I was wounded and...

FIRST MP   Hande Hoch! Was ist Ihre Kampfgruppe?

[LORACK *raises his hands. The* MPs *glance toward each other, as the German command is the first one* LORACK *has obeyed.*]

LORACK   I'm not German!

FIRST MP   Kampfgruppe Peiper?

LORACK   Clark Gable.

FIRST MP   Heinrich Himmler!

SECOND MP   [*Reacting to the sarcasm.*] You're an American?

LORACK   That's what I've been trying to tell you. I'm Matt...Matt Lorack.

SECOND MP   OK. We got a question for ya. Who won the World Series last year?

LORACK   [*He has no idea; guessing.*] I don't know. The New York Giants?

[*The* SECOND MP *raises his weapon.*]

SECOND MP   Nice try, Jerry.

LORACK   Wait a minute! I'm from Brooklyn, New York. Coney Island, Steeplechase Park...

SECOND MP   And?

LORACK   And what?

SECOND MP   You gonna tell me you're from Brooklyn, and you don't know who won the World Series?

LORACK   I don't follow baseball.

FIRST MP   Oh, sure, some American. The Yankees... it's always the Yankees. Murphy, let him have it!

[*The* SECOND MP *takes aim at* LORACK.]

LORACK   Wait... the Brooklyn Dodgers... Ebbets Field... Du-Ducky Medwick!?!

SECOND MP   Sure. They teach you Ducky Medwick but you don't know nothin' about the Yankees? Say auf wiedersehen, Fritz!

[*The* SECOND MP *aims his weapon at* LORACK. LORACK, *his hands raised in the air, closes his eyes and waits for the gunshot. Suddenly,* LIEUTENANT FITZGERALD *and* PAULIE, *an enlisted man, appear on the stage.*]

FITZGERALD   Hey, what the hell is going on here?

FIRST MP   [*Saluting.*] An execution, sir. We found ourselves one of Skorzeny's commandos!

FITZGERALD   You found yourselves one of my men! Lorack, what the hell are you doing here?

LORACK   [*Blankly.*] They're going to shoot me, sir.

FITZGERALD   [*To the* MPs.] Good job, you idiots. Next time, try killing the real enemy! Lorack, come with us!

[LORACK, *quite relieved, lowers his arms and walks offstage with* FITZGERALD *and* PAULIE, *leaving the bewildered* MPs *behind.*]

FIRST MP   Ducky Medwick.

SECOND MP   Yeah. Think we messed up, Sarge?

FIRST MP   I dunno, Murph. I got the feeling we just sent three Jerries back to the Fatherland.

SECOND MP   The Major is gonna have our asses in a sling.

FIRST MP   The Major ain't gonna know nothin', cuz nothin' happened. Got it?

SECOND MP   Got it. I didn't see nothin'.

FIRST MP   That's what I thought you'd say. Good. Won't happen again.
[*A beat.*]
Ducky fucking Medwick. Pfft.

[*Blackout.*]

scene 4

[*Same forest, later that morning.*]

Projection 9: "December 17, 1944"

Projection 10 (still): the snow-covered forest.

[LORACK, FITZGERALD, *and* PAULIE *make their way slowly through a snow-covered farm road. As the men round a curve in the road, they suddenly pale and come to a stop. They encounter an SS roadblock, and several Waffen-SS soldiers armed with machine guns are there to greet them.*]

FIRST SS MAN   Halt! Hande hoch!

[*The Americans are trapped. They glance briefly at each other, and then raise their hands in the air as the SS troops surround them.*]

[*Blackout.*]

scene 5

[*"The Three Points" Junction at Malmédy. A bit after noon the same day.*]

Projection 11 (still): A road sign at the crossroads has opposing arrows; one labeled "Malmédy" and the other "St. Vith." There is a cafe at the crossroads and a small shed a few hundred yards behind it.

Projection 12 (still): A few other farmhouses are sparsely distributed; otherwise there are wide fields, bordered by forest. The snow is heavy. The only indication that all is not right is the presence of several German tanks and armored vehicles. The men are all SS.

Projection 13 (footage): Near the cafe stand over fifty American prisoners grouped tightly together.

Sound: a general hubbub of confusion is heard.

[LORACK, FITZGERALD, *and* PAULIE *are led to the group of other prisoners (who appeared in Projection 13), one of whom is the soldier who ran from the hospital tent earlier. A total of eight to ten men onstage represent the many prisoners. They stand tightly grouped together.*]

LORACK   So...Paul...Paulie!

[PAULIE, *about the same age as* LORACK, *turns to his friend. However, his greeting is as solemn as it is happy, for a black cloud of poor fate is on his countenance. His eyes are focused straight ahead, fixated on the SS troops guarding them.*]

PAULIE   [*Emotionless.*] So, Matt. Whaddya hear and whaddya say?

LORACK   What do you hear and what do you say? Hell of a day, huh? Hey, it's good to see you; it's been a long time since Fort Dix, no? How's Ruthie?

PAULIE   [*Resigned to his fate.*] Good. Only I won't be seeing her again.

LORACK   Hey, Paulie, don't talk like that!

PAULIE   Take a good look around you. That's the SS lined up along that road—not regular army...they're not going to play games.

LORACK   [*Cheerfully naïve.*] Hey, look. We'll get out of this. Hell, I woke up dead yesterday.

PAULIE   What do you...

[PAULIE *is interrupted by the appearance of the* SECOND SS MAN, *gun in hand.*]

SECOND SS MAN   All right, all of you men! Into that field with the others! Move!

[*The prisoners are marched over to a field away from the crossroads and behind the cafe. They huddle together, talking anxiously.* LORACK *finds himself alone in the middle of the group, and looks around trying to find* PAULIE *or* FITZGERALD.]

FIRST US SOLDIER   This ain't good.

SECOND US SOLDIER   We should make a run for it…

FIRST US SOLDIER   Stand fast. You're going to get us all killed!

[*The prisoners continue to stand huddled together, like fish in a barrel. They stamp their feet in the snow, trying to keep warm. Suddenly, the* SECOND US SOLDIER *starts to break away from the others.*]

FIRST US SOLDIER   Don't move!

SECOND US SOLDIER   You do what you want. I'm getting out of here!

[*The* SECOND US SOLDIER *begins to run, just as the* SECOND SS *man enters, pistol drawn and starts in the direction of the prisoners, shouting unintelligibly. One prisoner tries to run. The* SECOND SS *man nears the group, shouting and firing his pistol. General mayhem ensues as the group of prisoners, reacting to the gunshots, breaks rank and disperses in several directions, but they do not get far.*]

[*Montage: inter-cut as necessary, ending with projection 14. This is the Malmédy massacre; the projections should go back and forth between the SS doing the killing (14) and the American prisoners falling (15).*]

Projection 14 (footage): Atop the hill, the other SS men fire machine guns into the group of prisoners.

Sound: Rapid machine-gun fire.

Projection 15 (footage): The prisoners attempt to flee, but most are mowed down immediately by gunfire. A very few seem to make it to the safety of the trees.

[*Onstage, the* SECOND SS *man, out of pistol ammo, raises his machine gun and fires. The Americans continue to drop like flies. Frightened screams are heard, only to be suddenly cut off as quickly as they began.* LORACK *finds himself in the middle of the small group. One by one, they are hit, and* LORACK *falls with the crowd, feigning death. A body lands on top of him, and then another. The top half of* LORACK's *leg is torn open by a bullet, and blood flows. Another body falls on top of him.*]

Sound: The SS men atop the hill are given a cease-fire order.

[*Fade projection 14.*]

[Onstage, the SECOND SS *man is out of bullets, but continues to dry-fire his weapon. It is not until another SS man slaps him back to reality that he stops, and stands silent, panting, his eyes filled with unsatisfied rage.]*

Sound: More orders are heard in German.

[The SS men begin to move through the prisoners' bodies, checking for survivors, kicking the fallen to see who is dead and who is alive, and administer "mercy shots" to the wounded and dying. The SS men move through the dead and they are approaching LORACK's *position. A single gunshot is heard.]*

[Blackout.]

scene 6

[The Malmédy crossroads, later that afternoon.]

[The SS are gone, and the crossroads are silent. The wind blows heavily, and the blown snow is beginning to cover the bodies of the prisoners. A pile of bodies begins to move, and with the sounds of a difficult, struggling task, LORACK *slowly appears from within the pile. As he does so, he realizes that he had been covered by the fallen bodies of* PAULIE *and* FITZGERALD, *and thus survived. As he extracts himself, he sees the expressionless faces on his friends, and each has, in addition to the machine gun wounds, a single bullet hole to the temple.]*

LORACK   Oh, Jesus…

*[*LORACK *surveys the carnage around him, shocked. He tries to stand, but falls and realizes that he has an awful leg wound. He begins to slowly crawl away from the scene and towards the forest. It is a most difficult task, and as he crawls, the heavy blood flowing from his leg creates a snail's trail in the snow behind him.]*

Projection 16 (footage): The bodies of the prisoners become buried deeper by the blowing snow.

Projection 17 (still): A small farmhouse.

*[*LORACK *crawls through the snow. He has been going for hours and is completely exhausted, beyond hope. Suddenly he spies the small farmhouse in the distance. He slowly makes his way to the farmhouse. As* LORACK *nears the farmhouse, he stops to survey the situation from the safety of the hedgerows. All seems quiet and safe, so*

LORACK *carefully crawls to the farmhouse and enters through the unlocked door, which he has great trouble reaching.*]

scene 7

[*The set revolves and reveals the interior of the farmhouse.*]

[*This is a simple Belgian farmhouse, recently lived in and with the look of having been abandoned in a hurry. The shelves are meagerly stocked with food, and a family portrait hangs crooked in its frame above the fireplace. This gives the farmhouse's interior the look of Miss Havisham's house on a much lower budget. There are bullet holes in the walls, which allow light and the occasional bit of snow to enter;* LORACK *manages to light a fire which provides the only other illumination in the room.*]

[*Fade projection 17.*]

[LORACK, *exhausted, lies near the fireplace and tries to nurse his wounds. As he struggles to do so, the door of the farmhouse suddenly swings open, and the wind blows snow through the doorway.* WERNER GRAF, *an SS Medic, appears.* WERNER *is a few years older than* LORACK *but under thirty. He is shorter than* LORACK, *and with his brown eyes, brown hair, and wire-rimmed eyeglasses, he is far from the Aryan ideal. He wears a white armband with a red cross indicating medical service. He sees* LORACK *and stands there for a moment, studying the situation.*]

LORACK   Oh, shit.

WERNER   You can relax; I'm not here to hurt you.

LORACK   Yeah. Why don't you just get it over with?

WERNER   I'm here to help.

LORACK   Don't touch me!

WERNER   Shut up, you idiot. I'm a doctor. You have lost a lot of blood.

LORACK   Your buddies fucked up, huh? So they sent you to finish the job. Go ahead. It doesn't matter anymore. This day can't get any worse.

WERNER   Those were not my buddies. Roll up your sleeve.

LORACK   What kind of poison is that?

WERNER Morphine. Now roll up your sleeve.

LORACK Don't I have to dig my own grave first?

WERNER No. You have to shut up first. If I wanted to kill you, you'd be dead already. Your arm, please.

[LORACK *acquiesces, and allows* WERNER *to administer the injection. He breathes a sigh of relief as the drug takes effect.*]

LORACK Well, at least I won't feel the bullet.

WERNER Stop it... listen to me! I am not going to kill you. I saw what happened at the crossroads... terrible.

LORACK You're SS.

WERNER I'm a doctor.

LORACK You're SS.

WERNER Your powers of observation are nothing short of amazing.

LORACK Look, I don't know anything. I don't know where I am. I don't know where my unit is. You can torture me...

WERNER If I was going to torture you, why would I give you morphine? Do you have any idea how short of supplies we are?

LORACK Oh, yeah. Wouldn't want the SS to run out of supplies! Look, why don't you just shoot me now? I had a bad enough day already—you'd be doing me a favor, really.

WERNER Just relax. You're still bleeding heavily.

[WERNER *applies a tourniquet to* LORACK's *leg.* LORACK *reluctantly allows this.*]

WERNER Here. Keep pressure on that.

[LORACK *holds the tourniquet in place.* WERNER *removes a stethoscope from his kit. He unbuttons* LORACK's *shirt, and as he does so, he notices* LORACK's *dog tag.* WERNER *is taken aback slightly. Rather than use the stethoscope, he leans back, looking at* LORACK *curiously.*]

WERNER   [*Somberly.*] A Jew. I can see it's the same in America.

LORACK   What is?

WERNER   Jews must identify themselves.

LORACK   Identi...this is my dog tag—my identity tag.

WERNER   And it says you are a Jew. It's the same in Europe...all Jews must wear yellow stars.

LORACK   It's not the same thing. This is just so they'll know where to send the body.

WERNER   Still, you are branded by your government. A label.

[LORACK *considers this as* WERNER *uses the stethoscope. As he listens to* LORACK's *heart, he cannot help himself; the words come out too quickly.*]

WERNER   You don't look Jewish.

LORACK   Well, what do you want me to do, take my pants off? You look more like a librarian than a Nazi yourself.

WERNER   I'm no Nazi. I'm only a doctor. I don't care if you are a Jew. Before the war, I knew many Jews.

LORACK   Knew?

WERNER   Yes.

[WERNER *continues to examine* LORACK, *who is uncomfortable with* WERNER's *last statement, yet allows* WERNER *to continue.*]

LORACK   Well, meet another Jew.

WERNER   [*Matter-of-factly.*] You think you are joking. You are not, though. You are the only Jew I've...uh...spoken with in years.

[WERNER *finishes examining* LORACK. LORACK *buttons his shirt. An uneasy silence fills the air between them. A strong wind blows; a rush of air comes down the chimney and causes the fire to flare up momentarily. A pile of ashes is disturbed by the wind and a gray cloud blows between the two men, whose gazes are interlocked.*]

[*Fade to black.*]

scene 8

[*Inside the farmhouse, about an hour later.*]

[LORACK *is asleep on the floor, his leg elevated by* WERNER*'s SS helmet.* WERNER *is busy in the kitchen area. He has cooked up some sort of hot meal in the fireplace and while it heats up, he rummages through the cabinets. He finds an old bottle of wine. He takes the wine with two glasses and he brings these over to the table. He hums the children's folksong "Little Hans" to himself, but is suddenly startled by* LORACK, *who is tossing and turning in his sleep, having a terrible nightmare.*]

LORACK   [*Asleep, screaming.*] No ... no! It's a fucking trap! They're gonna kill us all ... run for it!

[WERNER *stops what he is doing and rushes to* LORACK*'s side.*]

WERNER   Hey ... hey! Wake up.

[WERNER *shakes* LORACK *to consciousness.* LORACK, *bathed in sweat, slowly wakes up and is startled when he first sees* WERNER. *His eyes focus on the SS runes on* WERNER*'s collar.*]

LORACK   SS—get away from me, you Nazi bastard!

[LORACK*'s eyes light up with fear at first, and instinctively he tries to sit up and escape.* WERNER *holds him firmly, and* LORACK, *as he gains full consciousness, remembers the situation at hand and relaxes slightly.* WERNER *holds him upright.*]

WERNER   You're having bad dreams.

LORACK   Awake and asleep, it seems.

[WERNER *walks to the fireplace and fetches a bowl of his cooking and a spoon for* LORACK. *He brings it back to* LORACK, *who props himself up on the floor with great difficulty.*]

WERNER   Here: have something to eat. It's warm.

        [LORACK *takes the bowl from* WERNER. *Hungry, he scoops up a large spoonful, but as he puts spoon to mouth, he hesitates momentarily.*]

        Shall I call your Beefeater, sire?

LORACK   No ... no, it's all right.

[LORACK *eats and, as he decides the food is probably not poisoned, ingests the contents of the bowl hungrily. As he does this,* WERNER *produces a pack of cigarettes from his coat. He takes one for himself and offers one to* LORACK. WERNER *lights* LORACK's *cigarette, and then his own.* LORACK *holds his cigarette "American style" while* WERNER *holds his "German style" (backwards, in between thumb and his first two fingers).*]

[*Coughing from the smoke.*]

What the hell is this? Now you're really trying to kill me.

WERNER   They're Russian.

LORACK   Send a few cartons of these to the Eastern front! They'll work better than your Panzers.

WERNER   No. These are like fine vodka to the Russians. Anyway, it's no use; kill one Russian and the next day three more will take his place.

[WERNER *brings an old chess set over and begins to set it up.*]

Do you play?

LORACK   Mmm.

[LORACK *takes another drag from the cigarette, coughing less this time. He feels his leg; neatly bandaged. He looks back at* WERNER, *who is busily setting up the chess set.*]

So what's a nice guy like you doing in a place like this?

[WERNER *half smiles, but does not reply.*]

Anyway, thanks for patching up my leg.

[*Extends his hand.*]

I'm Matt. Matt Lorack.

WERNER   Werner Graf.

[*They shake hands.*]

LORACK   Thanks.

[WERNER *gets up, walks over to the table, and pours two glasses of wine. He returns to* LORACK, *and hands him one of the glasses. They begin to play chess.* WERNER *eyes* LORACK *curiously.*]

WERNER   I saw you arrive late to the field. You were not part of the captured unit.

LORACK   No. Wrong place, wrong time. So, Herr Untersturmführer Graf, why'd they do that...? All those men...our guys...

[*His voice trails off.*]

WERNER   Wrong place, wrong time. You were all in big trouble anyway. The Panzer divisions are not to take prisoners.

LORACK   So it was Peiper's men!

WERNER   Peiper, Peiper. You Americans make someone a movie star and soon you speak of no one else. Peiper was nowhere near the crossroads. He passed through here before it happened.

[*The chess game continues as the two men talk.*]

LORACK   Yeah. I guess he destroyed what he had to here and just moved on.

WERNER   Hey, let me tell you something about Colonel Peiper: I've met him; he's a good man.

LORACK   And so's Hitler, right?

WERNER   Wrong. The Führer is different. A madman filled with hate. Peiper is a good soldier and a respected commander...

LORACK   ...in the SS. Another Nazi.

WERNER   Nazi? No, Peiper is not a Nazi. He never joined the party even though they asked him to. He refused.

LORACK   Oh, so he just said "no" and that was it, just like that? I don't believe it for one minute.

WERNER   Listen. They don't bother Peiper. His combat record is good, so they respect that; he can get away with being an officer in the SS but not a member of the party. It...everything's crazy in Germany, you know? In the Luftwaffe, Field Marshal Milch is a Jew, but he keeps his rank and his power.

LORACK   A Jew in the Luftwaffe high command? Sorry, that's hard to believe.

WERNER   Maybe, but it's true. I tell you, things are crazy. Milch is a friend to Göring, and Göring says, "I decide who is Jewish." Milch and his family are safe.

LORACK   That makes no sense. Hitler hates the Jews. It was all in his book; I read *Mein Kampf*...

WERNER   Some of us think even the Führer might have some... Jewish blood. He...

[WERNER *stops himself.*]

...never mind. It's not important.

LORACK   "Hitler the Jew?" Oh, this is getting better and better...

[*He moves a piece on the chessboard.*]

...check.

WERNER   It doesn't matter. The corporal from the first war is now the Führer. We don't speak of this or ask questions. Peiper is a decent man.

LORACK   Decent. Kills everything in his path.

WERNER   Decent. A fine soldier. He does only what he needs to do. It is the units who follow that kill without mercy.

[*Ignoring* LORACK's *skeptical look.*]

I'll tell you something I heard. When we... when the SS were in Italy, Peiper saved some Jews.

LORACK   Oh, he did, did he?

WERNER   I was not there at the time. It's just a story I heard... and more than once.

LORACK   Well, if it is a true story, it was an honorable thing to do.

WERNER   Who knows what is true and what is a lie anymore?

[*He moves a chess piece.*]

Anyway, the war cannot last much longer... not with the Allies in

Europe and the Russians coming from the other side. The war is already lost.

LORACK   What's your story?

WERNER   SS Punishment Battalion.

LORACK   So you're the executioner; the punisher.

WERNER   No. Me, and the men who were with me, are the punished ones. Most of us are here because we did or said things the high command did not approve of. I was an army doctor. A few comments, the wrong people heard, and they transferred me into the SS, then off to the Eastern Front, and now here. The high command knows we are likely to die before the war is over. Such terrible things I have seen.

LORACK   Some of those guys were having a great time.

WERNER   The young ones, new conscripts. They have blood in their eyes. We just marched here from Germany, and they have seen the destruction of the Allied bombings. They want revenge. Not all are Germans, though. Some come from the foreign units of the SS. It's not what it used to be.

[*A sudden burst of cannon fire rattles the house. Snow, jarred loose, falls through holes in the roof. The battle-worn men stop momentarily to assess the threat and then each other. A beat. They shrug in unison and continue with their game.*]

LORACK   None of it makes sense. I'm not going back...

WERNER   Listen, I must tell you something. Your leg. I have done what I could, but you will never walk again.

LORACK   Somehow, I kinda knew that. First I get shot. Then I wake up in a morgue, get out of the morgue, and almost get executed by my own troops, even though I tell them Ducky Medwick... Ducky fucking Medwick! Then I wind up in a field and next thing I know everyone's dead. Now I got an SS doctor helping me out and a bum leg. This keeps getting better and better.

WERNER   What's a Ducky? Is it made of rubber?

LORACK   Wha? Oh, he's a baseball player. Joe Medwick. They call him "Ducky." It's a nickname. They ask baseball questions if they catch you. Supposed to prove you're American, if you know sports.

WERNER   And you did not?

LORACK   Me? No. I don't know anything about sports. I read. A lot. Always did; came from a big family. The library was the only place to hide.

[LORACK *moves a piece.*]

WERNER   Is that where you learned to speak German? At the library?

LORACK   [*Quizzically.*] What do you mean?

WERNER   Your German is quite good. You've been speaking it since I got here.

LORACK   No I haven't; have I?

WERNER   Yes. Perfectly.

LORACK   Shell shock? I didn't realize that till just now. Weird.
[*Changing the subject; it is too much for him to comprehend.*]
Anyway, I spent most of my time there, reading. Ducky Medwick played ball for the Brooklyn Dodgers; that's how I knew the name; my hometown . . . check.

WERNER   [*Laughs.*] Baseball questions. Why not the names of your presidents?

LORACK   Nah, most of these Joes are lucky if they know what day it is. I know the names of the presidents. Trust me, that wouldn't work.

WERNER   Games and more games.
[WERNER *focuses deeply, and handles a piece as he contemplates his next move.*]
This war, just a game as well. A bad game. I'm not going back either.

[LORACK *looks at him, stunned.*]

LORACK   Where can you go? They'd kill you.

WERNER   They don't expect the men of the punishment battalions to
   live anyway.

   [WERNER *moves his piece.*]

   Check.

Sound: In the distance, sounds of cannon fire are heard.

[*Fade to black.*]

Projection 18 (footage): An SS motorized platoon is traversing the snow-
covered road. As it travels along, there are explosions and near misses.

Sound: The platoon; many trucks driving on the snowy road. Explosions
and gunfire.

scene 9

[*Inside the farmhouse, about ten minutes later.*]

[LORACK *and* WERNER *are still playing the chess game. Only a few pieces remain
on the chessboard.* WERNER *ponders his next move for a while and then, with no
move to make, he knocks over his white king. The king falls, and rolls across the chessboard into* LORACK'*s black king, which also topples.*]

WERNER   Stalemate.

[LORACK, *with difficulty, extends his hand.*]

LORACK   Good game.

[*The two shake hands. Suddenly, a shell lands close to the farmhouse, knocking several
roof timbers loose. A loud explosion is heard. The two men maintain their handshake
throughout. Another, closer blast separates the two men.* WERNER *crouches back while*
LORACK, *unable to move, lies still and stares at the ceiling. The sound of engines grows
louder, closer.*]

WERNER   [*Listening carefully.*] Those are German troops. We haven't
   much time. They will stop here.

LORACK   Go. Get out of here; save yourself. You've done all you can for
   me.

WERNER   They'll kill you if they find you here.

LORACK   I'm moose meat anyway. You go. You've done what you can.

WERNER   I'll get you out of here.

LORACK   Cut it out—just go!

WERNER   I must carry you, then.

[WERNER *tries to lift* LORACK *to his feet, but is unable to do so; the leg wound and* LORACK's *struggling to stay on the floor cement him in place.*]

LORACK   Stop it!

WERNER   Hey, will you just…

Sound: A loud explosion very close by.

[WERNER *is cut off by the explosion, the force of which knocks him to the floor. As he tries to get up, he freezes in position as the farmhouse door opens. A highly decorated* SS LT. COLONEL *enters, accompanied by an* AI ADJUTANT. *They immediately see* WERNER, *but do not notice* LORACK *at first.*]

SS LT. COLONEL   Untersturmführer, are you wounded?

[WERNER *does not reply. The* COLONEL *approaches him.*]

We saw the trail of blood. Come. You must hurry. The Americans are not far behind.

[*The* COLONEL *notices* LORACK *on the floor.*]

What is this?

[*His mood changes suddenly for the worse and he draws his pistol.*]

You have been aiding the enemy? The punishment is death.

WERNER   No. This man was already here.

SS LT. COLONEL   [*The* COLONEL *looks at* LORACK's *fresh leg bandage. His eyes focus on* WERNER, *who now has a pistol pointed at him.*]

Shoot him. Now.

WERNER   Herr Obersturmbannführer, I…

[*The* COLONEL *walks over to* LORACK *and digs the heel of his boot into* LORACK's *leg.* LORACK *screams.* WERNER *instinctively steps forward, but the*

COLONEL *levels his pistol at* WERNER, *who stops in his tracks. The* COLONEL *continues to dig his boot heel into* LORACK's *wounded leg as he speaks.*]

SS LT. COLONEL   You are familiar with the rules of engagement, yes?

WERNER   Yes.

SS LT. COLONEL   You will shoot this man now. Perhaps I will spare you.

[WERNER *realizes this is a no-win situation. He swallows hard, draws his pistol, and approaches* LORACK. *The* COLONEL's *pistol is still aimed at* WERNER.]

WERNER   [*To* LORACK.] I'm sorry.

LORACK   I know.

[*The two men make eye contact. They understand each other.* LORACK *slowly closes his eyes and waits for a gunshot.* WERNER *raises his pistol, aims carefully at* LORACK *and then suddenly turns, firing two shots into the chest of the* COLONEL *and then immediately shoots and kills the* ADJUTANT *(rank of SS-Untersturmführer). As the* COLONEL *falls, his pistol discharges, fatally wounding* LORACK. *The* COLONEL *is dead before he hits the floor.* WERNER *drops his gun and cradles* LORACK *in his arms.*]

LORACK   Nice shot.

[*He passes out.*]

WERNER   Hold on. You'll be all right.

[WERNER *looks down at* LORACK's *stomach, which has been torn open by the bullet and is bleeding heavily. He realizes that* LORACK *is dying.* LORACK's *eyes turn to* WERNER, *then they close.* WERNER *crumples his coat and places it beneath* LORACK's *head. He removes his woolen SS cap and places it on* LORACK's *head, removes his scarf and wraps it over* LORACK's *shoulders. He reaches deep into a pocket and extracts a tiny yellowed piece of paper, which he unfolds carefully. Then he kneels beside* LORACK *and slowly begins to recite the Hebrew prayer for the dead.*]

WERNER   Yis ga dal v'yis kaddush . . .

[LORACK's *eyes suddenly open, surprised, he struggles to speak. As he speaks, blood spurts from his mouth.*]

LORACK But...how...

WERNER [*Forcing a weak smile.*]...the library. It's best you don't know, and "they" don't find out. Friends come in all shapes and sizes. Rest, take your sleep now.

[LORACK *is too weak to respond, but his eyes show understanding and acceptance. He dies, eyes wide open.* WERNER *holds his dead friend and continues.*]

Sh'may rabau....

[*Lights down, then up.*]

scene 10

[*The farmhouse, a few minutes later.*]

[LORACK *lies on the floor in his underwear.* WERNER, *already wearing* LORACK's *boots and pants, struggles to get into* LORACK's *shirt, which doesn't quite fit. He succeeds in buttoning the shirt only to discover that he has the buttons lined up wrong.* LORACK's *body, though lifeless, appears to be watching him, and this causes him to improperly button the shirt. Sighing, he unbuttons the shirt and starts to button it again.*]

WERNER My friend, I am sorry. I can feel you watching me. I can do no more for you. Your death is the only chance I have to save my life.

[WERNER, *now in full American uniform, kneels by* LORACK's *body and removes his GI dog tags. He stands up and begins to put the dog tags over his head. Halfway on, he pauses, removes them, kneels down again, and puts the dog tags back around* LORACK's *neck.*]

[*Tenderly.*]

So they'll know where to send the body.

[WERNER *stands silently over the body of* LORACK *for a moment. Then he dons the American helmet and exits the farmhouse. Before the door closes behind him, a strong breeze enters the room, blowing the chess set off the table. The two kings roll away from the table and into the pool of blood next to* LORACK's *body.*]

[*Blackout.*]

scene 11

[*The Belgian forest, later that night.*]

[WERNER, *now dressed as an American GI, makes his way through the forest adjacent to the road. He suddenly comes to a stop and crouches down. The* TWO MPs *are at a roadblock up ahead; their jeep blocks the road diagonally.* WERNER *surveys the situation; he will be seen no matter what he does. He lights a cigarette, holding it "American style" and assumes a limp to match the bloodstains on his pants leg.*]

WERNER   Hey! Over here!

[WERNER *approaches the* MPs, *who raise their machine guns.*]

FIRST MP   Stop and identify yourself, soldier!

WERNER   I'm a GI.

FIRST MP   Where you coming from, soldier?

WERNER   Malmédy. I escaped. They killed everyone...

[WERNER *continues to approach.*]

SECOND MP   Hold it, buddy. Let's see your dog tags.

WERNER   I... they took them. They took everything.

[WERNER *extends his arms palms up to demonstrate this. But* LORACK's *jacket is too loose on him, and the sleeve rolls up, exposing* WERNER's *wristwatch.*]

SECOND MP   They didn't take your watch. Nice try, Jerry.

WERNER   Matt. Matt Lor...

[WERNER *realizes his mistake too late.*]

SECOND MP   What?

FIRST MP   Hey...

   [WERNER *turns to see that he is facing a machine gun.*]
   Who won the World Series in '39?

[WERNER *takes a final drag from his cigarette and puts it out in the snow. He stands at attention, as a man before a firing squad. He thinks for a moment before he responds.*]

WERNER   Ducky Medwick.

[*The two MPs simultaneously open fire on WERNER, who drops to the ground in a hail of bullets.*]

FIRST MP   Ducky fucking Medwick.

[*The two MPs return to their post at the jeep. One lights a Lucky Strike cigarette as the other gets on the radio set.*]

SECOND MP   Easy-Bravo 14. One down at this location, dressed to kill. Repeat…

[WERNER *lies dead, face up in the snow. A lone last tear streams from his unseeing eye, and carves a trail through his blood-covered face before it drips onto the white snow.*]

[*As the lights dim, music:* "Ich Hatt' Einen Kameraden" *can be heard softly, Legato.*]

Projection 19: "Over 80 men were killed at Malmédy on December 17, 1944. The exact cause for the shooting remains a subject of fierce debate to this day."

Projection 20: "SS Colonel Joachim 'Jochen' Peiper was nowhere near Malmédy when the massacre took place. After ten years in prison as a war criminal, his death sentence was overturned and Peiper lived peacefully in France until his murder by French communists in 1976."

Projection 21: Joe Medwick baseball card or photograph in Dodgers uniform.

Superimpose: "Joe 'Ducky' Medwick played for the Brooklyn Dodgers in 1940–43 and 1946. He had a lifetime batting average of .324 and was elected to the Baseball Hall of Fame in 1968."

• • •

Amouresque
and **Arabesque**

Victor Gluck

**Two companion
comedies of courtship**

Adapted from stories
by Anthony Hope

Victor Gluck

Victor Gluck has been a playwright, drama critic, arts journalist, teacher, and actor. He studied acting and stagecraft with Sarah and Lincoln Stulik at the Emerson College Center for the Performing Arts at the Deertrees Summer Theatre, Harrison, Maine, and appeared onstage in *You Can't Take It with You* and *Finian's Rainbow*. He wrote his first one-acts for a year-long creative writing class at the Bronx High School of Science. At City College, he was the chairman of the Film Committee and later the chairman of the Program Agency of the John H. Finley Student Center. At New York University, he worked on an unfinished doctoral dissertation on the plays of D. H. Lawrence.

His double bill, *Amouresque* and *Arabesque*, "two Edwardian comedies of courtship," was presented as part of the Lunchtime series at the Quaigh Theatre. *Amouresque* went on to be a finalist in the Samuel French Short Play Festival and was presented at the Theater at St. Clements Church, again under the direction of Francine L. Trevens. He attended the Playwrights/Directors Lab at the Gene Frankel Theatre, where he wrote and directed two plays, a contemporary drama, *Achilles' Heel*, and *Come Kiss Me, Sweet and Twenty*, a third Edwardian comedy of courtship. He studied playwriting with Curt Dempster at Ensemble Studio Theatre, where his fourth Edwardian comedy of courtship, *Love Before Breakfast*, was given a reading. The four comedies of courtship were presented by the Ryan Repertory Company as a full-length evening called *Weekends in the Country* as part of their Summer Playwright's Festival. His only other full-length play to date is the unproduced musical, *Side Show*, written with composer Ira Singer and lyricist Allen Deitch, completed in 1973.

Gluck is best known as a drama critic for his twenty-seven years with *Back Stage*, the theatre trade paper, and Back Stage.com. He has also had his own theatre column in such weekly publications as *New York Guide/Wisdoms Child*, *East Side Express*, *The Brooklyn Spectator*, and *The Brooklyn Times*. His reviews have also appeared in *Our Town*, *The Native*, *Night and Day*, *Downtown Manhattan*, *C.A.B.*,

Stages Magazine, and *The Shakespeare Bulletin*. His drama reviews can currently be read at TheaterScene.net. Three of his cover stories for *Back Stage* were reprinted in the first two editions of the *Back Stage Handbook for Performing Artists*.

A member of the Dramatists Guild since 1981, Gluck is also a voting member of the Drama Desk, the Outer Critics Circle, and the American Theatre Critics Association. He has been a fellow critic of the National Critics Conference of the Eugene O'Neill Memorial Theater Center during the summer that introduced playwright August Wilson to the theatre community.

characters

(*in order of appearance*)

> **MRS. MARGARET HUDSON**, a middle-aged widow
>
> **MAY MORTIMER**, her niece, a beautiful young girl of nineteen
>
> **MR. FREDERICK JERNINGHAM**, an intense professor of
> philosophy, in his early thirties

scene one

time

1907

setting

The verandah of Margaret Hudson's country house, outside of Boston, Massachusetts. It is eleven-thirty on a Sunday morning in late spring. A table is set with three places for breakfast. There is a sideboard heaped high with breakfast delicacies. Behind the railing of the terrace can be seen a perfectly kept lawn and an orchard in the near distance. It is a radiant morning and the sunlight streams in.

[*At Rise:* MRS. HUDSON *is discovered at the table preparing a carafe of tea that has grown cold.* MAY MORTIMER, *her niece, a girl of nineteen, dressed in a white dress with a blue sash, enters from the house, stage left, reading from a copy of* Sonnets from the Portuguese. *She is so enraptured by the sonnet and her mood that she does not at first see her aunt.*]

MAY   If thou must love me, let it be for naught
      Except for love's sake only. Do not say
      "I love her for her smile . . . her look . . . her way
      Of speaking gently, . . . for a trick of thought
      That falls in well with mine, and certes brought
      A sense of pleasant ease on such a day"

MRS. HUDSON   [*Amused.*] For these things in themselves, Beloved, may

be changed, or change for thee, —and love, so wrought
May be unwrought so.

MAY [*Smiling now that she is awake.*] Good morning, Aunt Margaret. Is Mr. Jerningham up yet?

MRS. HUDSON Yes, he had breakfast early and walked off in the direction of the orchard. Would you like some breakfast?

MAY I'll just take some coffee, thank you.

[*As she speaks she gets herself a cup of coffee from the sideboard. She speaks with passion and irony that betray a great deal of emotion.*]

Do you know what that man has been doing all this week while he has been down here? Each mild and balmy day, he has been sitting in the orchard, where a light breeze stirs the boughs of the old apple tree under which he sits protected from the radiant, sun filled sky.

MRS. HUDSON Surely that can not be faulted on such a gorgeous day.

MAY He's been reading a treatise on ontology written by a friend of his, another philosopher, and it bristles with fallacies. There in the orchard my philosopher sits discovering them, all of them, mind you, and noting them on the fly leaf.

MRS. HUDSON [*Scarcely heard by May who is working herself up into a passion.*] You grow too agitated, my dear!

MAY He's not going to review the book, as you'd think from his behavior, or even to answer it in a work of his own.

MRS. HUDSON No?

MAY [*Her exasperation getting the better of her.*] No, it's just that he finds pleasure in stripping any poor fallacy naked and crucifying it. All he notices is if the wind turns his page, and he has to find his place again. Then he shuffles the pages until he's got the right one and settles back to his reading.

MRS. HUSDON I know, my dear, Mr. Jerningham is exasperating.

MAY I mean to have a word with him before I leave today.

MRS. HUDSON   You know where you can always find him. Good luck!

[MAY *is taken by surprise at* MRS. HUDSON's *last remark. Then she smiles and exits into garden.*]

scene two

setting

A corner of the orchard, immediately following.

[*At Rise:* MR. JERNINGHAM, *an attractive professor in his early thirties, is seated under a tree deeply engrossed in his book. He might be wearing a soft hat and steel-rimmed glasses. He has a very intense look—the look of those who can give themselves up completely to whatever they are doing.* MAY *enters from stage left.*]

MAY   Mr. Jerningham, are you very busy?

MR. JERNINGHAM   No, Miss May, not very.

MAY   Because I want your opinion.

MR. JERNINGHAM   In one moment.

[*He returns to his book, makes a couple of further notes with his pencil, closes his book with a snap, and gives his attention to the girl who waits nervously.*]

Now, Miss May, I'm at your service.

MAY   It's a very important thing I want to ask you, and it's very difficult, and you mustn't tell any one that I asked you; at least, I'd rather you didn't.

MR. JERNINGHAM   I shall not speak of it. Indeed, I shall probably not remember it.

MAY   And you mustn't look at me, please, while I'm asking you.

MR. JERNINGHAM   I don't think I was looking at you, but if I was, I beg your pardon.

MAY   Suppose a man—no, that's not right.

MR. JERNINGHAM   You can take any hypothesis you please, but you must verify it afterwards, of course.

MAY   Oh, do let us go on! Suppose a girl, Mr. Jerningham—I wish you wouldn't nod.

MR. JERNINGHAM   It was only to show that I follow you.

MAY   Oh, of course you 'follow me,' as you call it. Suppose a girl had two lovers—you're nodding again—or, I ought to say, suppose there were two men who might be in love with a girl.

MR. JERNINGHAM   Only two? You see, any number of men *might* be in love with—

MAY   Oh, we can leave the rest out; they don't matter.

MR. JERNINGHAM   Very well. If they are irrelevant, we will put them aside.

MAY   Suppose then that one of these men was, oh, *awfully* in love with the girl, and—and proposed, you know—

MR. JERNINGHAM   A moment, please! Let me take down his proposition. What was it?

MAY   Why, proposed to her—asked her to marry him.

MR. JERNINGHAM   Dear me! How stupid of me! I forget that special use of the word. Yes?

MAY   The girl likes him pretty well, and her people approve of him and all that, you know.

MR. JERNINGHAM   That simplifies the problem.

MAY   But she's not in—in love with him, you know. She doesn't *really* care for him—*much*. Do you understand?

MR. JERNINGHAM   Perfectly, it is a most natural state of mind.

MAY   Well then, suppose that there's another man—what are you writing?

MR. JERNINGHAM   I only put down "B"—like that.

[*He holds out his notebook to show her.*]

MAY   Oh, you really are—. But let me go on. The other man is a friend of the girl's; he's very clever—oh, fearfully clever; and he's rather handsome. You needn't put that down.

MR. JERNINGHAM   It is certainly not very material.

MAY   And the girl is most awfully—she admires him tremendously. She thinks he's the greatest man that ever lived, you know. And she—she—

MR. JERNINGHAM   I'm following.

MAY   She'd think it better than anything in the world if—if she could be anything to help him, you know.

MR. JERNINGHAM   You mean become his wife?

MAY   Well, of course I do—at least I suppose I do.

MR. JERNINGHAM   You spoke rather vaguely, you know.

MAY   Well, yes. I did mean become his wife.

MR. JERNINGHAM   Yes. Well?

MAY   But he doesn't think much about these things. He likes her. I think he likes her.

MR. JERNINGHAM   Well, doesn't *dislike* her? Shall we call him indifferent?

MAY   I don't know. Yes, rather indifferent. I don't think he thinks about it, you know. But she—she's pretty. You needn't put that down.

MR. JERNINGHAM   I was about to do so.

MAY   She thinks life with him would be just heaven; and—she thinks she would make him awfully happy. She would—would be so proud of him, you see.

MR. JERNINGHAM   I see. Yes!

MAY   And—I don't know how to put it, quite—she thinks that if he ever thought about it at all, he might care for her; because he doesn't care for anybody else, and she's pretty—

MR. JERNINGHAM   You said that before.

MAY   Oh dear, I dare say I did. And most men care for somebody, don't they? Some girl, I mean.

MR. JERNINGHAM Most men, no doubt.

MAY Well, then, what ought she to do? It's not a real thing, you know, Mr. Jerningham. It's in—in a novel I was reading.

MR. JERNINGHAM Dear me! And it's quite an interesting case! Yes, I see. The question is, Will she act most wisely in accepting the offer of the man who loves her exceedingly, but for whom she entertains only a moderate affection.

MAY Yes. Just a liking. He's just a friend.

MR. JERNINGHAM Exactly. Or in marrying the other man whom she loves exceed—

MAY That's not it. How can she marry him? He hasn't—he hasn't asked her, you see.

MR. JERNINGHAM True. I forgot. Let us assume, though, for a moment, that he has asked her. She would then have to consider which marriage would be productive of the greater sum total of—

MAY Oh, you needn't consider that.

MR. JERNINGHAM But it seems the best logical order. We can afterwards make allowance for the element of uncertainty caused by—

MAY Oh, no. I don't want it like that. I know perfectly well what she'd do if he—the other man—you know—asked her.

MR. JERNINGHAM You apprehend that—

MAY Never mind what I "apprehend." Take it just as I told you.

MR. JERNINGHAM Very good. "A" has asked her hand, "B" has not.

MAY Yes.

MR. JERNINGHAM May I take it that, but for the disturbing influence of "B," "A" would be a satisfactory—er—candidate?

MAY Ye-es. I think so.

MR. JERNINGHAM She therefore enjoys a certainty of considerable happiness if she marries "A."

MAY   Ye-es. Not perfect, because of—"B," you know.

MR. JERNINGHAM   Quite so, quite so; but still a fair amount of happiness. Is it not so?

MAY   I don't—well, perhaps.

MR. JERNINGHAM   On the other hand, if "B" did ask her, we are to postulate a higher degree of happiness for her?

MAY   Yes, please, Mr. Jerningham—much higher.

MR. JERNINGHAM   For both of them?

MAY   For her. Never mind him.

MR. JERNINGHAM   Very well. That again simplifies the problem. But his asking her is a contingency only?

MAY   Yes, that's all.

MR. JERNINGHAM   My dear young lady, it becomes a question of degree. How probable or improbable is it?

MAY   I don't know. Not very probable—unless—unless—

MR. JERNINGHAM   Well?

MAY   Unless he did happen to notice, you know.

MR. JERNINGHAM   Ah, yes. We suppose that, if he thought of it, he would probably take the desired step—at least, that he might be led to do so. Could she not—er—indicate her preference?

MAY   She might try—no, she couldn't do much. You see, he—he doesn't think about things.

MR. JERNINGHAM   I understand precisely. And it seems to me, Miss May, that in that very fact we find our solution.

MAY   Do we?

MR. JERNINGHAM   I think so. He has evidently no natural inclination towards her—perhaps not towards marriage at all. Any feeling aroused in him would be necessarily shallow and in a measure artificial—and in all likelihood purely temporary. Moreover, if she took steps to arouse his attention, one of two things would be likely to happen. Are you following me?

MAY Yes, Mr. Jerningham.

MR. JERNINGHAM Either he would be repelled by her overtures—which you must admit is not impossible—and then the position would be unpleasant, and even degrading, for her. Or, on the other hand, he might, through a misplaced feeling of gallantry—

MAY Through what?

MR. JERNINGHAM Through a mistaken idea of politeness in a mistaken view of what was kind, allow himself to be drawn into a connection for which he has no genuine liking. You agree with me that one or the other of these things would be likely?

MAY Yes, I suppose they would, unless he did come to care for her.

MR. JERNINGHAM Ah, you return to that hypothesis. I think it's an extremely fanciful one. No she needn't marry "A," but she must let "B" alone.

MAY You think "B's" feelings wouldn't be at all likely to—to change?

MR. JERNINGHAM That depends on the sort of man he is. But if he is an able man, with intellectual interests which engross him—a man to whom women's society is not a necessity—

MAY He's just like that.

MR. JERNINGHAM Then I see not the least reason for supposing that his feelings will change.

MAY And you would advise her to marry the other—"A"?

MR. JERNINGHAM Well, on the whole, I should. I think we made "A" a good fellow; he is a suitable match, his love for her is true and genuine—

MAY It's tremendous!

MR. JERNINGHAM Yes, and—er—extreme. She likes him. There is every reason to hope that her liking will develop into a sufficiently deep and stable affection. She will get rid of her folly about "B" and make "A" a good wife. Yes, Miss May, if I were the author of your novel, I should make her marry "A," and should call that a happy ending.

[*Pause.*]

Is that all you wanted my opinion about, Miss May?

MAY Yes, I think so. I hope I haven't bored you?

MR. JERNINGHAM I've enjoyed the discussion extremely. I had no idea that novels raised such psychological interest. I must find time to read one.

MAY Don't you think that perhaps if "B" found out afterwards—when she had married "A", you know—that she had cared for him so very, very much, he might be a little sorry?

MR. JERNINGHAM If he were a gentleman, he would regret it deeply.

MAY I mean—sorry on his own account that—that he had thrown away all that, you know?

MR. JERNINGHAM I think it is very probable he would. I can well imagine it.

MAY He might never find anyone to love him like that again.

MR. JERNINGHAM He probably would not.

MAY And—and most people like being loved, don't they?

MR. JERNINGHAM To crave for love is an almost universal instinct, Miss May.

MAY Yes, almost. You see, he'll get old and—and have no one to look after him.

MR. JERNINGHAM He will.

MAY And no home.

MR. JERNINGHAM Well, in a sense none. But really you'll frighten me. I'm a bachelor myself, you know, Miss May.

MAY [*Whispering.*] Yes.

MR. JERNINGHAM   And all your terrors are before me.

MAY   Well, unless—

MR. JERNINGHAM   Oh, we needn't have that "unless." There's no unless about it, Miss May.

> [MAY *jumps to her feet. For an instant she looks at the philosopher. She opens her lips as if to speak, and her face grows red. The philosopher gazing past her does not notice.*]

A beautiful thing, sunshine, to be sure.

> [MAY*'s blush fades into paleness; she closes her lips. Without a word she turns and walks slowly away. The philosopher watches her for a moment.*]

A pretty, graceful creature.

scene three

setting

The verandah, same as Scene One. It is two o'clock and the table is set for lunch.

[*At Rise:* MRS. HUDSON *is seated at the table with her sewing as* MR. JERNING-HAM *enters from the direction of the garden, carrying his hat, his book, and his notebook.*]

MRS. HUDSON   Everything's cold. Where have you been, Mr. Jerningham?

MR. JERNINGHAM   Only in the orchard—reading.

MRS. HUDSON   And you've missed May.

MR. JERNINGHAM   Missed May? How do you mean? [*Pause.*] I had a long talk with her this morning—a most interesting talk.

MRS. HUDSON   But you weren't here to say good-bye. Now, you don't mean to say that you forgot that she was leaving by the two o'clock train? What a man you are!

MR. JERNINGHAM   Dear me! To think of my forgetting it!

MRS. HUDSON   She told me to say good-by to you for her.

MR. JERNINGHAM   She's very kind. I can't forgive myself.

MRS. HUDSON   Did you see much of her while you were here?

MR. JERNINGHAM   More than I should have expected of someone so much younger.

MRS. HUDSON   You're not as old as you pretend to be, Mr. Jerningham.

MR. JERNINGHAM   I will grant you that she *is* very pretty; however, she's quite young.

MRS. HUDSON   In time that will change.

MR. JERNINGHAM   Imagine, the other day she didn't know the meaning of the word "ontology."

MRS. HUDSON   May is eager to learn. She'll soak up knowledge with an eagerness that would surprise you.

MR. JERNINGHAM   Yesterday I had to explain to her Nietzsche's theory of the superman.

MRS. HUDSON   Isn't that what you do at the college?

MR. JERNINGHAM   Surely, but there I am on call like a doctor at a hospital. It's a terrible strain in one's private life to play teacher to one's friends and acquaintances twenty-four hours a day. Even a doctor gets time off to be himself periodically. Being a mentor *all* the time would be terribly wearing.

MRS. HUDSON   Professors have been known to marry their star pupils.

MR. JERNINGHAM   True enough—but there must be complete compatibility.

MRS. HUDSON   Pray tell, how does one measure that?

MR. JERNINGHAM   That *is* a question.

MRS. HUDSON   In my experience, it is not the couples who share everything in advance that make the happiest marriages.

MR. JERNINGHAM   Alas, I am not likely to find out. I never meant to, but I seem to have dwindled into a confirmed state of bachelorhood.

[MRS. HUDSON *looks at him for a moment, then sighs, and says with a wry smile.*]

MRS. HUDSON   Have you everything you want?

MR. JERNINGHAM   Everything, thank you; [*Enumerating what is before him.*] my favorite cheese, cucumber sandwiches, a white wine, the Sunday paper, and a sympathetic ear.

[*Smiles at her.*]

Yes, everything in the world that I want, thanks. You've been most kind . . . I'm sorry I missed Miss May. That was an interesting case of hers. But I gave her the right answer. The girl must marry "A."

MRS. HUDSON   And the girl will, you know.

[MR. JERNINGHAM *stares at her as the curtain falls.*]

• • •

characters

(*in order of appearance*)

MRS. MARGARET HUDSON, a middle-aged widow

JULIAN LOWELL, her cousin, witty and intellectual essayist in his
thirties

AUDREY LISTON, vivacious and effervescent, successful novelist of
popular fiction, age 28–30

GERALD GARDINER, tall, handsome, athletic millionaire, 27–29, his
temperament both amiable and placid

PAMELA MYLES, beautiful, capricious, proud debutante, in her early
twenties

• • •

scene one

time

1907

setting

The verandah of Mrs. Hudson's country house. It is five o'clock on a Friday
afternoon in late spring. Behind the railing of the terrace can be seen a perfectly well-kept lawn and an orchard in the near distance. It has been a
beautiful day, which is still evident from the sunlight.

[*At rise:* MRS. HUDSON *and* JULIAN *are discovered having tea. From* JULIAN's
*outfit it may be correctly surmised that he has just arrived from the city, although it
should also be obvious that he is financially well off.*]

JULIAN   Who do you have staying with you this weekend? When you
wrote to me you only indicated that I would know several of your
other guests.

MRS. HUDSON   Well, my dear, there's my sister and her husband. My
niece May, Gerald Gardiner, Pamela Myles, and that absentminded

philosophy professor Frederick Jerningham, and because I knew you were coming, Anthony, I've invited your novelist friend Audrey Liston.

JULIAN   Miss Audrey Liston is a very pleasant young woman whose company I enjoy—except on paper!

MRS. HUDSON   And I thought it would be nice for you to have someone to talk to about books and so on. Gerald and Pamela probably won't suit your taste, and if I remember Mr. Jerningham's character correctly, he has only his own topic of conversation.

JULIAN   You've noticed Audrey's habit of describing herself as an "authoress in a small way"? I've pointed out to her that three bestsellers in six years could hardly be called "a small way."

MRS. HUDSON   Do I detect the slightest bit of jealousy in your tone? Or is it simply that she has become a household name in so short a time while you, on the other hand, have had to overcome your academic inclinations in order to conquer the reading public?

JULIAN   [*As if he has not heard a word she has said.*] When I've told her that the English language embraces no such word as "authoress," she smiles and says that it ought to— although with a nod in the direction of correctness, I confess, I sympathize to some degree.

MRS. HUDSON   [*With an amused smile and an arch look.*] You were always the purist!

JULIAN   Now I'm not saying that she is not very diligent. I know that she will work from ten to one every day that she is here. How much she will write, of course, is between her and her conscience.

MRS. HUDSON   I hope you two have not had a falling out, Julian?

JULIAN   And finally as Audrey would hardly deny she "takes her characters from life!"

[*Mimicking her voice.*]

"Surely every artist must!" And she will proceed to maintain that people rather like being put into books—

MRS. HUDSON [*Who has been holding back her laughter during the last speech, finally lets it out.*] You're suffering from a case of wounded pride! You haven't recovered from figuring in her latest book as the misogynistic genius with the drooping mustache.

JULIAN How everyone knew it was me I shall never understand. That Audrey lengthened and thickened my hair and invested my very ordinary work-a-day eyes with a strange, magnetic attraction, availed nothing. I was at once recognized, and may I remark in passing, an uncommonly disagreeable fellow she made me.

MRS. HUDSON You have passed though the fire, Julian, you may be tolerably sure that from the point of view of art, you present to Miss Audrey Liston no other aspect of interest, real or supposed.

JULIAN It will assuage my wounded pride if Audrey serves all the rest of her acquaintance as she has served me.

MRS. HUDSON How long do you reckon they will last her?

JULIAN At her present rate of production? About five years! And if fate is kind to her, this weekend will provide her with most suitable patterns for her next piece of work.

MRS. HUDSON However, we must save this conversation for later as here she is!

[AUDREY LISTON *enters from stage left. She is an intense, energetic young woman of about twenty-nine years old. She is dressed for traveling and appears rather breathless. When she talks she is both vivacious and irrepressible.*]

AUDREY [*Putting out her hand.*] Mrs. Hudson, so nice to see you again— and Julian, you naughty boy, you never even told me you were coming.

[*As* JULIAN *gets up to protest his innocence.*]

MRS. HUDSON My dear young lady, on this score my cousin is entirely innocent. He did not know until this moment that he would have the pleasure of your company. Won't you sit down and take some refreshment?

AUDREY [*As she settles herself at the tea table.*] You are forgiven, Julian, but sometimes I have the notion that you have been avoiding me lately.

JULIAN [*Dryly.*] Whatever could have given you that idea, Audrey?

AUDREY At any rate, I want to tell you how opportune your invitation was, Mrs. Hudson. I'm hoping fate will be kind to me this weekend and provide me with suitable patterns for my next piece of work. Take your characters from life, I always say! Surely every artist must.

[JULIAN *and* MRS. HUDSON *exchange glances.* AUDREY *catches* JULIAN *throwing his eyes up to heaven.*]

I see Julian disagrees with me as usual. I have found that people rather like being put into books! Yes, just as they like being photographed, for all they grumble and pretend to be afflicted when either process is levied against them.

JULIAN What I only meant, Audrey, is—

AUDREY I know you, Julian. Anyway, Mrs. Hudson, who is that attractive couple I observed on the tennis court when I drove up from the station. That charming young girl and that tall, handsome young man.

MRS. HUDSON Ah, you have discovered my little secret. I wondered how long it would take someone of your discerning eye. Julian, with his attention on higher things, would never have noticed. I have invited Pamela Myles and Gerald Gardiner down here this weekend so that they might get to know each other better. If an engagement should take place...

JULIAN [*Interrupting her, with a frown.*] Matchmaking again, Cousin Margaret?

MRS. HUDSON [*Ironically.*] You must allow an old woman her few pleasures in life!

AUDREY [*Delightedly.*] A possible romance? I must begin a study of the protagonist!

[PAMELA *and* GERALD *come into view across the lawn carrying tennis racquets. They are deep in conversation.* MRS. HUDSON *waves to them. They wave back.*]

MRS. HUDSON [*Getting up.*] I see that Pamela and Gerald have finished their game. I must leave you two together while I tend to the arrangements for dinner. Dinner will be at six this evening. Don't be late! Miss Liston, I hope this weekend should prove fruitful for you, and Julian, I hope the country will improve your disposition.

[MRS. HUDSON *exits into house stage left.*]

JULIAN Cousin Margaret!

[*He gives up his protest.*]

AUDREY Whatever did that mean? Now, Julian, I'm looking for some new types for my next novel and I think I have found them in Gerald Gardiner and Pamela Myles. What do you think?

JULIAN I don't know, Audrey, if you are asking my opinion or if you have made up my mind. However, as to the former, he appears to my jaded eye to offer no salient novelty as a protagonist for a work of fiction. To do him justice, he is tall, broad and handsome but he possesses a manner of enviable placidity.

AUDREY I always like your perceptions even when I disagree with you. I must make some notes. Go on, Julian.

[*She takes out a small notebook and a pen.*]

JULIAN Pamela, I will allow is exactly the "type" that you love. She is haughty, capricious, "difficile," but sound and true at heart. And there you have volume I.

AUDREY I never know when you are joking! I agree with you in your conception of Pamela, but you do not do justice to the artistic possibilities latent in Mr. Gardiner.

JULIAN Whatever can you see in such a dull fellow?

AUDREY You miss his curious attraction, which will tax my skill to the utmost to reproduce.

JULIAN [*With irony.*] You do yourself an injustice.

AUDREY   I propose that you should also make a study of him—

JULIAN   Pray leave me out of this! I am not writing a three-volume novel but putting together a book of essays—more my line, don't you think?

AUDREY   I attribute that to a shrinking from the difficulties of the task. You really ought to stop reading your Flaubert and that Mr. Henry James and try some really important authoresses like Mrs. Henry Wood and Ouida.

[JULIAN *looks askance at the very idea.*]

Now to get back to the task at hand.

[*With another glance at* PAMELA *and* GERALD, *who are laughing at the other side of the lawn.*]

They must have a misunderstanding of course!

JULIAN   But of course! What should you say to another man?

AUDREY   [*Her mind racing ahead.*] Or another woman?

JULIAN   It comes to the same thing—about a volume and a half!

AUDREY   [*Swatting him lightly.*] Julian! But it's more interesting. Do you think she'd better be a married woman?

JULIAN   [*Pointedly.*] The age prefers them married.

[*Music cue. At this point,* PAMELA *and* GERALD *come up to the terrace.* AUDREY *and* PAMELA *greet each other, while* AUDREY *can't take her eyes off of* GERALD.]

GERALD   [*Addressing* JULIAN *when he recognizes him.*] How are you, old chap?

[GERALD *and* JULIAN *shake hands.*]

JULIAN   Nice to see you again. How have you been since the Stanhopes at Christmas?

GERALD   I can't complain, Lowell.

[*Looking at* JULIAN *with the eye of the college crew coach.*]

Keeping fit, are you?

[GERALD *takes a pencil from* JULIAN's *jacket pocket and pretends to use it as a barbell or punches him on the stomach to suggest that he is getting too much avoirdupois.*]

JULIAN [*Quickly changing the subject.*] Audrey, I'd like to introduce you to Gerald Gardiner.

[*To* GERALD.]

This is Miss Audrey Liston.

AUDREY [*Who can't take her eyes off of* GERALD.] Charmed.

GERALD Delighted, I'm sure.

AUDREY Don't I know your Aunt Isabella?

GERALD [*Bored with hearing about his famous aunt.*] And haven't I been told that you also have a hobby?

PAMELA Don't be silly, Gerald. Don't you recognize the author of *Flame to the Candle*? Everyone has been talking about it for months.

GERALD [*Bowing slightly in the direction of* PAMELA.] I stand corrected. The sun must have temporarily addled my brain. Have you met Miss Pamela Myles?

[JULIAN *and* PAMELA *shake hands. The ladies turn to each other.*]

JULIAN Miss Myles.

PAMELA I have heard such wonderful things about your new novel, Miss Liston, but, alas, with this year's social season I haven't had a moment to even cut the pages of your book.

AUDREY I have been so lionized this season since my little effort came out that I haven't even had a chance to consider a sequel. I wonder if this weekend will give me some archetypes.

JULIAN Cousin Margaret said that dinner is early this evening. Shall we go in?

[JULIAN *ushers them toward the house.*]

GERALD Whatever does that author lady mean? I can't make head nor tail of anything she says!

PAMELA Hush, Gerald, she'll hear you!

MRS. HUDSON [*Entering dressed in her evening frock.*] I see you have all met. Professor Jerningham and my niece May have already gathered in the library. Won't you come in?

[MRS. HUDSON *exits into house.*]

AUDREY   [*As she puts out her arm to* GERALD *so he can take her in.*] Have
     you shot any lions lately, Mr. Gardiner?

[AUDREY *and* GERALD *exit into house.*]

[PAMELA *continues to sit staring ahead.* JULIAN, *taking pity on her, goes over, puts
out his arm, she takes it and They exit into house.*]

[*Blackout.*]

scene two

[*It is sometime after dinner. The terrace is bathed in moonlight. It is a beautiful
evening.* JULIAN *and* GERALD *come out of the billiard room. They are attired in
evening clothes and are either smoking,* JULIAN *with his pipe, or drinking whiskey—
and—soda.* GERALD *is in a talkative mood;* JULIAN *is in a reflective mood. Obviously
pondering a serious matter.* GERALD *has the handsome, open countenance, candid
blue eyes, and blond good looks of the young man who has always had everything and
has no cares in the world except how to idle away his next hour. Although his self-
assurance is obvious, he is very pleasant company. Even tempered and seeming to enjoy
himself whatever he is doing.*]

GERALD   You play a good game of billiards, Lowell, for a man who
     leads such a quiet sort of life.

JULIAN   [*Amused.*] You don't play such a bad game yourself considering
     you beat me three games to two.

GERALD   [*Modestly.*] I play to win. There's no point in playing otherwise.
     Where do you ride, Lowell? I don't recall seeing you at the
     Brookline Country Club.

JULIAN   I don't ride, Gardiner.

GERALD   But you do belong to the Brookline?
     [JULIAN *shakes his head no.*]
     We must do something about that. I'll see that your name is put
     up for nomination.

JULIAN Thank you, I'm flattered. However, my work keeps me much occupied. I don't find time for recreation of that kind.

GERALD But you must keep fit in any event. I say, Lowell, if you work hard, you have to play hard too. Take this crowd Mrs. Hudson has asked down here this weekend. Not a very jolly lot on the whole. Mostly a bookish sort of people.

JULIAN That shouldn't surprise you with our proximity to Cambridge. Besides, Mrs. Hudson's late husband was a professor, and I myself was at one time associated with the university.

GERALD No, I didn't mean you. And then there's Miss Myles.

JULIAN I should have thought that Miss Myles was exactly the sort of girl to help beguile the long, pleasant hours of a holiday in the country.

GERALD I never know how she'll be treating me from one minute to the next.

JULIAN However, you must admit that she is most agreeable to look at!

GERALD Then there is your fellow author, Miss Liston.

JULIAN Concerning Miss Liston, there is something I feel it my duty to warn you about, Gardiner. I wonder if you are aware of the risk you run at Miss Liston's hands.

GERALD Risks? You mean of making Miss Myles jealous?

JULIAN There's that too surely, but I meant that if you are not very careful, you will find yourself the hero of her next novel. She's on the prowl here this weekend for new material, so she has told me in confidence.

GERALD [*Seriously.*] You know, old chap, I've always sort of imagined myself as the hero of an adventure. We're all the hero of our own life so to speak. Whenever I've had my picture taken with one of my trophies for sailing or boxing or riding or polo, I've often thought that this will make a fine illustration in a privately printed biography someday.

[*Pause.*] But what does she know about me?

JULIAN   She's very quick. She'll soon pick up as much as she wants.

GERALD   She'll probably go all wrong.

JULIAN   There is such a thing as poetic license. She'll change the color of your hair or your eyes, in any case.

GERALD   If one's portrait is to be painted, the artist ought to do one justice. I must give Miss Liston every chance of appraising my character.

[AUDREY LISTON *comes out of the house. Her eyes light up when she sees* GERALD. *She comes up to the two men.*]

AUDREY   There was something else I wanted to discuss with you, Mr. Gardiner. I'm sure Julian won't mind if I take you away for a moment, will you, Julian?

[*She takes* GERALD*'s arm and begins to lead him to the other side of the terrace as* JULIAN *looks on amused.*]

I'm thinking of altering the scheme of my story.

[*Pause.*]

Have you ever noticed how sometimes a man thinks he's in love when he isn't really?

GERALD   [*Pondering seriously.*] Such a case sometimes occurs.

AUDREY   Yes, and he doesn't find out his mistakes—until—

GERALD   Till they're married?

AUDREY   Sometimes, yes. But sometimes he sees it before—when he meets somebody else.

GERALD   [*Gravely.*] Very true.

AUDREY   The false can't stand against the real. If someone comes along who can appreciate and draw out what is best in him—

GERALD   That's all very well, but what of the first girl?

AUDREY   Oh, she's—she can be made shallow, you know; and I can put in a man for her. People needn't be much interested in her.

GERALD   [*Nodding seriously.*] You could manage it that way.

AUDREY She will really be valuable mainly as a foil. I shall make her nice, you know, but shallow—not worthy of him.

GERALD And what are you going to make the other girl like?

AUDREY I haven't quite made up my mind yet, Mr. Gardiner. I thought on that account you could help me.

[*She leads him into the garden and they exit.*]

[JULIAN *takes a book out of his pocket and settles down at the table to read.* PAMELA MYLES *enters. She is looking even more beautiful. She's dressed alluringly.*]

PAMELA Have you seen Gerald Gardiner, Mr. Lowell? He promised to take me boating in the moonlight but he seems to have forgotten his promise. Miss Liston also seems to have disappeared since dinner.

JULIAN They were both here a while ago, Miss Myles, but I don't know where they were headed. They may be out looking for you.

PAMELA And you're not much better—reading an old book on a beautiful night like this.

[*Putting out her hand for the book.*]

Give it here!

[JULIAN *hands her the book sheepishly. She turns a few pages.*]

The House of Mirth by Mrs. Wharton—horrid stuff!

[*She flings the book on the table.*]

Now that I've finished at Miss Francis Academy I've promised myself never to pick up a book again.

JULIAN You will put both Miss Liston and myself out of business. Of course, it would give you more time for other things.

PAMELA [*Sharply.*] There are other things to do, you know. You and Miss Liston are no fun at all, locking yourself up in your rooms all day "writing" as you call it—just as we need a fourth for tennis.

JULIAN I had no idea I was ruining your weekend. I'll have to make a greater effort.

PAMELA You could start by being more attentive to the ladies. Take dinner for instance, you were in one of your far-away moods.

Miss Liston, on the other hand, couldn't seem to detach herself from poor Gerald for one moment.

JULIAN   On that score I think I should warn you—

PAMELA   I am fully able to take care of myself, Mr. Lowell, despite any false notions you may have acquired concerning the weaker sex.

JULIAN   In that case I won't tell you of the risk you run.

PAMELA   But aren't Gerald and Audrey Liston funny? If I didn't know better, Mr. Lowell, I would suspect that they are writing a novel together!

[*She bursts into peals of laughter at the very idea.*]

JULIAN   Perhaps Mr. Gardiner is giving her the materials for one.

PAMELA   I shouldn't suppose that anything very interesting has ever happened to him.

JULIAN   I beg your pardon. I gathered the impression that you liked him. You're always out riding together or playing tennis or going boating. You are together so much that you don't give anyone else much of an opportunity.

PAMELA   I do like him. What's that got to do with it? One can count a person among one's friends, Mr. Lowell, and yet be aware of his failings.

[*Pause.*]

[*In a milder mood.*]

He's very conceited, isn't he?

JULIAN   [*Severely.*] Then you ought to snub him.

PAMELA   So I do—sometimes. He's rather amusing, though.

JULIAN   Of course, if you're prepared to make allowances—

PAMELA   Oh, what nonsense.

JULIAN   Then you've no business to amuse yourself with him.

PAMELA   Dear, dear! How moral you are, Mr. Lowell.

[*Pause.*]

I think it is getting cold. And it's rather slow tonight. I shall go to bed.

JULIAN [*With a wicked gleam in his eye.*] Oh, won't you wait and bid Miss Liston and Mr. Gardiner good night?

PAMELA I don't know what you mean, Mr. Lowell.

JULIAN No?

PAMELA No.

[*She turns away. Then she says over her shoulder.*]

Wish Miss Liston good night for me, Mr. Lowell. Anything I have to say to Gerald will wait very well till tomorrow.

[*She exits into house.*]

[JULIAN *looks perplexed for a moment and then smiles in the direction* PAMELA *has gone. He takes a tentative look in the direction of the garden, where* AUDREY *and* GERALD *presumably are. Then he settles down in his reading chair, reopens his book that* PAMELA *had so idly flung on the table, finds his place, and becomes absorbed.*]

[*The lights dim and the leaves can be heard rustling. Suddenly* AUDREY *and* GERALD *come out of the shrubbery.* GERALD *wears his usual passive look but* AUDREY'*s face is happy and radiant.* AUDREY *goes over to* JULIAN.]

AUDREY Have you been reading all this time?

GERALD [*Looking around as though he's lost something.*] You'll both excuse me for a moment, won't you?

[*He exits into house.*]

JULIAN Why, you look as if you'd invented the finest scene ever written.

AUDREY [After a dreamy pause.]

I think I shall stick to my old idea in the book.

[GERALD *comes out of the house frowning.*]

GERALD I say, Lowell, where's Miss Myles? I promised to take her boating.

JULIAN She's gone to bed. She told me to wish you good night for her, Miss Liston. No message for you, Gardiner.

[GERALD *stands frowning a moment, then with an unheard exclamation under his breath, he strides back in the house.* AUDREY *never takes her eyes off* GERALD *but he never looks in her direction. A door can be heard slamming.* JULIAN *quickly looks at* AUDREY'*s altered face.*]

AUDREY [*In agitation.*] What does he want her for, I wonder? He said nothing to me about wanting to speak to her tonight.

[*She begins to walk slowly towards the house, her eyes on the ground, the light gone from her face. Suddenly she turns back in* JULIAN'*s direction as though she has made a decision.*]

I—it's—I don't quite know what I shall do with the book.

JULIAN I thought you'd settled?

AUDREY So I had, but—oh, don't lets talk about it, Julian.

[*Pause, then she continues talking as though to herself.*]

I don't know why I should make it end happily. I'm sure life isn't always happy, is it?

JULIAN Certainly not. You mean your man might stick to the shallow girl after all?

AUDREY [*In a whisper.*] Yes.

JULIAN And be miserable afterwards?

AUDREY I don't know. Perhaps he wouldn't.

JULIAN Then you must make him shallow himself.

AUDREY I can't do that. Oh, how difficult it is!

[*Fast blackout, leaving the two characters as if frozen in time.*]

scene three

[*The verandah the next morning about eleven o'clock. It is a radiant spring day.* MRS. HUDSON *and* JULIAN *are having breakfast. He is examining a newspaper.* MRS. HUDSON *looks dreamingly into the distance over her tea cup.*]

MRS. HUDSON   I think we shall have some good news about my niece May and Professor Jerningham.

JULIAN   Has May decided to attend his college?

MRS. HUDSON   You know perfectly well that Harvard only takes men! Guess again.

JULIAN   I can't imagine.

MRS. HUDSON   I think May has a romantic interest in the professor.

JULIAN   Is it reciprocated?

MRS. HUDSON   I don't see why it shouldn't be. She is beautiful, intelligent, poised, and shall have a great deal of money someday.

JULIAN   And then there is the age difference. How many years are between them?

MRS. HUDSON   I don't see why that is a problem. My late husband, you may recall, was a good deal older than I.

JULIAN   [*Wryly.*] And you never had a day of less than bliss with George Hudson.

MRS. HUDSON   [*Flustered.*] Yes, well, the past is the past, as they always say.
[*Quickly.*]
I haven't seen as much of your friend Audrey Liston as I usually do. How is she enjoying her time here?

JULIAN   Would it surprise you to hear that she has taken a fancy to young Mr. Gardiner?

MRS. HUDSON   No! Really? I wouldn't have dreamed of that. Is this in a literary way?

JULIAN   I have a sinking feeling that for her it goes beyond that. Although she should get a book out of this weekend in any case.

MRS. HUDSON   Does she realize that his father expects him to present the family with a suitable engagement in the next year? I don't think the Gardiners would approve of a writer of romantic novels in the family.

JULIAN   I thought Gerald's grandfather left him his own money. Will the family wishes count so much in his decision?

MRS. HUDSON   I don't think poor Teddy Wharton likes Edith's books, although you can almost call her an artist, so it may be different . . . Gerald is no intellect like your friends or Edith's circle but he has a sense of tradition and family history.

JULIAN   What sort of bride will satisfy the family?

MRS. HUDSON   His wife will be expected to take her place in Back Bay society. He will want a hostess that will do him proud. But why are we talking as if Cupid hasn't already been good to us this weekend? Mr. Gardiner and Miss Myles are planning to announce their engagement when they return to their families. I thought you knew!

JULIAN   I did hear something like that.

MRS. HUDSON   You have been teasing me all along! It is a good thing I understand your ironic sense of humor. Well, you will have to be particularly nice to Miss Liston when you see her and make none of your usual witty bon mots at her expense—though, to tell the truth, I've never seen her take you seriously!

[*Standing up.*]

I must get my garden hat before this Massachusetts sun defeats us all.

[*She starts for the garden where she sees* AUDREY LISTON, *who has heard the last speech.*]

[AUDREY *enters from house right. She is dressed in an outfit suitable for traveling and is buttoning a pair of gloves. Her mood is somber and the vivacity is gone.*]

My dear Miss Liston, have you heard the good news? Miss Myles and Mr. Gardiner became engaged last night! I felt certain that this weekend would prove fortuitous for engagements.

AUDREY   Yes, your niece May came into my room this morning with the news. Even Mr. Jerningham had heard when I met him on his way into the garden just now. I must extend my best wishes before I depart this morning.

MRS. HUDSON   Are you going already? You will deprive Julian of your charming company.

AUDREY   [*Meaningfully.*] I find that I must return to town on business related to my new novel. I hope you will forgive my rushing away so suddenly.

MRS. HUDSON   If it is the call of the muse, then I understand perfectly. However, you must promise to stay longer next time. Won't you take some breakfast before you go?

AUDREY   I'll just have time for some tea and toast. I believe that there is a twelve o'clock train.

MRS. HUDSON   In that case, let me arrange for your carriage. Julian can see that you have everything you want. I hope you have enjoyed your stay. Will half an hour be sufficient?

AUDREY   My valise is packed. That should give me just enough time to have a word with Julian before I go. Thank you for everything. It has proved a most—productive weekend.

MRS. HUDSON   I'm so glad, my dear. Then I'll see you around at the drive shortly, Julian, don't make Audrey late now, do you hear?

[*She exits.*]

JULIAN   [*Hands* AUDREY *a cup of tea as a peace offering.*] Have you solved the problem of your story?

AUDREY   I have adopted your suggestion. The man doesn't find out.

JULIAN   Then you've made him a fool?

AUDREY   No, I—think it might happen though he wasn't a fool.

[*Pause.*]

I'm going to make him find out afterwards.

JULIAN   What! After he's married the shallow girl?

AUDREY   Yes.

JULIAN   Rather too late, isn't it? At least, if you mean there to be a happy ending.

AUDREY   [*As she enlaces her fingers.*] I haven't decided about the ending yet.

JULIAN   If your intent is to be tragical—which is the fashion—you'll do best to leave it as it stands.

AUDREY   [*Slowly.*] Yes, if I'm tragical, I shall leave it as it stands.

[*Pause.*]

Of course, I could—

[*She stops and looks apprehensively at* JULIAN.]

Of course, the shallow girl—his wife—might die, Julian.

JULIAN   [*With a smile.*] In novels, while there's death, there's hope.

AUDREY   Yes, in novels.

[*The carriage is heard on the gravel. She turns away overcome with emotion.*]

I must see to my hand luggage. Look me up when you get back to town, Julian, and you must tell me all about your next book.

[JULIAN *takes her extended hand and she rushes out. He returns to his newspaper with a sigh. A pause and then* MRS. HUDSON *comes onto the terrace from the garden path.*]

MRS. HUDSON   The carriage is ready. Where is Miss Liston?

JULIAN   She has gone upstairs to collect her belongings. I imagine that she will be down shortly. Can you keep a secret?

MRS. HUDSON   I see you have a story for me. I'm all attention.

JULIAN   I predict that Audrey Liston's next bestselling novel will be called *The Riddle of Love*. It will concern a handsome, rich young man who marries a beautiful but superficial heiress. He then meets the love of his life. The shallow wife turns out as badly as possible and dies unregretted. He is then reunited with his lost love, and all ends joyfully. It will be a simple story, prettily told in its little way, and the scene of the reunion will be written with genuine feeling—nay, with a touch of real passion.

MRS. HUDSON   The new Mrs. Gardiner would do best to see that her husband never meets Miss Liston after they are married, or life may prove to copy art.

JULIAN   True art demands an adaptation, not a copy, of life. I read that somewhere the other day. It seems correct, if Miss Audrey Liston, authoress, be any authority.

[*Curtain falls.*]

• • •

The Birth of Theater

Jules Tasca

Jules Tasca

Through I.U.P., Jules Tasca has taught playwriting at Oxford University in England, and he has performed with a Commedia dell'arte group in Central Italy. He is the author of over 125 (full-length and one-act) published plays that have been produced in numerous national theatres, from the Mark Taper Forum to the Bucks County Playhouse, as well as abroad in England, Ireland, Austria, Germany, South Africa, Canada, and Australia. He has also written for radio and television. He scripted *The Hal Linden TV Special*. His plays *La Llorona* and *Maria* were produced on National Public Radio. Other one-act pieces were broadcast in Los Angeles and abroad in Germany and his play *The Grand Christmas History of the Andy Landy Clan* was broadcast on 47 national Public Radio Stations.

He was the national winner in New York's Performing Arts Repertory Theater Playwrighting contest for his libretto, *The Amazing Einstein*. He has adapted the stories of Oscar Wilde, Guy de Maupassant, Mark Twain, Robert Louis Stevenson, and Saki; modernized Aristophanes' *Ecclesiazusae* (Women in Congress); and written new versions of *Hamlet* and *Macbeth*.

His libretto for C.S. Lewis's *The Lion, the Witch and the Wardrobe* had its world premiere in California and played in London and New York and is currently touring nationwide. For his play *Theater Trip*, he was the recipient of a Thespie Award for Best New Play, and *Old Goat Song* won a Drama Critic's Award in Los Angeles. His plays *The Spelling of Coynes*, *The Death of Bliss*, and *Deus-X* have been included in the Best American Short Plays anthologies (his most recent play *The Rapture of Mammon* appears in the 2005–2006 volume). His tragic piece *The Balkan Women* won the prestigious Barrymore Award for Best Play and another tragic play *Judah's Daughter* received the Dorothy Silver International Playwrighting Award. Tasca won first prize in the Bucks County Writers' Club Screenwriting Contest. His piece, *Live Drawing*, is about the relationship between Leonardo da Vinci and the *Mona Lisa*, and has been published by the Dramatic Publishing Company. Tasca's play *The Mission*, which played at New Theatre in Florida, received a Carbonelle nomination by the South Florida Theatre League for Best New Play. The author is a member of New York's Dramatist Guild.

cast

Four young hunters:

YIL

PENO

DEN

ENGO

time

Prehistoric

place

An open field

setting

Black box

[YIL, PENO, *and* ENGO *clean and comb a large bear skin.*]

YIL   Everyone says bears are good-luck animals.

ENGO   How much good luck did the bear have, Yil?

PENO   Yes. Once he walked the world. He was king of the wide plains. Now, he's a rug...king of nothing.

[DEN *enters and paces.*]

YIL   Den? Den, what's the matter?

DEN   We are tasked by the elders.

PENO   The elders?

ENGO   To do what?

YIL   Yeah. The bear meat's on the fire.

PENO   Food for all.

DEN   Food for all, Peno, but they want...

PENO   What?

DEN   The elders say that life here is mundane. They say...

YIL   Go on, Den.

DEN   They say that we hunters have all the excitement.

ENGO   Oh, sure, excitement. Look at the scars all over us.

DEN   Be that as it may, they believe we live on the danger edge of life and therefore our lives are...are...are more meaningful.

PENO   So...let them take spears and go up against a 12-foot feral bear.

DEN   You know they can't, Peno. The elders are old. The women are women and the children are young.

PENO   What is it they want us to do?

YIL   Yes. Tell us, Den.

DEN   They want us to reenact the kill.

ENGO   Reenact the kill?

DEN   For the whole clan at fireside tonight.

YIL   Tonight?

DEN   Yes. They want us to show the killing of this bear.

YIL   Why us?

ENGO   Yeah. Why? There are more than 10 other hunting teams in the clan.

DEN   I asked them that right off, Engo. They said they wanted this team, because we are the smartest, craftiest, most daring.

[*The others groan in displeasure.*]

PENO   Because we're the smartest, craftiest, and most daring, we draw extra work?

DEN   Peno, the elders have spoken. I have an uncle in that group. There's no way to refuse the gray ones.

[*Pause. A beat.*]

ENGO   This is a stupid request. How do you do a reenactment of killing a bear with no bear?

YIL   Good point, Engo.

[*The four ponder this for a few beats.*]

DEN   The answer is...

PENO   What?

DEN   There can be no live bear, so...so we can't give them the real thing.

PENO   You're saying the obvious, Den.

YIL   We can't do it real unless...unless we took them all on a hunt.

DEN   Which is impossible, so...

ENGO   So?

DEN   So we...we pretend there's a bear.

YIL   Pretend?

ENGO   A man pretending to be a bear?

[ENGO *laughs.*]

YIL   Den, that's so...so...so...

PENO   Childish...

ENGO   That's true, Peno, only children would pretend to be animals. We're men. We're hunters.

DEN   Has anyone got a better suggestion?
   [*They all ponder once again.*]
   Well?
   [*They all shrug at* DEN. DEN *crosses to the bear skin.*]
   Who wants to be the bear?
   [*The other three laugh.*]
   Come on. Who wants to be the bear?

YIL   You do it, Engo, you have more hair on your chest than I do.

ENGO   But, Yil, you smell more like a bear.

[PENO *laughs.*]

DEN   Be serious. One of us has to get under this skin and try to act like a bear.

YIL   Don't look at me. I think it's bad luck to pretend to be a bear, a bear we killed at that.

DEN   Whoever said it was bad luck, Yil?

YIL   Nobody, but it seems to be...to be...yes, an unnatural act.

ENGO   For a man to pretend to bring back to life a dead...a dead... Yil's right. It is against nature.

PENO   Bad luck. Good luck. That's not the point. The fact is it's not true to life.

DEN   You're right, but...we...we have to make it look true. The clan's not stupid. They know we're not really killing a bear before their eyes.

PENO   Why would our clan want to watch something that is false?

DEN   They'll see something that...that...that was true when we did it.

YIL   Give them something that is false to show them something true? Huh?

ENGO   I don't understand you either, Den.

PENO   It's double talk, Den. That's why nobody understands it.

DEN   Look, when they tell stories around the fire, we love to hear tales of great deeds, don't we?

PENO   That's different, Den. That's storytelling. This thing they're asking us to do is...is...

DEN   It's storytelling, too. Except...except they want us to...to take different parts of the story.

YIL   I don't know.

DEN   Why can't we show the clan as closely as we can what a true hunt is like.

PENO   The truth of the hunt is the hunt.

YIL   Peno's right.

ENGO   All else is false.

DEN   The children do such things and call it play.

PENO   We're hunters, not eight-year-old act-it-outers.

DEN   Then … then no one can give the hunt truth like hunters. Hunters showing the hunt.

ENGO   Well, I wouldn't pretend to be a bear in front of my whole family.

YIL   Nor I. I still think it's bad luck.

DEN   Men, what do you want to do with this task? Tell me. Who wants to go before the elders and refuse?

[*A pause. They look at each other.*]

PENO   I'll take the bear's part.

YIL   Peno?

ENGO   Peno, what are you saying?

DEN   He said he'd take the part of the bear.

PENO   Yes.

YIL   He's kidding …

PENO   No. I'll take the bear's part, only to show how false is the idea of reenacting a hunt. I'm the bear. You there are the hunters.

YIL   All right. We're stuck with this. The craftiest and smartest will look the silliest and dumbest.

ENGO   So how do we do this? How do we begin?

DEN   Peno …

[DEN *points to the bear skin.* PENO *crosses to the bear skin and puts it on himself.* YIL *and* ENGO *look at* DEN.]

DEN   What?

YIL   It's strange to see the . . . the bear . . . I mean, the skin quicken . . .

ENGO   Yeah . . .

DEN   Where are we? How was it, the killing, I mean?

Engo   Peno . . . the bear . . . lies down asleep . . .

DEN   That's right . . .

YIL   Then we four—it'll be three in this untrue telling—we three . . .

DEN   Pick up our spears.

[*The three pick up spears and creep up on the sleeping bear.*]

ENGO   We spear Peno to death through his eyes in his sleep like so . . .

[*They simulate stabbing until* PENO *rolls over to play dead.*]

YIL   [*After a pause.*] That's all there was.

ENGO   One growl and a knee jerk and the bear was done.

PENO   Then we thanked the bear for giving up his life so that we and
our families could survive.

DEN   Hmmm . . . no . . .

PENO   No what?

DEN   No, it won't do.

ENGO   That's how this bear was killed.

DEN   We can't show the clan a bear we killed in his sleep.

YIL   There wasn't much to it—this time. Of all the dangerous hunting
trips we've been on, once—once—we get lucky and find a
sleeping bear.

DEN   Yil's right. This hunt was not a regular normal hunt, because there
was no—what am I trying to say?

PENO   No contest.

DEN   Yes. That's it, Peno. There was no fight.

YIL That's so. For all we know this bear might've been sick. We might've killed a bear already half dead.

ENGO We got lucky. That's how it went. With this bear there was no fight.

DEN Then we can't show them this hunt.

PENO What's this?

DEN We can't go before the group and show them a kill with no fight.

YIL Why not?

ENGO It would be boring, Yil.

YIL So we don't have to do it?

DEN No. We have to do...do something.

PENO What?

DEN We...we reenact the bear hunt before this one.

ENGO Where I almost got mauled to death?

DEN Don't you think the crowd would love something like that?

PENO Would you listen to him?

DEN What?

PENO Den, that's dishonest to the core.

YIL They'll all be eating the meat of a bear we killed in his sleep and we show them a pretend kill they ate three weeks ago.

ENGO The further we go the more false we become, Den.

PENO Engo's right. We'd be telling an out and out lie.

DEN If we show ourselves slaying a slumbering bear or a sick bear, it will make us look like old women.

YIL Den's right there.

PENO If we pretend the other bear hunt for this one, we are deceiving our people.

DEN   All right. What you say is true...Let's just look at it another way. The elders requested this to break apart the ordinary, nothing-ever-happens day. The elders want us to give everyone a...a bit of...a bit of excitement. All most of them do is gather nuts, sew skins, chase two-year-olds.

PENO   I prefer telling the truth.

ENGO   I too.

DEN   So do I. I'm asking you all to look on this another way.

PENO   What way?

YIL   You look at a lie from all directions, it's still a lie.

DEN   Let's forget about lying. Let's just say that our reenactment shows...

ENGO   Shows what?

Den   Give me a second...please . . . Let's say that our reenactment—whenever it took place and with whatever bear—shows...shows the truth of the hunt.

YIL   Huh?

DEN   We're giving the clan a truth: the truth of the hunt.

YIL   The truth of the hunt?

PENO   Which is what, Den?

DEN   I'm not sure. We hunt all the time. There's an honesty to what we do when we hunt.

ENGO   I'm still wondering. What is the truth of the hunt?

DEN   Yes. We need to know, so...so we'll know what we are trying to say.

YIL   The truth...

ENGO   Of the hunt...

[*They ponder the question, even examining the bear skin, hopeful that an answer will come.*]

PENO   The hunt can only have one outcome—the death of the animal.

YIL   Or the death of the hunter.

ENGO   Which has happened. Remember poor Eslo?

YIL   Lost so much blood.

DEN   And Eslo was maybe the best hunter of us all. So...death...

ENGO   Yes. The truth of the hunt is death.

DEN   In this case the bear. But...

PENO   What?

DEN   The other truth of the hunt is...is life.

ENGO   I can see what Den means. We...we always thank the dead animal for his life that we might live.

YIL   How can there be two truths to the hunt?

DEN   No. It's not two truths. It's one. Life and death. That's what the hunt's all about. Isn't it?

PENO   The truth of the hunt is life and death.

YIL   The truth of the hunt...

ENGO   Is life and death.

YIL   If a hunt has a truth, I would agree it's life and death.

DEN   We don't lie when we reenact the hunt. No. We...we...we show the clan as truly as we can what it is to hunt.

ENGO   Den's starting to make sense.

PENO   Or are we talking ourselves into making sense?

DEN   Can we at least try it, Peno?

PENO   Pretend we're doing the hunt before this one?

YIL   I don't mind trying it here in private.

ENGO   I don't either. How do we begin?

DEN   We need...we need a plan. If I remember, we...we sneaked up on the bear, who was pawing the stream for fish. We saw him before he caught our scent. We quietly moved in on him.

YIL Fishing. Yeah. He hunted fish to survive the same as we hunted him.

PENO What's that got to do with anything?

YIL It was just...just a thought.

DEN Maybe we can use Yil's thought. Yes. We can...we can have the bear catch and swallow a fish before we go after him...

PENO But the bear didn't catch or swallow a fish.

DEN So what? It tells our story of the hunt. Yil's idea. Life and death of the fish. Life and death of the bear.

ENGO Life and death of one of us...

DEN Maybe...

PENO I'm the bear, remember? Where do I get a fish and how do I swallow it?

[*They think about this question.*]

DEN We use a dried fish...

YIL We can get that. Yes. Yes.

ENGO And you could pretend to swallow it, but...but just tuck it into the folds of the bear skin.

PENO You're full of ideas for me to do.

YIL You have fast hands. You could do that. After Peno—that is, the bear—eats the fish, we sneak up on him.

DEN Then he caught our scent. He turned. We froze.

ENGO Then he attacked us.

YIL That's how it was. Yes. The four of us went at him...

DEN It'll have to be three in our reenactment.

PENO Less and less true.

DEN It's a display of a hunt, not a hunt, Peno. It's a story we're telling to show the way of the hunt.

ENGO I can agree to calling it a display and not a hunt.

YIL If we announce it tonight as a display, yes, then I think we're telling them the truth.

DEN Good idea. We'll announce it as such. A display. Agreed?

YIL Agreed . . .

DEN The bear fishing takes and swallows a fish. Then he attacks us.

ENGO Yes.

DEN Yil and I jabbed at the beast from the left to divert his attention . . .

YIL I remember . . .

DEN Engo and Peno went to the right and struck the first blow.

[ENGO *stabs the air with his spear.*]

ENGO I did.

PENO Engo enraged the beast and the bear lunged at Yil and grabbed and clawed him.

YIL Den freed me—yes—by sticking his spear in the bear's chest.

ENGO I'm starting to sweat just talking through it.

DEN That's good, Engo.

PENO It is?

DEN Yes. If Engo's getting worked up about it, maybe the people around the fire tonight will. What happened after Yil broke loose?

PENO I pierced the bear's stomach.

DEN In our display, Engo will go for the stomach.

YIL But it was Peno who—

PENO I'm the bear, Yil. You want me to stab myself? Make it look like a suicide?

YIL I forgot, all right?

ENGO But wait, Den. Then the bear pounced on Peno.

DEN Just make it... make it you, Engo. In our display, the bear falls on you.

ENGO If that's how you want to do it.

YIL The rest of us warded the bear off with jabs to his neck and face.

DEN Yes... those jabs made the bear stand up. He got my shoulder in his jaws.

ENGO Half blind, that wounded one fought before Yil freed Den. Then he caught me. His jaws still clutched my ankle when we finished him.

DEN When the animal's blood stopped ours still ran.

YIL Wait.

ENGO What?

YIL How do we show blood?

DEN Hmmm...

[*They all ponder this query.*]

ENGO I have it!

PENO What?

ENGO In our water bags. We'll fill them with animal blood. We'll leave the stoppers out. While we fight and move, blood will splatter.

YIL That's a good idea.

DEN That's... that's really exceptional thinking, Engo...

PENO I still question all of this. I've seen madmen think they were beasts.

DEN But you're not a madman, Peno. You must always be in control.

PENO Madmen think they're in control, too.

DEN But you really are in control, Peno. We have a plan. Now... now we have to train...

YIL Train?...

DEN Practice. The way we do for the real hunt. We must go over and over and over it, until our display of the hunt is perfect. Our reputation as hunters and as act-it-outers hangs in the balance.

ENGO Den's right. We don't want to look like fools out there.

YIL No.

ENGO How do we begin?

DEN I guess from the point where the bear is fishing.

PENO Yes.

DEN You need to put on the skin...Peno...

[PENO *puts on the bear skin.*]

PENO It could've been worse. We could've killed a jackass.

[*The others laugh.*]

Let's say...let's say the stream is here.

[PENO *crosses across the stage. The others pick up their spears. The bear, PENO, makes an unconvincing move to grab a fish and pretends to swallow it. The bear turns and sees the hunters. The bear gives out an unconvincing growl. The hunters move forward a step.*]

YIL I say stop!

ENGO Why?

YIL It's...it's just...it's just...

DEN I know what Yil's trying to say.

YIL I say this is all untrue...not to...not to be believed...I say, Peno is not a bear. I say we look foolish...

PENO [*Throwing off the skin.*] You're blaming me?! You're blaming me for this failure?! I told you from the outset that this wouldn't work!

DEN Maybe...maybe we could try someone else to play the bear.

PENO Someone else?! I can play a bear as convincingly as any of you!

YIL Peno...

PENO   No. Den's trying to take my part away!

DEN   I'm not. We just need some effort here.

PENO   Oh? Who put you in charge?

DEN   Somebody has to guide us along. Do you want to do that and I'll play act the bear?

PENO   I can pretend a bear as well as anyone, thank you.

DEN   All right! Then be a bear!

ENGO   Stop this bickering! Let's try it again.

YIL   We understand, Peno, it's harder for you to be a bear. It's easier for us to be hunters.

DEN   Agreed. Peno has the most difficult part.

PENO   I think so. The bear...why, the bear is...is the main player.

YIL   Let's just all try to do better.

DEN   Let's try to do it true, the way we do the real hunt.

ENGO   Yes.

DEN   And talk it up. The way we do when we run into a bear. Let's see...the bear...Peno where you were before...

[PENO *puts on the bear skin and moves to his position left.*]

DEN   Let's start. The bear's hunting in the stream. Don't be shy, hunters. Talk it up.

[*The hunters pick up their spears and observe the bear fishing. The bear makes a growl, grabbing for the fish, which is slippery in his paws. The bear swallows the fish. After a beat, the bear turns and sees the hunters. The bear raises his arms and lets out an enormous roaring growl.*]

DEN   Careful now!

YIL   Look at the size of him!

[*The hunters back up a step as the bear steps forward.*]

DEN   Yil and I'll go to his left! Engo, go right!

ENGO   Not too close! Not too close!

[DEN *and* YIL *prod the bear from the left.* ENGO *moves in on the right. The bear rages throughout the ordeal. The bear grabs* YIL *and claws him.*]

YIL   I'm hurt!

DEN   [*Stabbing at the bear's chest.*] Move away!

YIL   I'm bleeding!

DEN   Move away! Engo, go for the stomach!

[ENGO *stabs at the bear's stomach. The bear pounces on* ENGO.]

ENGO   Help me! Den! Yil! Help me!

[YIL *and* DEN *stab away at the bear's head and neck. The bear rises at the pain and* ENGO *slips out. But the bear takes hold of* DEN'*s shoulder.*]

DEN   Keep stabbing at him! Get him! Harder! Deeper!

[ENGO *and* YIL *on either side of the bear stab away at the beast over and over.* DEN *frees himself and delivers the penultimate blow to the bear's chest.*]

YIL   Good one, Den!

ENGO   He's reeling!
      [*The bear falls, grabbing* ENGO'*s ankle.*]
      He's not dead! Kill him! Kill him! My leg!

[YIL *and* DEN *stab away with deep thrusts.*]

YIL   Die! Die! Die! Why don't you die?!

[*Finally the bear succumbs. The three hunters stand there and look at the kill.* ENGO *kicks the animal to see if he moves.*]

DEN   Thank you, bear, for giving up your life that man might live.

[*A long beat.*]

YIL   That's . . . that's it then.

[PENO *slowly casts off the bear skin and rises. He joins the other three looking down at the bear skin.*]

PENO   Watch the spears.

ENGO I know. We have to be careful. A couple of times we almost cut Peno...

YIL Because...because we...we got into it.

PENO You know...

DEN What, Peno?

PENO You know...for a minute there...I...I...

ENGO Peno?

PENO Strange...just strange...In the heat of the fight just now—I don't know what it was—I felt...I felt this animal. I mean to say, I felt this bear...I mean, in me...I felt...

YIL You did?

PENO It's scary. I felt like a bear.

ENGO Felt like...

PENO The bear. Yes. I think...I think the bear knows it's going to die.

DEN It does?

YIL How do you know?

PENO I don't know how. But I know now that a bear knows it's going to die. I mean, I felt that.

ENGO I think I can understand, Peno. For a while there, I felt as if I were really hunting. I did.

YIL I too. This is amazing strange. Yes.

PENO I hate to admit it, but there is a magic to what we did. Yes, a magic.

DEN And a truth. I mean, it looked like a hunt. I think we can show them what a hunt is like. I do.

YIL If we could only get it perfect, you know, without looking at one another to see what we do next.

DEN We will get it perfect.

ENGO   Make it look like it's just happening.

DEN   We must do it the same way every time we go through it. Every spear thrust measured. Every move the same.

PENO   Yes. Let's try it again.

DEN   We must. Yes. Of course. Take up your positions then.

[PENO *puts the bear skin back on. The others pick up their spears and take the aggressive stance of the hunters. The bear again catches his fish, eats it and turns to the hunters. The bear lets out his savage sound of aggression. The hunters take a step forward and raise their spears. All four actors freeze. The lights slowly fade on the tableau.*]

• • •

acknowledgments

For their support of this edition and my position with Applause Books, I would like to thank my agent, June Clark, as well as the people at Applause Books/The Hal Leonard Performing Arts Publishing Group, including my publisher, John Cerullo, and editor, Bernadette Malavarca.

Furthermore, I'd like to thank my colleague at RRC Rick Pulos, my graduate assistants Nichole Arvin and Liliana Almendarez, and the administration of LIU—Dean David Cohen, Associate Dean Kevin Lauth, and Assistant Dean Maria Vogelstein.

I'd also like to express my gratitude to all the theatres around the country and their literary managers, as well as all the playwrights whose work I read, enabling me to compile this theatre series. A very, very special thanks to Michael Messina.

I follow in the footsteps of a wonderful project—The Best American Short Plays/The Best Short Plays series published by Applause Books, and I would like to thank all the previous editors of this series: the late Stanley Richards, Ramon Delgado, Howard Stein, Mark Glubke, Glenn Young, and anyone I may have left out who came before these fine editors, who've helped make this series a success since 1937.

A quote from the 1989 edition of The Best Short Plays edited by Ramon Delgado:

> From the beginning of this series the past and present editors have sought to include a balance among three categories of playwrights: (1) established playwrights who continue to practice the art and craft of the short play, (2) emerging playwrights whose record of productions indicate both initial achievements and continuous productivity, and (3) talented new playwrights whose work may not have had much exposure but evidences promise for the future. An effort has also been made to select plays not anthologized elsewhere and, when possible, plays that are making their debut in print.... The value of these considerations is to honor the artistry of the established playwrights, encourage the emerging, acknowledge the promising, and offer a varied selection of new plays in one volume.

As the editor of this series, I plan to keep the tradition moving into the future.

—Barbara Parisi